COMMUNICATIONS POLICY

D1744106

Communications Policy

Theories and Issues

Edited by

Stylianos Papathanassopoulos
and
Ralph Negrine

First published 2010 by
PALGRAVE MACMILLAN

Palgrave Macmillan in the UK is an imprint of Macmillan Publishers Limited, registered in England, company number 785998, of Houndmills, Basingstoke, Hampshire RG21 6XS.

Palgrave Macmillan in the US is a division of St Martin's Press LLC, 175 Fifth Avenue, New York, NY 10010.

Palgrave Macmillan is the global academic imprint of the above companies and has companies and representatives throughout the world.

Palgrave® and Macmillan® are registered trademarks in the United States, the United Kingdom, Europe and other countries.

ISBN: 978–0–230–22458–2 hardback
ISBN: 978–0–230–22459–9 paperback

This book is printed on paper suitable for recycling and made from fully managed and sustained forest sources. Logging, pulping and manufacturing processes are expected to conform to the environmental regulations of the country of origin.

A catalogue record for this book is available from the British Library.

A catalog record for this book is available from the Library of Congress.

10 9 8 7 6 5 4 3 2 1
19 18 17 16 15 14 13 12 11 10

Printed in China

Contents

List of Tables and Figures

Tables

Figures

Notes on Contributors

Bram Abramson is a lawyer specializing in communication policy with McCarthy Tetrault in Toronto.

Johannes M. Bauer is Professor in the Department of Telecommunication, Information Studies and Media at Michigan State University, where he is also the co-director of the Quello Center for Telecommunication Management and Law. His research covers policy and management issues in communications and information industries, in particular the design and effects of public policies towards next-generation networks and services, as well as business strategies for the design and deployment of advanced services. Dr Bauer has served as an adviser for public and private sector organizations in North America, South America, Europe and Asia.

Sandra Braman has been studying the macro-level effects of the use of informational meta-technologies since the mid-1980s. Currently a Professor at the University of Wisconsin, Braman has held visiting professorships at the University of Bergen (Norway), Federal University of Rio de Janeiro (Brazil), the University of South Africa (South Africa) and the University of Colorado (USA). Her work includes *Change of State: Information, Policy, and Power* (MIT Press, 2007/9) and the edited volumes *The Emergent Global Information Policy Regime* (Palgrave Macmillan, 2004), *Biotechnology and Communication: The Meta-technologies of Information* (Lawrence Erlbaum, 2004) and *Communication Researchers and Policy-making* (MIT Press, 2003).

Dom Caristi is Associate Professor of Telecommunications in the College of Communications, Information and Media at Ball State University, Muncie, Indiana, USA. He is a founding member of the Digital Policy Institute, an interdisciplinary research group. He was a Fulbright Professor in Communication and Mass Media of the National and Kapodistrian University of Athens in 2009 and in Journalism at the University of Ljubljana, Slovenia, in 1995. He has authored more than two dozen articles, chapters and books and is often quoted in the popular media. Caristi received his PhD from the University of Iowa.

Alistair Duff is Reader in Information and Journalism at Edinburgh Napier University, where his main teaching areas include the information society, freedom of information and political columns. He is author of *Information Society Studies* (Routledge, 2000) and articles in journals such as *Information, Communication & Society* and *Journalism Practice*;

he has contributed to *The Independent*, Talk 107 and other media outlets. Dr Duff has taught summer school at the University of Zurich and was a 2006/7 visiting fellow at Oxford.

Gisela Gil-Egui is Assistant Professor of Communication at Fairfield University (USA), where she teaches courses on new information technologies, mass media and international communication. She obtained her MA (1999) and PhD (2005) degrees in communication from Temple University. She also holds a BA in journalism from Universidad Central de Venezuela (1992). Her research focuses on telecommunications policy and economics, e-government, Latin American media and institutional regimes for the governance of international communication. She has published articles in *New Media & Society*, the *International Communication Gazette* and *Information, Communication & Society*.

Alison Harcourt is Senior Lecturer in Politics at the University of Exeter and Jean Monnet Chair in the information society. She is programme coordinator for the European MA programmes. Her primary focus of research is regulatory change in communications markets. She has written on the regulation of traditional and new media markets at EU and EU member state levels, contributing to the literature on regulatory competition, committee governance, Europeanization, policy transfer and policy convergence.

Jackie Harrison is Professor of Public Communication, Head of Department Journalism Studies and Chair of the Centre for Freedom of the Media at the University of Sheffield. She is currently researching the architecture and culture of European media and information policy in terms of its civil, social (welfare) and political (democratic) roles, as well as European-wide risks, failures and abuses of news media freedom and standards. She is the author of *News* (Routledge, 2006) and *European Broadcasting Law and Policy* (Cambridge University Press, 2007), and is editor of *Mediating Europe: Mass Media in Contemporary European Culture* (Berghahn, 2009).

Robert W. McChesney is the Gutgsell Endowed Professor in the Department of Communication at the University of Illinois at Urbana-Champaign. His work concentrates on the history and political economy of communication, emphasizing the role media play in democratic and capitalist societies. He is the President and co-founder of Free Press, a national media reform organization. McChesney has written or edited numerous books. He has also written more than 150 journal articles and book chapters and another 200 newspaper pieces, magazine articles and book reviews. His work has been translated into twenty-one languages. Since launching his academic career in the late 1980s, McChesney has made some 500 conference presentations and visiting guest lectures as well as more than 600 radio and television appearances.

Ralph Negrine is Professor of Political Communication in the Journalism Studies Department, University of Sheffield. His most recent book is *The Transformation of Political Communication* (Palgrave Macmillan, 2008) and he is now working on a study of aspects of the media in Europe.

Stylianos Papathanassopoulos is Professor in Media Organization and Policy at the Faculty of Communication and Media Studies at the National and Kapodistrian University of Athens. He has written extensively on media developments in Europe and especially on television issues. His research interests are European communications and new media policies, as well as political communication. His recent books include *Television in the 21st Century* (Kastaniotis, 2005); *Media and Politics* (Kastaniotis, 2004); *European Television in the Digital Age: Issues, Dynamics and Realities* (Polity Press, 2002); *European Communications: The Policies of European Union in the Communication Domain* (Kastaniotis, 2002).

Serge Proulx is Professor in the École des médias at the University of Quebec at Montreal, where he is also the director of two research groups. He is a sociologist specializing in the study of the uses of media and communication technologies, and author of more than a dozen books and over 100 journal articles. His current research looks at changing media practices and the social appropriation of new technologies.

Marc Raboy is Professor and Beaverbrook Chair in Ethics, Media and Communications in the Department of Art History and Communication Studies at McGill University in Canada. He is the author or editor of 16 books and more than 100 journal articles or book chapters, as well as numerous research reports for such organizations as the World Bank, UNESCO, the Japan Broadcasting Corporation and the European Broadcasting Union. He is a member of the international council of the International Association for Media and Communication Research (IAMCR), past president of the Canadian Communication Association and member of several editorial boards. He is also a founding member of an international advocacy campaign for Communication Rights in the Information Society.

Concetta M. Stewart is the Dean of the School of Art and Design at Pratt Institute in Brooklyn, New York. Previously, Stewart served as the Dean of the School of Communications and Theater at Temple University in Philadelphia. She holds a PhD from Rutgers University in Communication and Information Studies and an MA from the New School for Social Research in Media Studies. Prior to joining Temple, Stewart worked at AT&T/Bell Labs. Her publications deal with the evaluation and impact of communication and information technologies on organizations, as well as broader social and policy issues related to these technologies.

Yan Tian is Assistant Professor in the Department of Communication at the University of Missouri-St Louis. She holds a PhD in Mass Media and Communication from Temple University. Her main research interests are in the effects of new communication technologies on individuals and society. She has recently published in journals such as *Health Communication*, *Patient Education & Counseling* and *New Media & Society*.

Roxanne Welters is a former graduate student in the Department of Communication at the University of Montreal in Canada.

PART ONE

Theories

1

Approaches to Communications Policy: An Introduction

Stylianos Papathanassopoulos and Ralph Negrine

Communications policy addresses a wide range of contemporary concerns regarding the structure and the organization of communications systems in the past, in the present and in the future. To discover the factors that influence communications policy, however, one has to go beyond the conventional view of media and communication studies and try to combine them with policy studies. This is because communications policy is a product of politics, economics and culture: interest groups and corporate bodies press for congenial policies, politicians and civil servants jockey for influence over outcomes, political problems occur during policy implementation, and so on. Explanations of communications policies must therefore be grounded in a broader view of the general determinants of state and corporate action.

This book aims to bring together theoretical analysis with empirical research findings. Not only does it introduce the key debates and developments currently taking place in Europe and the USA, but also it hopefully adds to our knowledge of the dynamics of communications policy in a rapidly changing communications environment. The present introductory chapter is devoted to the contemporary analyses of various political models and tries to find ways of fitting media sociology and policy studies into these frameworks.

Policy and communications: in search of definitions

In seeking to make sense of this body of knowledge, it is worthwhile beginning with some attempt to discern how some of the key terms are conceived

3

and used. In this section, we comment briefly on how such matters as 'policy' and 'communications policy' – herein incorporating something that can also be referred to as 'information policy' (see Duff's chapter in this volume) – and 'the public interest' are generally used. Whilst the object of this discussion is to highlight points of interest, it is useful to note that 'policies', however conceived, do usually make some reference to sometimes explicit, sometimes implicit notions of 'the public interest'. Subsequent sections of this chapter will explore the multidisciplinary character of communications policy, the role of the state in the communications policy process and how these procedures have been approached by various communication and policy perspectives.

Defining policy

'Policy' can refer to a set of explanations and intentions, to the realization of intentions (Hall and McGinty, 1997: 439), to a series of actions and their consequences, or to all of these together. As for 'policy analysis', Wildavsky (1979: 15) reminds us that there can be no single definition. Instead, there are many approaches that highlight such things as 'the output of policy-making', 'a pattern of responses', 'cluster of decision-making' arrangements and 'a structure or confluence of values behaviour' (Kerr, 1976: 351) that reflect the complexity of such work. Moreover, policy is made in a variety of different contexts, each producing different outcomes. We prefer, therefore, to consider policy analysis as a general description of the subject matter under scrutiny. This avoids an unnecessary review of what policy is/is not (and could be), as well as trivial repetition of the literature.

In practice, it is difficult to conceptualize policy, even as a term, because it usually involves a wide range of issues, actors and aspects. Ideally, a policy is derived from a central authority, which, through a rational review process, sets clear objectives. But on occasions policies are not visible or set down anywhere; for example, statements by a government minister about matters under discussion may be considered important as well as delicate or controversial. Yet this kind of policy communication is important because it allows for citizens and interest groups to be informed about policy intentions and thus become involved in the policy-making process (Gelders *et al.*, 2007). Inaction may also be a kind of policy; an absence of a policy is therefore a positive decision in favour of non-intervention in media industries, as in the sector of the print media in Western Europe (Siune, 1998: 18). Policies can also often have unintended consequences, and these may be critical for certain media. Policies are often incremental, building on past rules (Bar and Sandvig, 2008; Storsul and Syvertsen, 2007), and may be contradictory in as much as they will deal with some sectors but not with others.

Thus, print policy may differ from broadcast policy, so creating anomalies. The internet, in many ways, offers challenges to policy processes that have traditionally dealt with separate media. Policies are, nevertheless, the outcome of an interaction between a government's approach to problem-solving and discussions, including bargaining, and other actors engaged in the formulation of policy outcomes.

Understanding a policy and its process should not require the invention of a new repertoire of concepts or taxonomies and it can begin by integrating the existing stock of knowledge. Therefore, an open-ended definition of policy and of policy analysis leaves much room for critical reflection. It also has the added advantage that it should be able to treat policy as a means to an end rather than an end in itself. Although this could be seen as a simplification, it may be preferable to detailed and possibly fruitless debates surrounding the details of decision-making mechanisms, of evaluation and of regulatory supervision.

Defining communications policy

Broadly speaking, communications policy seeks to examine the ways in which policies in the field of communications are generated and implemented and their repercussions for the field of communications as a whole. Although this is admittedly a broad definition, it has to be remembered that 30 years ago the term 'communications policy' was not widely used (Halloran, 1986: 47) and there was little discussion about the need to develop policies for the field of communications as a whole. Although, in practice, there were often specific policies relating to particular media, there was no real attempt to seek to coordinate activities for the entire media landscape, either within one country or across a group of countries. Part of the reason for this was that different media had different histories and therefore regulatory traditions: the press was, by and large, less regulated, if at all, compared with the medium of radio and, later, television, which developed within a particular setting. Another reason was that different national cultural and political traditions led to the development of different policy-making approaches.

Consequently, until recently there were different traditions of media policy in Europe. Whilst these could always be contrasted with US approaches as being restrictive and dampening innovation, limiting consumer choice and paternalistic, it was always acknowledged that there was 'no single or uniform West European approach to communication policymaking' (Homet, 1979: 3). In reality, then, different policy regimes existed in the countries of Europe: some were politically motivated; others drew on laissez-faire approaches, still others on paternalistic considerations (see Siune, 1998).

Public (service) broadcasting developed out of the state sector and was often considered to be something that the authorities should be involved in: it would thus be controlled, guided or gently regulated. By contrast, the press belonged to the private sector; it was thus less heavily regulated and oversight was minimal, although it could face other pressures given the overwhelming interest in, and concern for, its political influence. Here, again, there were significant differences between countries within Europe as between the northern European countries and those of Southern Europe (see Hallin and Mancini, 2004; Hallin and Papathanassopoulos, 2000).

Technological developments such as cable television and satellite broadcasting and the convergence of media – in effect the convergence of computers, telephony and the television screen – created an environment in which one could no longer simply consider communications media in isolation and as separate elements of a yet ill-defined whole. Developments in cable and satellite clearly impacted on public broadcasting, developments in these impacted on the press and radio, and so on. Hence, the growing appreciation of the need for more inclusive policies towards the communications landscape as a whole. The problem faced by policy-makers, though, was how precisely to create such policies and how to regulate the media. Should governments themselves exercise degrees of oversight? Should different bodies regulate different media (press, radio, television, etc.)? Or should specially designated bodies be set up to deal with media policy and regulation? The British government, for instance, has set up a regulatory body, OFCOM, the Office of Communication, whose task is to develop policies and regulate the media. This model, similar to the FCC in the USA, may be one that other countries in Europe could adopt for the purposes of dealing with communications issues at the national level.

However, these sorts of issues do not simply stop being important when one reaches national boundaries, especially since media do not remain within such boundaries. Dramatic changes in communications systems and technologies have drawn nation states and international organizations such as the European Union and the International Telecommunications Union into a consideration of the need for strategic approaches to managing technological (and implicitly communication) change for national, regional and/or international benefit. Whilst this has not meant that all previous policies are redundant, it has forced policy-makers and others to consider their usefulness in the more global and converged landscape. As pointed out above, new policies are not written on a *tabula rasa*; they occupy a rather crowded space inhabited by existing laws, organizations and interest groups. In the 1970s, May and Wildavsky (1978: 13) suggested that past policies become an important part – sometimes the most important part – of the environment to which the future must adapt; whether this is still the case in a context wherein the internet has forced 'older' means of communication to implode (e.g., newspapers) or reconfigure themselves (e.g., broadcast services) is arguable. That said, much policy-making is often no more than *policy-succession*, whereby an existing policy or programme is succeeded by another. This policy succession is recognized in most communication policies, especially regarding the introduction and absorption of new media and communications technologies. Policies in respect of IPTV, for instance, could be viewed as drawing on policies for the development of optical fibres in the 1980s and 1990s and those as a succession of various cable development programmes of the 1980s, such as the *Plan Câble* in France. Similarly, the *Digital Britain* report is reminiscent of discussions surrounding the cabling of Britain in the 1970s.

Implementing a policy

The implementation of a policy is often the most important and most difficult phase in the policy process (see deLeon and deLeon, 2002) and it could be argued that due to the complex socio-political, cultural and economic character of such policies it is a particularly problematic area of study. It is at the point of implementation that deficiencies – or unintended consequences – of policies often materialize. It is also at this stage that one can pass judgment on the success, or failure, of a policy. Nevertheless, implementation is a phase that needs to be paid much attention and it is often overlooked in accounts that look at the generation of policy. Yet one of the problems with the implementation phase is the need for coordinated action: the complexities of the communications system require joint action by those involved in the social, economic, political, cultural, even foreign affairs of a country. A lack of coordination is, therefore, problematic. Equally problematic is the fact that as circumstances change, for example, with deregulation, globalization and convergence altering the nature of communications systems and processes, the difficulties of implementing policies can become more acute because the set of instruments available for implementing policies may no longer be adequate. For instance, convergence and digitalization have forced regulators to reconsider how best to deal with telecommunications operators who now deliver both old and new content, alongside traditional content providers.

The 'public interest' as a consideration in policy

In communications policy the issue of the public interest is a critical consideration. As Mike Feintuck (1999: 57) has noted: 'much regulatory activity, not only of the media, but also for example, for utilities, is justified by reference to a claim of the public interest'. Although the history of the public interest goes back to classical times, as a concept it remains ambiguous and not only in the media field. When applied to the mass media, according to Denis McQuail (2003: 47):

> its simple meaning is that [policy-making bodies] carry out a number of important, even essential, informational and cultural tasks and it is in the general interest (or good of the majority) that these are carried out well and according to the principles of efficiency, justice, fairness and respect for current social and cultural values. At the minimum, we can say that it is in the public interest that the media should do no harm, but the notion entails many positive expectations as well as restrictions and forms of accountability.

A simple way to distinguish the meaning of the public interest is among the three main rival concepts: utilitarianism, unitary and common interest approaches.

Utilitarianism or majoritarian approaches aggregate individual values and preferences. The public interest is merely the sum of individuals' wealth, happiness and avoidance of pain. Therefore, the state's role must be limited to maximizing individuals' benefit according to the overall popular vote. In the case of the media, the public interest will be best achieved by giving more freedom to media market forces. Its main proponents would argue that, broadly speaking, media systems governed by market forces tend to the maximization of benefit for both producers and consumers and to the society as a whole (McQuail, 1992).

Unitary concepts base the public interest on some collective moral imperative that transcends particular or private interests. In other words, the public interest necessarily takes precedence over the interests of individuals, in order to pursue a vision of an ideal society (Berki, 1979). It requires individuals, if necessary, to sacrifice their individual interests and lives in the pursuit of a greater collective interest or ideal. In the media field, the public interest is decided by reference to some single dominant value or ideology. This would only work in a paternalist system in which decisions about what is good are decided by guardians or experts. Its main application could be considered the foundation of 'public service broadcasting'. This is because public service broadcasting is often defined in terms of benefits which it is supposed to deliver to society: universal provision and wide-ranging appeal; services to regions and minorities; attention to national interest, identity and culture; the provision of informational and educational services beyond what the market would require, etc. (cf. McQuail, 1992: 3). The claim for media freedom is another good example of the invocation of unitary theory in relation to communication, but there are many other claims which invoke normative support for control of the media. These relate to matters such as education, protection of the young, national language and culture (see Blumler, 1992). In each case, a well-established and fundamental value principle is at stake.

Between these two approaches there is the common interest theory (McQuail, 2003). This refers to cases where a common interest is not an aggregation of individual interests, but it is a shared interest, with little scope for dispute over preferences. Typical examples are: basic services of transport, power, water, etc. In the media field basic features of national media structures and the services they provide (for example, technical standards, press subsidies, frequency allocations, access to political parties, rules for advertising) are often justified on grounds of a wider 'common good', transcending individual choices and preferences, with more reference to experts or to tradition than to the balance of popular opinion. The principle of freedom of speech and publication may itself have to be supported on grounds of long-term benefits to society which are not immediately apparent or clear to many individuals. In the political communication area the demand for an informed citizenship by the media is regarded as a necessity in a democratic political system and thus in every citizen's interest.

In his study of the foundation of communications policy in the USA, Philip Napoli (2001: 22–8) has presented a conceptual model in which the 'public interest is shown to be achieved by way of five media policy principles: localism, the free marketplace of ideas, universal service, diversity and competition'. He also notes that these principles represent the key guiding principles, but they lack a broad consensus in terms of stable, explicit and coherent interpretations. Patricia Aufderheide (1999) has also identified several interpretations of the public interest in US communications policy. The public interest during the New Deal era was equated with 'the economic health of the capitalist society, associated with peace and prosperity' (1999: 5), a little later with social welfare and the notion of the universal service. In the 1970s, it was associated with competition and with the 1996 US Telecommunications Act the public interest was thought to be better served within a competitive marketplace.

In spite of these discussions, the idea of the 'public interest' remains problematic. First, it has never been explicitly defined. Second, even if this is done, it is impossible in practice to identify where the public interest lies and, third, analysts of communications systems have doubted whether the practices and institutions of modern politics and the media are such that the public interest is pursued. Recently, there has developed a new approach that relates the public interest to an interactive process (from pragmatic political discourse, to utopian open dialogue and consensus) among concerned stakeholders and affected parties. At one pole it includes the Madisonian concept that gives the public interest a substantive content, but one which can only be determined *ex post facto*: the actual result of political conflict, bargaining and compromise between particular sectoral or private interests. But in one way or another, in the age of globalization and deregulation, as Smith (1989: 10) has pointed out, 'the interests of the public may not coincide with the interests of a particular nation state'. Moreover, in an era that witnesses the rise of individualism, and neo-liberalism and neo-conservatism's increasingly dominant managerialist ideology, there is a wide belief that only by adopting commercial practices can governments and public institutions achieve efficiency and effectiveness and thus best serve the public interest.

The multidisciplinary character of communications policy

One of the field's main characteristics is its multidisciplinary and multi-dimensional approach. Sociology and politics are given priority in most relevant studies because policy issues mature within a societal context, determining the nature of political actors, decision-making structures and processes, as well as policy outcomes; but economics and industrial/technological considerations do not lag far behind. In fact, the multidisciplinary character of communication policy and its analysis permits anybody from any discipline to be involved (see Rowland, 1993; Galperin, 2004b). Economists (see Mueller and Lentz, 2004), lawyers (see Reinard and Ortiz, 2005), sociologists and political scientists have all contributed to, and interpreted, communication policy science and/or analysis and research. Even media studies, with its macro-perspective on media matters, can provide 'research [that] might be useful for policy makers' (Braman, 2003: 11). Communications policy is multidimensional by nature because the problems concerning public policy analysis are simply too complex to permit solution from a single disciplinary base. Much of this echoes what Wildavsky (1979: 15) stressed a long time ago, namely, that policy analysis is an applied subfield whose content cannot be determined by disciplinary boundaries, but by whatever appears appropriate to the circumstances and nature of the problem.

The communications field is also influenced by the emergence of new technologies (see also Goggin, 2003). Three decades ago, Ithiel de Sola Pool (1973) argued that new developments in communications technology challenge existing industry and legal arrangements and shape the regulatory aspects of the communications domain, since the new technologies, the ICTs, blur the distinctions between communications media and make previous arrangements obsolete. A decade later, it was widely recognized that communications policy analysis was rather inadequate 'for an environment that had qualitatively changed as a result of technological innovation' (Braman, 2003: 1). More recently, Denis McQuail (2007a: 9) noted that communications or media policy 'is now a familiar category for a branch of public administration and law that has grown in significance and for a branch of inquiry in the social sciences that has also acquired a clear identity as a field of teaching, research and publication'. It is, though, something that 'is still guided ultimately by political, social and economic goals' even though 'they have been reinterpreted and reordered' (McQuail, 2005: 240).

In sum, communication policy research aims to provide policy-makers, among others, with a better understanding of the changes in the field and to evaluate their policies. Besides, as Sandra Braman (2004a: 158) has argued, 'policy makers are most comfortable making law when they feel they understand what it is that is being regulated'. In other words, communications policy research and analysis aims to provide us with useful guides or suggestions for the policy-maker facing an uncertain future. The task of determining what 'the' policy should be/is, and therefore also how it came into being, is thus not a simple or straightforward exercise. It requires searching various sources of information as well as looking into the relationships between interested parties, connections between events and the context within which all this takes place. Moreover, since that contextualization is nowadays increasingly of an international character, the task before the researcher gains added complexity.

Communications policy and the state

As Paul Sabatier has noted, 'any theory of the manner in which governmental policies get formulated and implemented, as well as the effects of those actions on the world, requires an understanding of the behavior of major types of governmental institutions (legislatures, courts, administrative agencies, chief executives), as well as the behavior of interest groups, the general public, and the media' (Sabatier, 1991: 147). The fact is that policy and the policy process cannot be examined with a unitary approach (Hall and McGinty, 1997). In seeking to comprehend the complexities of the communications and policy process, scholars from both fields have worked with a number of different approaches to analyze the growing impact of communications and the new technologies on socio-political and economic life and the role of the state and state action in modern society in general, and in the communications field in particular. This section describes briefly some of these approaches of state action and/in the communications field.

Analyzing communications policies in terms of the state, directs our attention to a single, general problem, namely, the interrelation between governing institutions within a nation state and other interests within that state vying to be heard when policy is under discussion. The centrality of the state is critical for understanding policy generation and implementation since state intervention in the communications area is widespread and ranges from facilitating industrial development through subsidies and tax concessions, to direct ownership of certain industries or companies. Our view is that the state needs to be considered as a primary unit of analysis and the basic unit for action and that it enjoys a 'relative autonomy' from both its internal and external – including international – environments.

Our key objective in this section is to present approaches that help us better understand how policy is generated, by whom and in what circumstances. Inevitably, we have been selective but we believe that our selection offers a sound way forward and an insight into how the state helps formulate, implement and evaluate communications policy.

Approaches

In setting out approaches to the study of communications policy, it is important to pay some attention to the place of the state in the process of policy formulation and implementation. Is the state a 'pawn' of interests as Dahl has suggested (1961: 50–1)? Does it impartially reflect the preferences of competing interests (Shipan, 1997) with no single interest capable of controlling policy-making? Or does the state act on behalf of particular groups and interests, as the political economists would suggest? Furthermore, are the individuals and groups vying for a share of resources *rational* actors maximizing their personal interests? Are there, by contrast, issues relating to the nature of *capitalist societies* and structures of determination within these that are in need of more urgent attention, as the *political economists* would suggest, whereby the focus is primarily on the relation 'between the economic structure and dynamics of media industries and the ideological content of the media' (McQuail, 2005: 99; see also Golding and Murdock, 1991)? The increased concentration of media interest around the world, the continuous relaxation of ownership rules, efforts to 'secure' private interests while managing the decline of the public sector of the media and telecommunications, as well as the growing importance of the communications industries underline the continuing relevance of this approach.

Beyond this approach for exploring the genesis of policy, there are three that seek to explain the development of policies by looking at the ways in which, in practice, groups and institutions haggle with state bodies. These are approaches that highlight the roles of group interests, of the state and of the interplay between the two. We explore each of these briefly below.

Group and interest approaches to communication policy

The focus of attention here is on collective, group or individual vested interests which enter a process of bargaining within the polity. Not surprisingly, more notice is taken of intensely influential groups than of those with weak preferences. Moreover, the policy process occurs temporally through the formal development process and spatially across linked sites of responsibility (Hall and McGinty, 1997). Communications in general and media structures in particular are influenced by the relevant interest groups more than by the government; the bargaining process among interest groups leads to the formation of general communications/media policies. Thus, the state is a *coding machine* – a passive vehicle through which input is processed. The state generally mirrors or responds to the balance of pressure groups in civil society (MacPherson: 1973).

In a modern complex society, institutions and organizations often mediate between power and its distribution. Deregulation in action could be seen as a form of intervention that advances managerial efficiency by overcoming the fragmentation caused by dominant interests' capture of state agencies (Mosco, 1988). One must therefore look at the organizational level to understand public policy. Accordingly, researchers need to be extremely cautious in going beyond actors' expressed preferences in analyzing power relations. Nevertheless, the picture provided by this approach assists our understanding of various developments in the communications sector. This perspective is particularly helpful in explaining how policy-making and state action are affected by interests and coalitions of interests.

State-centric approaches to communications policy

'State-centric' approaches have become important in determining public policy. Although there are two variations, left and right, both argue that public policy is not primarily a reaction to pressure from interested groups. On the contrary, state preferences are at least as important as those of civil society in accounting for what the democratic state does and does not do. The state is not only frequently less subject to societal pressure than previously imagined, insofar as it regularly acts upon its preference, but it also becomes *relatively autonomous* when its preferences diverge from the demands of the most powerful groups in civil society and it imposes those preferences against societal resistance (Nordlinger, 1981; Hall, 1986; Saunders, 1981: Ham and Hill, 1984). The state's strength consists of its capacities to be autonomous and to act (Hoffmann, 1983). The latter depends on the state's organization and the balance between its scope and resources. For example, the deregulation and liberalization of the British telecommunication sector was not an outcome led by the pressure of vested interests but from the willingness of the Thatcher government to offend against the 'bastions of the state' (see Vogel, 1996).

From a pluralist perspective, the state is regarded as a broker (Dunleavy and O'Leary, 1987). State administrations, agencies, politicians, parties and governments have their own preferences. Moreover, in our interdependent and complex world, one could say that the transfer of policy authority to the EU level has increased economic interests' uncertainty over who decides and what is decided and thus it enhances the authority of the state in shaping policy (Sadeh and Howarth, 2008).

The state as a broker, as an intermediary, might be constrained by clients and other interests, but it is more autonomous than a cipher, a machine or mirror. It is an autonomous and active actor, formulating independent preferences and objectives that cannot be reduced to an aggregate of private preferences or the interests of the dominant class. Concerning the transition to digital television in the USA and the UK, Galperin (2004a: 26) notes that at 'the same time long-established industry rules were being relaxed, critical decisions about digital TV standards, the timing for the introduction of equipment and services, and the allocation of radio spectrum, to mention a few examples, emerged from a political rather than a market-driven process'.

This approach highlights variables such as the territorial and functional centralization of the executive branch, the domination of the executive over the legislature and the control of material and informational resources by the ability of policy instruments to change civil society. This approach also provides a tool for understanding the policy process and corrects other approaches that underestimate the state's role. The main problem with this approach is that it disallows societal influences, including the often *unintended consequences* of past policies. Similarly, theories about a state's capacities to carry out a range of policies do not assure us of the state's effectiveness since success or failure of a policy depends largely on a range of factors – organizational, cultural, etc. – within society. The approach has limitations that relate to the management of change. In short, a pure state-centric approach, although providing a promising line of enquiry, needs to be placed within a wider framework or environment before it can explain a state's action and behaviour. The state affects, but is also affected by, the societal and international environment. Modern states do not appear to be as independent of societal influence as state-centric theories suggest.

State–society approaches and the institutional approach

Policy analysis within the wider framework of state–society relations does not necessitate returning to pressure groups' influence models to explain state action. There are likely to be structural consistencies behind the persistence of distinctive national patterns of policy. In 'strong' states, particularly, intermediation between state and society may not be confined to pluralist and corporatist options. Rather, states may selectively recognize only some mobilized interests concerned with a policy issue. Segmented policy patterns result, co-opting a limited range of compatible interests into the policy process. As Everard (2000: 8) has noted, the state is not a 'unitary identity, it is multifaceted' and such approaches provide us with a framework that integrally connects economy and policy.

Working within this framework, it is possible to explain historical continuities and cross-national variations in policy. Galperin (2004a: 284) shows that in the case of the communications sector 'governments have considerable autonomy to shape the transition in consonance with domestic policy agendas and protect established arrangements in the communications sector'. This resonates with what Peter Hall (1986: 13–14) has referred to as the 'institutional approach to state–society relations'. He argues that this approach better explains policy by emphasizing the institutional relationships – both formal and conventional – that bind the state's components together and structure its relations with society. This approach uses the concept of institution to refer to the formal rules, compliance procedures and standard operating practices that structure the relationships between individuals in various units of policy. As such, they have a more formal status than cultural norms, but this is not necessarily derived from legal (as opposed to conventional) standing. This approach emphasizes the *relational character of institutions*, using 'organizations' virtually as a synonym for 'institution'. This approach is interesting because it asserts that organizations affect the degree of power that any one set of actors has over policy outcomes. This is extremely useful when trying to explain, for example, the problems of co-coordinating various units in new media policies.

A variation of this is the 'new institutionalism' approach and is a middle-range rather than a fully blown grand theory (Blom-Hansen, 1997). All that really connects the different approaches is a notion that 'the organization of political life makes a difference' (March and Olsen, 1998: 944) and, hence, that the role of institutions should be considered in an explicit and systematic way. Hallin and Mancini (2004), for example, have also shown that the differences of the media systems in Western societies can be traced to their political history and societal arrangements.

In respect of these issues in the context of *media governance*, Donges (2007: 327) notes three points that need to be emphasized:

1. Actors such as media organizations (institutionalized as private or public companies) or regulatory authorities etc. cannot be considered decoupled from the institutional setting they emerged from. Moreover, institutional rules define how organizations observe and evaluate their environment. Organizations bear their institutional history inside and cannot shake

it off. They are path-dependent in the sense that it is hard to change their structures.

2. Institutional rules are the basis of media regulation, and all forms of regulation are always rooted in institutional arrangements. That is the reason why we can distinguish different models of media and politics (e.g., Hallin and Mancini, 2004) or different 'ideas' or regulatory cultures even within Europe (e.g., Cuilenburg and McQuail, 2003; see e.g., Napoli, 1999).

3. Institutional rules are always the products of decisions made by media, political, or economic actors.

The institutional approach also helps us to understand policy process and output, and according to Herman Galperin, it 'has much to offer to communication and information policy scholars at a time when the governance regime for new technologies is growing in complexity. Today, the rules created and enforced by traditional regulatory bodies on a national scale are now only part of a multilayered regime that includes international treaties, voluntary self-regulation and semi-public cooperative arrangements under the umbrella of a vast collection of organizations' (2004b: 166). Individual states and societies in the age of globalization have become increasingly interdependent economically, industrially and culturally. Communications systems in the age of the internet are part of a global communications system, necessitating policy guidelines to enable the national system to work well within an international system. In effect, policy and regulation in the communication sector have moved away from being essentially part of a domestic political process and towards becoming part of a new complex international dimension of technological, industrial and economic governance (see also Dyson and Humphreys, 1990).

Political systems and policy processes are influenced more and more from abroad, meaning that old orthodoxies about boundaries of the state as a country need re-examining. Converging computing, telecommunications and television have brought not only new actors, but also they brought international actors into the communications field and intensified the trends of globalization of production, investment and distribution. Satellite technology and the internet breach aspects of national sovereignty. In fact, there are many bodies nowadays such as the International Telecommunications Union (ITU), World Trade Organization (WTO), UNESCO, WIPO (World Intellectual Property Organization), ICANN (Internet Corporation for Assigned Names and Numbers), EU, etc., which deal with various aspects of international systems and at the same time affect national regulations (McQuail, 2005). One has also to take into account the non-governmental organizations which have in the last decades gained increasing importance as actors in the international relations, world politics and global governance (Beyer, 2007).

Such a 'complex interdependence' (Keohane and Nye, 1998: 81) in the information age generates distinctive political processes and the communications technology revolution continues to lend support to this trend, bringing more and more activities within an international agreements framework. In effect, the international arena is increasingly characterized by competition and cooperation among states, reflecting internal and external conflicts over national versus global solutions to problems. It is unlikely that many contemporary technological/communications phenomena could be identified as solely internal or solely external. Nonetheless, this distinction helps us gain a perspective on the role of the state in the international context and its interaction with other sovereign states. In this formulation, the state, even in its regulatory role, does not act merely as a mediator between internal demands and external constraints and pressures, but as a shaper, capable of moulding its own preference between domestic and international policy determinants. For example, although the governments in Europe have almost everywhere withdrawn from any directly *dirigiste* role, they 'retain the right and sometimes the obligation to react or restrain market developments on behalf of a public (sometimes national) interest and also to establish and maintain conditions for efficient and fair operation of a free market' (McQuail, 2007a: 11).

As well as being the primary unit of analysis, the state is generally also the foremost unit of action, although the environment – whether domestic, international or both – may constrain state action. Globalization, for example, imposes structural imperatives on states, so limiting their action. This does not, however, contravene the idea of the 'relative autonomy' of the state from both society and global economy (Bailey and De Ruyter, 2007). According to Hyder (1984), the tentacles of international cooperation are deep and widespread, but its impact depends on the extent to which negotiated agreements are actually carried out. The lack of any established legal and political arrangements causes problems for implementing policies. The EU is a prime example because its specific business is to complement, supplement and even replace individual policies of its member states without being a political union (see Chakravartty and Sarikakis, 2007; Knill and Lehmkuhl, 2002). Moreover, within Europe the integration process has been inextricably bound up with the transformation of both the traditional system of 'nation states' and of the role of individual member states. This transformation has not been 'solely the product of integration but has derived from other developments such as globalization, new developments in economic management, notably the move towards the regulatory state, and domestic moves towards "new public management" as a way of better administering policy' (Bulmer, 1998: 366). In other words, European integration is seen as a dependent variable of state development at the *national* level (Bulmer, 1998; see also Featherstone and Radaelli, 2003) and this has produced new forms of governance, and new institutions of government shaping what Castells (2000: 340–8) has called the 'network state'. In fact, there are still wide margins for strategic behaviour by politicians to pursue their 'national interest' policies (Jordana *et al.*, 2006: 460).

To conclude, regardless of global pressures and influences, the communication system will continue to be dominated by the nation state and it remains a useful mechanism for collective control over communications media. Even in the case of the internet, the regulation of the new medium which crosses frontiers, nations tend to regulate the internet in their own way (May *et al.*, 2004). A recent example is the failure of the European Commission to establish an EU telecommunications agency that would ensure consistent regulatory decisions by national authorities. The original plan called for giving the commission more power over national authorities but both the European Parliament and the Council of Ministers rejected the commission proposal. As Denis McQuail notes (2005: 270), 'for the foreseeable future, mass communication will continue to be dominated by the nation-state and the small group of rich and powerful countries that arbitrate world events'. Indeed, in the current era of the financial, monetary and *traditional mainstream media* crises the role of the state becomes more critical as a provider of solutions to problems: as the failures of market mechanisms become apparent, guided state-inspired solutions may need to come to the fore.

The organization of this book

Following the introductory chapter, this book is divided into two parts. The first part aims to deal with the theoretical aspects of communications policy, not as the introductory chapter does, but to address the various dimensions of communications policy. The second part of the book is devoted to the issues related to communications policy, such as the consolidation of the communication industry, the future of public broadcasters in the digital era, the role of the European Union in the whole communications sector. Inevitably, space restrictions have meant that we have not been able to include other areas, such as a discussion of intellectual property rights and piracy in the age of the internet (Perelman, 2002) or issues related to young people (Livingstone, 2002).

In the first part of this volume, Sandra Braman argues that the number of laws and regulations dealing with information and information technologies has increased considerably. As a result, the boundaries of the field of media policy are increasingly difficult to discern. Problems raised by technologies, media practices, the nature of policy-making processes and the unique characteristics of media as a policy issue area confound the effort. Braman critically reviews approaches to resolving the problem of defining media policy and proposes a definition as the subset of the larger domain of information policy that includes those laws, regulations and policy principles that have the effect of mediating the public itself. She concludes by exploring a few examples of non-traditional types of media policy issues from this perspective.

Alistair Duff seeks to provide a clearer picture of information, building on useful groundwork in information science and other disciplines. He traces the history of 'information policy' and describes the present state of 'information policy', with particular reference to some salient themes of the current literature: issue inventories (i.e., the scope of information policy); academic identity (including a critique of attempts to appropriate information policy for one discipline); and the ideal – or, it is argued, illusion – of a 'national information policy'. In the final section of his chapter he makes some suggestions for the future direction of information policy. He argues that information policy should engage much more thoroughly with the tradition of political philosophy and that information policy may benefit from more forays into the field of futures studies. He also proposes that information policy could be positioned as a subset of the interdisciplinary specialism of information society studies, in which case its definition might be resolved in terms of the 'normative theory of the information society'.

Marc Raboy, Bram Dov Abramson, Serge Proulxa and Roxanne Welters note that changes in the technological and economic environments have been accompanied by a series of policy developments at international and national levels. An important implication of these changes has been an impasse for policies that articulate public interest with respect to the media. To address this, they propose a research agenda centred on the idea of 'social demand'. This refers to the range of expectations with respect to media that exceed economic (market) or political (state) considerations – that is to say, expectations as they can be extrapolated from what people say about their media use, as well as the efforts of organized social and cultural groups to influence the direction of media policy.

This part of the book concludes with Jackie Harrison's attempt to examine current communication policy dimensions under the heading of the emerging communicative spaces in Europe. She argues that the European Union has to develop a European civil society. Specifically, she is interested in the conditions under which the expression of European public opinions can be communicatively facilitated in an audiovisual way which is both European-wide and which is independent of the various political and economic institutions that currently govern and regulate the EU. She argues that the EU once more needs to engage in some institution building. This time the EU should build a pan-European organization of public service communication (EU PSC) consisting of two distinct but related audiovisual institutions united in their concern for the facilitation of the EU's civil and social aims: one, an audiovisual institution of European public news journalism and, two, an institution of European social communication.

The second part of the book deals with various distinct issues in communications policy analysis and research. Robert McChesney chronicles the uprising of 2003 when media policy exploded into the public consciousness as millions of Americans registered their opposition to the relaxation of long-standing media ownership rules. In effect, he offers an overview of the resistance of civil society groups as well as some political leaders to the efforts to restructure and reduce media ownership and cross-ownership caps in the USA. This raises the question of the role of civil society groups in a field of investigation usually dominated by public sector actors and national and transnational private sector companies.

Alison Harcourt investigates the processes through which the European Union has become a major actor in national media regulation. She examines the processes through which the EU has become a salient actor in national regulation. Under observation are the actions of the European Commission, the Merger Task Force and the European Court of Justice. In her chapter, Harcourt shows how these institutions have pursued *Europeanization* with intersecting but different agendas. The ensuing pattern is one of policy convergence – a result that is surprising in a policy area which is considered to be deeply seated at the national level.

Papathanassopoulos and Negrine try to point out the challenges faced by public broadcasters in the digital competitive market and discuss the role of public broadcasters in the new European communications landscape. More precisely, their chapter describes the challenges public broadcasting faces in an increasingly competitive digital television market. The chapter provides an account of the current situation of public broadcasters in Europe. Then, it explores the two major challenges they are going to face – the fiscal crisis and the threats posed by convergence and digitalization. Finally, it discusses the role of public broadcasters in the new European television landscape.

On the other hand, Johannes M. Bauer reviews changes in the state's involvement in the communications sector by using the example of the telecommunication services. In effect, he reviews these transformations of the state from heavy involvement in the provision and regulation of telecommunication services to its more indirect role as a regulator to the more recent return of the state. The chapter notes that the role of the state has adapted in response to a multitude of forces, including new challenges faced by the sector, the evolving economic and technical conditions, changing political conditions, and shifts in the configurations of relevant stakeholders attempting to shape communications policy.

Dom Caristi examines the changing landscape for communication law in a digital, global environment. He argues that two major issues need to be addressed. First, digital media regulation can no longer be effective if it regulates only within one nation. International agreements exist in some areas, yet national laws are often circumvented by those operating 'offshore'. Second, digital media are distributed – and altered – much more easily than physical media. Whereas copying books once required expensive equipment and large amounts of time, an e-book can be copied in just seconds using equipment found in most homes in developed countries. Thanks to ubiquitous distribution, the World Wide Web has allowed what used to be minor infractions to take on major consequences. A scheme needs to be implemented that deals broadly with these issues. The International Telecommunication Union has started a process that needs to adopt a more assertive role.

In the last chapter, Gisela Gil-Egui, Yan Tian and Concetta M. Stewart explore key contemporary US and European Union policy documents so as to identify the similarities and differences in the way that the digital divide has been defined in both contexts. They present the results of a multimodal exploration of key policy documents produced by the US government and the European Commission between 2004 and 2008, on issues related to access to, and harnessing of, information and communication technologies for purposes of economic growth and development. Findings from their study suggest a shift, from the openly neo-liberal, market-oriented discourses that dominated both sets of documents in our previous study, to a more nuanced framing of ICT policies – one that considers broader structural factors affecting the effectiveness of strategies in this regard and proposes a more active role of the public sector in the implementation of such policies. The authors discuss the contextual elements intervening in this gradual move towards a new ICT policy-making paradigm.

Underpinning all these chapters is a common view, namely, that communications policy is a problem-oriented field of study and that it is multidisciplinary in character. Furthermore, and as these chapters also seek to demonstrate in their different ways, work in this field draws on a whole range of disciplines in order to seek to better understand how we have arrived at the present and how best to deal with the challenges of the future.

CHAPTER

Mediating the Public through Policy

Sandra Braman

Introduction

Around the world, policy-makers are struggling to cope with the myriad legal issues raised by digitization by making new laws and regulations or by adapting, reinterpreting, or replacing those already in place. Because so many of these laws and regulations are directed at technologies used not only by the media, but also for numerous other purposes, it can be difficult to discern the boundaries of the domain of media law and policy in this environment. Indeed, when almost all of our activities, including face-to-face conversations, include a technological element, it is no longer even clear what it is that is being mediated in any given situation.

Resolving these issues matters because the path taken will frame the analysis, making, implementation and evaluation of law and policy in future. This is significant because of the constitutional and constitutive functions of media law as that which determines the conditions under which all other decision-making takes place. The distinction between the two functions – the constitutional and the constitutive – is critical. The former refers to the abstract principles expressed in the texts of constitutions or constitution-like documents upon which laws and regulations that deal with information, communication and culture rest; there are 20 such principles in the US Constitution and additional principles are found in other constitutions around the world. The latter refers to the actual structural and other effects of laws and regulations dealing with information, communication and culture on society, irrespective of intentions or abstract ideas upon which they may have been based.

While the US Constitution protected communication because it was believed necessary to democracy, much current law for information technologies and content is intended to serve quite other purposes. How a policy issue area is identified is political because it determines who participates in decision-making; the rhetorical frames, operational definitions and value hierarchies involved in decision-making; the analytical techniques and modes of argument used; and the resources considered pertinent. When an information technology problem is defined as an economic, industrial or trade issue rather than as media policy, protections for speech and other constitutional principles important to the media may not apply. An overemphasis on what is 'new' about digital technologies exacerbates the danger that fundamental principles developed over centuries to protect civil liberties and promote effective democratic processes will be lost in the electronic environment. Turning away from technologies and towards that which is being mediated – the public – keeps both constitutional and constitutive matters in view.

This chapter reviews the evolution of the definitional problem, identifies analytical challenges, critically reviews extant approaches to resolving the problem and proposes a definition of media policy as the subset of the larger domain of information policy that includes those laws, regulations and policy principles that have the effect of mediating the public itself. The chapter concludes by exploring a few exemplars of issues that were not on the traditional media policy agenda but are of critical importance today.[1] The case used to ground the discussion here is US law, but related stories appear in the history of other countries. The literature referenced includes not only contemporary works, but also important items from the past in a conversation that has now been underway since the 1950s.

The definitional problem

When the US Constitution and Bill of Rights were written, what we refer to as media law and policy was intended to ensure that citizens could use oral and print means of expression to communicate with each other and with their government. Because content must be distributed in multiple directions in order to be useful for political purposes, the synchronous and co-present sharing of ideas through assembly and asynchronous and distributed communication through publishing and the postal system were both protected.[2] Because in order to meaningfully discuss shared matters of concern citizens need access to information and freedom to form their own opinions on the basis of that information, these were also protected.[3] And because to be effective ideas and opinions must be communicated to those who can act, the First Amendment further protected the right to ask specific things of government.[4] While general ideas about human rights had been around for a while, at the time this was the most highly articulated treatment of communication principles from a legal perspective.

It didn't take long, however, to become more complicated. Technological innovation created truly mass media, expanding the set of regulatory subjects. New technologies of the second half of the 19th century, such as the electrified printing press that made mass consumption of newspapers possible for the first time, stimulated development of privacy law because it was felt that reporters intruded on personal privacy. Social concerns about uses of the telephone in the 19th century were trumped by government desire to intervene in the structure of the telephone system as a social networking technology by World War I. Other stimuli to the development of media law and regulation around the turn of the 20th century and during its first decades included attention to propaganda, distributed during war by the new communication distribution medium of the airplane. Distinctions among types of political speech received in-depth legal analyses when World War I pamphleteers – again dependent on the electrified printing press – were able to take advantage of windows of skyscrapers as a distribution medium to flood the streets with their messages. Perhaps not coincidentally, the word 'media' itself came into use during the period in which the first regulatory systems were being put in place for broadcasting, in the 1920s.

The cycle of innovation and legal reaction continued with each new development. Over time, judicial interpretation of constitutional law for the mediated environment in the USA articulated a number of dimensions along which rights and responsibilities were differentiated: *context* (public v. private); *content* (political v. economic v. cultural v. personal); *genre* (fact v. fiction, fact v. opinion, news v. history); *speakers* (public v. private, and individual v. corporate v. governmental); *receivers* (voluntary v. involuntary, adult v. minor, and competent adult v. incompetent adult); and *political condition* (war v. peace, elections v. between elections).[5]

In the 21st century, the field within which the media operate has broadened yet again. The directly communicative functions of the media are now a relatively small proportion of the overall role of information technologies in society. The distinction between public and private communicative contexts has become one of choice and will, rather than ownership, control and history of use. And we have come to understand that both non-political content and the infrastructure that carries it can have structural impact.

These historical factors make bounding the domain of media policy problematic. Conceptually, the field of media policy can be considered co-extant with that of information policy, broadly defined as all laws and regulations pertaining to information creation, processing, flows and use. The distinction between information and media policy remains important, however, in order to ensure that pertinent constitutional principles will underlie those activities by which citizens perceive themselves as members of a shared public and engage in public discourse about political affairs. Several classes of problems, however, confound the effort to carve media policy as a distinct domain out of the larger universe of information policy: those raised by technologies, media practices, features of the policy-making process and characteristics of the media as a specific issue area.

Technology-based problems

The phrase 'the convergence of technologies' conflates several analytical issues pertinent to the problem of bounding the domain of media policy. New information technologies are qualitatively different from those with which media policy has historically dealt; blur medium, genre, function and industry; are ubiquitously embedded in the objects of our material world; and replace slow-changing structuration processes with more rapid processes best described as 'flexible'.

From technology to meta-technology

The law has not historically distinguished between tools, technologies and meta-technologies, even though these differ along dimensions of legal importance:

1. *Tools* can be made and used by individuals working alone and make it possible to process matter or energy in single steps. The use of tools characterized the premodern era. Because communication is an inherently social act it may only be when marks are made for the purposes of reminding oneself of something that it can be said there are communication tools.
2. *Technologies* are social in their making and use; that is, they require a number of people to work together. They make it possible to link several processing steps together in the course of transforming matter or energy, but there is for each technology only one sequence in which those steps can be taken, only one or a few types of materials can be processed, and only one or a few types of outcomes can be produced. The shift from tools to technologies made industrialization possible, and the use of technologies thus characterizes the modern period. The printing press and the radio are examples of communication technologies.
3. *Meta-technologies* vastly expand the degrees of freedom with which humans can act in the social and material worlds. Meta-technologies enable long

processing chains, and there is great flexibility in the number of steps and the sequence with which they are undertaken. Meta-technologies can process an ever-expanding range of types of inputs and can produce an essentially infinite range of outputs. They are social, but enable solo activity within the socially produced network. Their use characterizes the postmodern world. Meta-technologies are always informational, and the internet is a premiere example of a meta-technology used for communication purposes.

The shift from technologies to meta-technologies affects the scope and scale of the policy subject, as in the transition from national telecommunications networks to the global network of networks that we refer to as the internet. The degrees of freedom offered by meta-technologies expand the range of alternative outcomes that must be considered by policy analysts, with those involved in information warfare and authors of malware marking the frontier, followed by those experimenting with social media and artists. Meta-technologies involve a causal chain that is potentially much longer and more variable than those with which policy analysis has historically dealt, requiring the development of both new policy tools and new methods for policy analysis. Policy-making is most effective when the subject of regulation is deeply understood, but few government officials understand the technologies that are being regulated or are familiar with what social scientists are learning about the ways in which those technologies are being used and the effects of those uses.

Convergence of communication styles

Media have been distinguished from each other by (1) the number of message receivers (one, a few, or many); (2) the nature of interactivity, if any, between sender and receiver; and (3) the difference between synchronicity and asynchronicity. These dimensions together may be described as a matter of style.

Historically, there has been experimentation with how to use each type of communication technology. The telephone was used as a mass medium in various ways from the 1870s through the 1920s (particularly in rural areas), and was used so again during the presidential election campaign of 2008. The radio is still used as a two-way medium for some specialized communities of users. The establishment of regulatory systems, however, also fixed the uses of each medium. As a result, specific media have become associated with particular styles of communication. Over the air (broadcast) television is mass communication, from one to many; it does not permit direct interactivity between viewers and programming; and it is experienced by its entire audience at the same time, synchronously. Wired telephony, on the other hand, is predominantly person to person (one to one), is by definition interactive and is synchronous. Personal letter writing is one to one and interactive, but asynchronous.

The internet blends communicative styles in all three dimensions. During a single session a user may communicate with a single person, small groups and the public *en masse*, often fluidly switching back and forth among the three. Similarly, one-way and interactive communications, both synchronous and asynchronous, can be mixed within a single session. This blending of communication styles is problematic for the definition of media policy because point-to-point communication with a single receiver can no longer be excluded from discussions of media law. Interactivity, too, must be included because it has been deemed constitutionally worthy of protection because of the way in which it changes a discourse and the nature of information exchanged.

Blurring of medium, function and industry

The impact of the convergence of communication and computing technologies does not stop with style. It further confounds any expectation that particular systems and industries will map onto each other in a stable way. This confounds efforts to apply laws and regulation that are industry-specific, as well as efforts to use law and regulation (largely but not exclusively via antitrust [competition] law) to keep industries separate from each other. It disrupts habits of policy analysis when methods used are based on assumptions about the social functions to be served by particular media industries. And it alters the economics of each of the industries involved.[6]

Ubiquitous embedded computing

We are accustomed to treating the media as an identifiable set of objects in which communicative capacity can be found and which serve only communicative functions, distinct from other objects and from ourselves. Increasingly, however, information technologies are ubiquitously embedded in the material world – in familiar objects such as cars and refrigerators; in the natural environment from soil, to the ocean, to trees; and even in people for security, aesthetic, or prosthetic reasons. This change presents a conceptual and operational challenge to those making, implementing and interpreting media law.

The media and flexible structuration

Constitutive processes involve structuration, the interaction between structure and agency, with the latter defined as the ability to effectively act on the basis of one's own intention. Constitutional protections for the media are intended to ensure that individuals have the communicative agency necessary to effect governance. Digital meta-technologies have added to our forms of possible agency and changed the nature of forms of power that have long existed. Political scientists typically distinguish among three forms of power. *Instrumental* power is the ability to control or shape behaviours through physical means. *Structural* power is the ability to control or shape behaviours through the design of institutions and rules. *Symbolic* power is the ability to affect behaviour through shaping perceptions and modes of thought. Informational meta-technologies have made a fourth form of power important. *Informational* power affects behaviour through manipulation of the informational bases of instrumental, structural and symbolic forms of power and through generating new forms of power. In addition to the actual and potential phases of power long familiar to political scientists, power can also now be exercised in its virtual phase, defined as tools of power that do not yet exist but that can be brought into being using extant resources and knowledge.[7]

Among the effects of informational power is a blurring of the distinction between agency and structure, for informational structure itself becomes agency. The notion that 'code is law' popularized though not originated by Lessig (1999), exemplifies acknowledgment of the structural importance of informational power. Breaking down the distinction between structure and agency makes structuration processes far more flexible, complicating media policy by dissolving the policy subject and introducing more complex modes of causality. There are agents that have not been recognized as such by the law, or there may be no identifiable agents at all. Causality may be indirect, indiscernible, affected by multiple intervening variables and involve causal chains that are beyond analytical reach. These changes in the nature of agency and causality are evident in practice-based problems faced by those seeking to define media policy.

Practice-based problems

Contemporary media practices make the problem of defining media policy more difficult not only because there is constant innovation, but also because genres are blurred, players have multiplied and policy subjects are now often networked rather than autonomous entities.

Blurring of genres

Genre distinctions – such as those between fact and fiction, fact and opinion, and news and history – are fundamental to such legal issues as libel, advertising regulation and postal rates. The blurring of genre thus adds conceptual problems to legal analysis. We continue to struggle with the application of standards of facticity that are important from the perspective of libel and fraud when they arise in mixed genres such as docudrama and infotainment. Arguments over whether to treat bloggers as journalists for legal purposes exemplify what this looks like in practice.

Tactical media

Tactical media practitioners work with the possibilities unleashed by the interchangeability of structure and agency. While mainstream and alternative media have historically used content to engage in political battles, the tactical media movement launched in the 1990s spurns struggles over content as a losing battle. Instead, these activists take seriously Marshall McLuhan's (1964/1994) insight that the medium *is* the message and have turned, instead, to manipulation of information production, processing and delivery systems. The goal is to alter the semiotic and electronic realities within which media operate, an exercise of informational power. Tactical media practitioners combine news and political commentary with art. Consumption, aesthetics and humour are viewed as opportunities to enact power, and the emphasis is on stand-alone events and ephemeral networks rather than persuasive campaigns and enduring social movements. Media law and policy focused on content are inadequate in the face of tactical media. Tactical media practitioners are quite self-aware that what they are doing, therefore, is 'pre-policy', stimulating legal innovation.

Everyone's a player

In the pre-digital era most areas of media policy affected professional communicators almost exclusively; libel law and problems of copyright infringement are good examples. In the electronic environment, however, everyone who communicates runs the danger of bumping into the same legal and regulatory issues, even when individuals perceive themselves to be involved solely in interpersonal communication. Traditional approaches to media policy that orient towards professional communications and established media organizations must be reconsidered in this context.

Competition law (antitrust) in a network society

Competition law has been used heavily in the USA since the late 19th century to restrain firms in the media industry; indeed, much of the current shape of the telecommunications industry still reflects antitrust decisions made in 1913 and 1956. Intertwined ownership of the infrastructure and the multidimensional networking of firms, however, can make it difficult to treat firms as distinct and autonomous units for the purposes of antitrust law. Constant innovation, the emphasis on services rather than goods and the interchangeability of goods and services make it difficult to conduct antitrust analysis of products; globalization makes it difficult to conduct antitrust analysis of markets.

Policy process-based problems

Some of the problems in defining media policy today derive from the nature of policy-making itself, such as the tension between incremental and radical change, the importance of latent as well as manifest policy, invisibility, policy interdependence and precession, and relationships between public policy and other types of influential decision-making.

Transition policy

Policy change can be radical, when an entire body of existing law is abandoned in favour of building anew from scratch during revolutionary periods, or incremental, in a series of small evolutionary steps. Incremental policy-making is necessary for working decision-makers in both the public and private sectors who must operate within existing law under severe time and resource constraints. Too, there is always a lag between the development of new ideas about and knowledge of social circumstances and their application in arenas as detailed and complex as the law – a lag reinforced by reliance upon precedent. It is not possible to understand all of the effects of new technologies in their entirety immediately; it took, after all, about 500 years to begin to fully comprehend the effects of the printing press. Those who analyze, make and implement media policy today face the problem of trying to achieve incremental legal change during a period of revolutionary change in the policy subject.

Latent and manifest policy

Not everything that falls within the domain of media policy is labelled as such. Thus, borrowing from the late Robert K. Merton (1955, 1981), it is useful to distinguish between media policy that is manifest – clearly directed at what has traditionally been understood as the mass media – and that which is latent. The general notion of latent policy first appeared in the 1920s, and has since gained currency in fields ranging from technology policy to political science. Latent policy includes that which is created as a side effect of decisions aimed at other subjects, as when Securities and Exchange Commission regulation of the financial markets mandates the distribution of particular types of information. It can develop when its subject matter is categorized under other names, as in the 'confidence- and security-building measures' (CSBMs) incorporated into arms control treaties of the 1980s and 1990s that required specific types of information collection and distribution in support of foreign policy. Latent policy can also appear synergistically when policy from a variety of decision-making arenas interacts to produce something quite different in combination, as when the use of alternative dispute resolution systems to reduce the burden on the courts results in a loss of public access to the kinds of information about deals made when conflicts are resolved that the Constitution recognized as so essential to a democracy. The effects of latent policy can be direct. Its importance adds to the definitional task by requiring inclusion within the boundaries of the field those matters that have not habitually been assumed to fall within the domain, placing new demands on the research agenda.

Invisible policy

Many types of media policy decisions are highly influential but little discussed, or even acknowledged. In the USA, the world of media policy includes such things as presidential signing statements through which a president unilaterally presents his or her own interpretation of a law just signed combined with a statement of the extent to which the law will be followed, decisions by federal and state attorneys general that guide policing practices and court decisions, and the practice of hiding statutory law directed at one issue within a piece of legislation commonly understood to deal with another matter. The significance of invisible sources of law and regulation to media realities makes it necessary to take such decision-making venues into account in the process of defining the field. Invisible policy is formal and is developed within government, but has largely escaped attention.

Policy interdependence

Media policy made at different levels of the social structure is highly interdependent, reflecting the emergence of networked forms of organization in all aspects of life and the interpenetration of political structures. Indeed, for many countries around the world, international organizations are as or more important than national governments in shaping their media policy, and it was in the area of the information infrastructure that the European Economic Commission (EEC) for the first time explicitly applied Commission law to member states. Though this interdependence is often necessary, and indeed inevitable, it can also create a 'policy trap'. Some efforts to extend US or European law outside its borders occur 'naturally', through harmonization of legal systems or the movement of decision-making into the realm of private contracts when there is a legal vacuum rather than through the excesses of extra-territoriality (unilateral efforts by a nation state to exert its law outside its borders). Numerous other forms of 'policy transfer' or 'policy convergence' are now underway, though relatively little studied in the area of media policy. The globalization of the information infrastructure and growing appreciation of the populations in developing countries as potential markets had been heightening developed country interest in enriching the infrastructure and technology access of developing countries over the last couple of decades, though that may be affected by responses to the global financial crisis.

Interdependence also characterizes media policy within each country. In the USA, there is a tension between the desire to support the national information infrastructure at the cost of state law and forces stimulating decentralization of decision-making. Influence runs from the bottom up as well as the top down, for even decision-making at the local level can have an influence on national policy.

Policy precession

Treatment of policy as a design problem must also take into account interactions among the effects of policies, what we can describe as policy *precession*, which requires analysts to link research on multiple laws and regulations as they affect each other rather than looking at issues in isolation. Precession, a concept derived from physics, occurs when two systems interact such that a decision or event in one changes the axis along which decisions or actions in the other can take place. The familiar notion of path dependence suggests precession but does not incorporate sensitivity to the number of precessive steps that may be linked, the degree of complexity precession adds to the analytical problem, or differences in the angles of change. When precessive links are understood by some players but not by others, it is possible to erect barriers to meaningful participation in decision-making on one issue by foreclosing options through filters or actions designed by a related piece of legislation or regulation. An example is provided by an interaction between patent and antitrust law. The ability to assert property rights in ways of doing business through patent law combined with the trend towards asserting property rights as early as possible in a processing chain in order to claim ownership of all products of that process means that antitrust law may no longer be able to reach some pertinent types of anticompetitive practices. In another example, the content, interpretation and implementation of privacy laws significantly changed in many countries when antiterrorism laws were put in place.

Public policy and other decision-making

Formal policy mechanisms unfold within a broader legal field as understood in the Bourdieuian sense. Public policy now also interacts with decisions made by private decision-makers, and there are purely private sources of decision-making with constitutive impact, informal aspects of decision-making processes that are highly influential but have received relatively little analytical attention, and technological and normative trends with enormous structural force. Decisions made in all of these arenas should be included within the definition of media policy. Some of these non-traditional types of media policy are relatively obscure and may require specialized knowledge in order to be comprehensible, such as those made by technical standards bodies. Others are easier to understand, like the role played by ISPs in determining speech conditions for the internet.

Issue-based problems

Political scientists group together issues related to the same subject into 'issue areas'. Compared to traditional issue areas, such as defence, agriculture and trade, media policy is relatively new and, for digital technologies, very new. Other unique characteristics of media policy include the multiplicity of players and decision-making arenas and the level of impact on other issue areas.

Multiplicity of players and decision-making arenas

An unusually large number of players, types of players and decision-making venues are involved in the making of media policy. While in other areas, such as tuna fishing, there is a natural limit to those with a legitimate involvement and few ambiguities regarding responsibilities, information technologies – and thus decision-making about them – are pervasive. As a result, literally dozens of entities – governmental, quasi-non-governmental and private – have a history of some type of involvement and, often, a stake. Within any single branch of government several different agencies can be involved, often in conflict with each other. The result can be gridlock, an inability to make policy at all. Because of this multiplicity, it is inadequate to use a venue-based approach (e.g., 'policy made by the FCC') to defining media policy.

Impact on other policy issue areas

Another unique aspect of media policy is the degree to which it influences decision-making in other issue areas through constraints on both decision-making processes and the lenses through which issues are viewed. Media policy creates the communicative space within which all public and decision-making discourses takes place; determines the kinds of information that will be available to inform those discourses; provides the stuff of the institutions within which and processes through which decision-making takes place; and offers many of the policy tools used to implement policy decisions directed at other types of social processes. The relative importance of media policy confounds the problem because it adds pressure to the politics of the definitional process discussed. To the degree that those involved with decision-making in other issue areas *understand* the importance to what they do, there will be efforts to subsume media policy within treatment of other issue areas or to define it as something other than media altogether.

Definitional approaches

The effort to keep media policy in sight in an expanding legal field for information and information technologies began several decades ago. A review of the literature reveals a variety of definitional approaches, some implicit and some explicit – by list, legacy legal category, industry, stage of the information production chain and impact on society. Each has strengths and weaknesses.

By list

Early efforts to think about media policy in the new environment simply listed areas to be included. In an influential governmental report of the 1980s, for example, policy analyst Leeson (1984) included technical knowledge and its diffusion, physical network components and structure, services offered and terms of network use, and regulation of content. Communication scholar Tunstall (1986) during the same period added industrial planning along with aerospace defence research and development because each of these affects the nature of the infrastructure available to the media. This approach has the appeal of being relatively easy, but lists are inevitably incomplete and rapidly obsolesce. Because they are not based on a coherent logic, they do not provide a foundation from which policy analysis can be conducted.

By legacy legal category

The legacy approach to defining media policy orients around the categories established by statutory and regulatory law, separately for each technology.

There are strengths in this approach: it is familiar; precedent is well developed; the terms of legacy law still govern daily activity and provide the conceptual, rhetorical and analytical frameworks for policy discourse; many traditional issues are still adequately addressed with legacy law – false advertising is still false advertising, and libel is still libel.

The phrase 'legacy law' has come into use because inherited legal categories often no longer fit empirical realities. Diverse legal and regulatory systems have developed over time in response to specific technologies, each defining rights and responsibilities differently. The right to editorial control provides an example: it is unlimited in print up to the boundaries determined by constitutional law, constrained in broadcasting and forbidden in telecommunications; in the digital environment the same message could easily travel through all three types of systems as it is produced and delivered, and thus be simultaneously the subject of all three types of regulation. The silo habits of legacy law also impede our ability to directly confront issues that span traditional legal categories, as in the problem of regulating privately owned interfaces with the public communications network. One such interface (the mailbox) is discussed in constitutional law, while another (CPE, or 'customer premises equipment', from the telephone to the computer) is a matter of telecommunications regulation within administrative law. Though the two simply present different faces of the same issue, well-developed discussions in each area of the law never reference or draw upon each other, nor are the outcomes of those discussions necessarily consistent with each other.

By media industry

Because policy issues often arise when they become problematic for the corporate world, there has been experimentation with industry-oriented approaches. Such approaches are appealing because they speak directly to immediate concerns and can form the basis of discussion and operationalization via 'best practices' within industry-specific contexts such as trade associations. There is, however, no longer any fixed map of industrial sectors, and there is not likely to be one for quite a while, if ever again. An industry-based approach also skews the discourse in favour of profit and efficiency at the cost of values such as equity, human rights and the protection of civil liberties. From an industry perspective, those who make media messages become 'producers' and those who 'receive' them are 'consumers', rather than 'citizens', or active participants in a culture. Focusing on industries also raises the risk that an approach to resolving a problem within one industry may be incompatible with techniques or interpretations used in other sectors.

By stage of the information production chain

Models of an information production chain are rife, though not always explicit. Such models may be explicit but are always at least implicit in the minds of media policy-makers. They are implicit in constitutional law, for example, as a means of distinguishing among types of communicative spaces for the purposes of differential application of the First Amendment.

The model of an information production chain described here has proven useful in the study of media policy in a wide variety of domestic, international and comparative arenas.

This approach includes the stages of information creation (*de novo*, generation and collection), processing (cognitive and algorithmic), storage, transportation, distribution, destruction and seeking. Relations between stages of an information production chain change when new linkages become possible between stages of the chain, as when the web makes it possible for producers and users of information to become directly linked; when parties at a stage of the chain lose their independent functions, as when the intermediaries between producers and users are no longer necessary; or when relations among parties change in such a way that there is reason for drastic reorganization, as multiple information providers choose to pool their resources. The entire information production chain can be seen as the subject of media policy: there are no messages to send without information creation and processing, information is often transported in the course of gathering inputs into message creation, storage may be combined with distribution (as in books, or records) and, while it has received less attention than other media policy matters, destruction of the historical record created by the media is an important political issue.

One advantage of defining media policy via reference to the information production chain is that doing so provides a meso-level theoretical link between the abstract and the empirical. Another advantage is that it permits exclusion of certain types of information, actors, or modes of processing from either specific or all stages of the chain, thus incorporating the sensitivities of those who resist the commoditization of all information. The model of an information production chain is useful in breaking down complex communicative processes into their elements for differential analysis and legal treatment of those elements. Thus, while interactive and non-interactive, synchronous and asynchronous, and intercast, narrowcast and broadcast communications may all be mixed by users of the internet, the concept of an information production chain can be of value in determining just how to distinctly apply legal principles. The heuristic utility of the approach has been demonstrated.

There are also problems with this approach as a boundary-defining mechanism, most importantly the lack of a consensus on ways of distinguishing among different types of information processing beyond the gross distinction suggested above between algorithmic and cognitive modes. The analytical problem it presents can be complex, for many media processes, phenomena and products involve more than one stage of the chain.

By impact on society

Some advocacy groups and scholars start not from the law, but from the social impact of the law. The Center for Media Education (CME) deals with any type of communication policy that affects children (from media violence to software filtering) (www.cme.org), for example, and the Electronic Privacy Information Center (EPIC) looks at any type of policy that has an impact on personal privacy (from encryption to the US Patriot Act) (www.epic.org). The value of this approach is that it turns attention away from the minutiae of existing law and regulation and towards the point of the policy-making exercise – building and maintaining the kind of society we want to live in. It offers a way of incorporating the entire range of values that need to be accommodated within the policy-making process. This approach makes it possible to bring the historically disparate medium-specific issues within a common framework, and in turn can enrich analysis of specific problems by bringing to bear upon them pertinent discourse irrespective of originary legal realm. It offers both justification and techniques for finding the best from legacy law as law, policy and regulation are adapted and transformed to meet today's circumstances. And it encourages the enrichment of policy thinking by theories and empirical knowledge derived from the social sciences and humanities. Often, however – as in much of the discussion about the 'digital divide' – concerns are expressed in such general terms that it is difficult to identify specific laws or regulation that might usefully be the subject of attention. Bounding the domain of media policy by social impact also places significant demands on communication theory. Because most who do this start with a single issue of concern, there is no overarching framework within which to relate one issue to another or to serve as a foundation for policy analysis. A theoretical response to this problem is possible, but would be a formidable intellectual task.

Defining media policy for the 21st century

With all of this in mind, how do we distinguish media law and regulation from other policy dealing with information technologies and the content they carry? To be useful, an approach to bounding the domain of media policy for the 21st century must have the following characteristics:

1. *Validity* – it must map onto empirical reality.
2. *Comprehensiveness* – it must include all matters of concern.

3. *Theoretically based* – it must rest on a theoretical foundation that can provide a basis for thinking through positions on media policy issues.
4. *Methodologically operationalizable* – it must use concepts that are susceptible to analysis via social science research methods, in order to facilitate the process of informing policy positions with the results of research and advances in theory.
5. *Translatable* – it must be cast in terms that make it possible to translate new policy principles, tools and specific policies into the language of legacy law in order to enable incremental legal change.

None of the definitional approaches reviewed above meets all of these criteria. Indeed, it may not be possible for a single approach to serve all of the functions that must be fulfilled – developing a theoretical framework for the field, identifying specific media policy issues for attention, analyzing those issues in ways that incorporate the range of pertinent types of social science knowledge and translating the results of that analysis into the language and genres of the legal system. An alternative is to accept a multiplicity of definitional faces, each of utility at a different stage of the policy-making process.

Stage 1: a broad vision

The first step is achieving a broad vision of the field within which media policy questions arise. Doing so is necessary in order to develop a theoretical stance from which to examine issues, place various issues relative to each other and understand interactions among issues. Information policy is used here as an umbrella concept to broadly define the field as all law and regulation that deals with information creation, processing, flows and use. Use of a model of an information production chain as a heuristic makes it possible to read across the categories of legacy law to determine what falls within the domain of information policy and what does not; its stages include the following.

Information creation

Information can be created in three ways: it can be the product of a genuinely original creative act and thus come out of nothingness, so to speak (creation *de novo*); it can be the outcome of systematic procedures for developing such as those referred to by the concept of facticity (e.g., the 'facts' of journalism) or the methodologies of statistics (e.g., 'data'). Information is also created when it is generated as a byproduct of other life activities and processes, such as when one interacts with an institution (e.g., registering for a class, getting a driver's licence) or changes one's status (e.g., gets married). Media policy questions involving information creation include matters of intellectual property rights and access to both information and infrastructure.

Information processing

Information processing can be algorithmic (undertaken through procedures describable in mathematical form and thus accomplishable by computers) or cognitive (undertaken through procedures only available to the human brain to date). Some forms of information processing may be exclusive to one or the other of these categories, while other forms of information processing (e.g., alphabetization) can be undertaken either way.

There is a plethora of ways of more finely articulating differences among types of information processing, a task of importance across policy-making venues and issues because more subtle distinctions are critical to the interpretation and implementation of the law. The work needed to develop a set of distinctions that can achieve consensual acceptance is therefore a critical item for the research agenda. Media policy issues in this area include restrictions on information that come from defining it as not speech and therefore not covered under the First Amendment (part of the debate over encryption), or as a result of the government's claim that access to information in the public domain does not include the right to process that information (a claim made in the *Progressive* case of the 1970s). Information processing also raises antitrust issues, as was seen in the legal challenge to Microsoft's treatment of the relationship between its browser and its operating system.

Information transportation

Information transportation takes place when a single message is transported (to one, a few or many). A conversation on the street, a letter or the production of a single documentary would be examples of information transportation. This stage of the chain involves single messages. Restrictions on content or communicative behaviours put in place by ISPs as well as in non-electronic environments, including surveillance, are examples of media policy issues that can arise here.

Information distribution

Information distribution is distinguished from transportation because it involves regular transportation of messages over time to either narrowcast or broadcast audiences, and often with a commercial aspect. Rather than messages, distribution involves channels. Media policy issues at this stage of the information production chain include trying to ensure a diversity of voices in all facets of the public sphere, access to the distribution network, anonymity and censorship via the chilling effect of surveillance.

Information storage

Information storage occurs through fixation in a medium and through archival and cultural practices. Storage is important because it enables the communication of ideas across space and across time and because it forms the basis of our social memory. From the media policy perspective, information storage and destruction issues are two sides of the same coin. Laws and regulation that mandate the creation, storage and destruction of public records create the public memory so are important as an input into policy-making and as a matter of identity. The reliability and security of the information infrastructure are also important.

Information destruction

Just as information can be produced essentially *de novo*, unlike matter it can be utterly lost or destroyed as well. The fragility of digital information, and the ease with which it can be altered, have increased the salience of issues raised by the risk of loss of knowledge and memory as policy issues. Loss of public memory through destruction of public records is the key media policy issue at this stage of the information production chain.

Information seeking

Sociologists and psychologists have brought information seeking to our attention as a distinct type of cognitive and social process worthy of attention in its own right. Information seeking has also been examined from an economic perspective, as its costs are of importance when considering research and development budgets, risk analysis and in a number of other arenas. Incorporating sensitivity to cultural, social, personal and cognitive differences in modes of information seeking into laws and regulations is one possible policy response. Positive support for education in media literacy is another. Surveillance is an issue here since government knowledge of information-seeking practices can have a chilling effect.

Media policy and the information production chain

Media activities typically involve at least two and often more of the above stages of the information production chain. These stages may be sequenced in any order in another difference from processing in the material world. Legal rights and responsibilities differ according to stage of the chain, however, as do the political, economic, cultural and social forces and effects of what is undertaken at each stage. Thus use of the information production chain in analysis of a media policy issue must:

1. distinguish between the different stages of the chain involved;
2. separately analyze the policy issues involved at each stage of the chain pertinent to a particular media event, content, or process; and
3. link analyses of the issues at each stage together in order to master the effects of interdependence and precession.

In summary, then, media policy, in its broadest sense, is co-extant with the field of information policy, which involves issues that arise at every stage of an information production chain that includes information creation, processing, flows and use.

Stage 2: narrowing the lens

Though media policy issues can be identified at every stage of the information production chain, not everything within the broad field of information policy involves the traditional media policy concerns with freedom of expression and participatory decision-making regarding the fundamental structures of society. To bound media policy in such a way that constitutional concerns remain focal, the question must be asked: what is being mediated? Typically, the media have been understood to mediate between sender and receiver, entities involved in the *process* of mediation. Alternatively, however, the word could be used to refer to the *product* of mediation – the public. Doing so provides a definitional principle for narrowly bounding the domain of media policy, and suggests three additional definitional principles as corollaries.

Definitional principle: mediating the public

The question of just what it is that is being mediated has not been addressed by media policy analysts in the past because it has been assumed that the answer is obvious: the media are technologies that come in between the sender(s) and receiver(s) of a message. Though this is accurate, it is also trivial, addresses only part of the mediation process and has little analytical utility. Focusing attention instead on the product of mediation, the public, provides a conceptual foundation for analysis of media policy in terms of its constitutional and constitutive functions. The *constitutional* functions of media policy, determined by constitutional law, address the conditions under which the public can actively engage in the production and reproduction of the society in which members of the public live. Within the constraints thus established, the media play the *constitutive* role of structurally shaping society through its facilitation of the constructive roles of the public. Thus:

> media policy as narrowly defined is that subset of information policy that deals with those technologies, processes and content by which the nature of the public is mediated.

Corollary 1: media in the public interest

Starting from this definitional principle makes it possible to narrow the field of media policy by excluding issues the resolution of which serves *only* economic or other purposes. Patricia Aufderheide has offered a definition of the public interest that may be useful here: it is 'discourse about shared problems that require shared solutions' (Aufderheide, 2002). This suggests a corollary: media policy is that policy which affects public discourse about shared problems that require shared solutions.

Corollary 2: media for all of the public

There is a temptation to restrict the domain of media policy to the mass media, those technologies and processes through which a message is transmitted from one point to many points. However, narrowcast communication (from one point to a few points) and 'intercast', or point-to-point communication (from one point to one point) are also important to the nature of the public and public discourse, and protections for these are also rooted in the Constitution. All three are mixed in the internet. Thus, media policy is that policy that affects discourse from and to the public and within the public sphere.

Corollary 3: media with either direct or indirect constitutive effect

Some existing media law requires a direct causal relation between a message and its effect, as in the 'imminence' requirement of the test for clear and present danger used by the judiciary in the USA.[8] The strengthening of constitutional protections for commercial speech because of its ultimate political importance in recent decades demonstrates growing appreciation for the constitutive role of indirect causal relations as well. The lengthening of the causal chain involving media technologies discussed increases the relative proportion of actions or decisions that may ultimately have an impact on discourse in the public sphere but do not directly do so; technical standards for the information infrastructure provide a vivid example of this. Thus a further corollary is suggested: media policy involves law and regulation of those matters that have either direct or indirect impact on the nature of the public.

Stage 3: analysis of media policy issues

The ultimate analytical criterion for any type of policy must be its constitutional effect. Other types of questions may usefully and appropriately be addressed along the way, involving feasibility, economic consequences, cultural impact, and winners and losers. The first and last question in any analysis must, however, be the impact of a decision on the nature of society – its identity, structure, borders and change of society. Social theory, as well as the results of social science research, has much to offer in response to such questions, though casting legal analysis solely in terms of legal precedent and economics has provided a conceptual barrier to policy use of such theory and data. To frame policy analysis in such a way that social theory and data become desiderata as decision-making inputs, and to ensure that analysis is oriented towards fundamental constitutional goals, then, the definitional face of media policy at the analytical stage must be oriented around society itself: media policy deals with issues that affect the identity, structure, borders and change of the society served by the nation state.

Stage 4: translation of analysis into law

In order to achieve efficacy, the results of society-oriented analyses must finally be translated into the language, and the genres, of legacy law. It is only in this way that theoretically and empirically informed analysis of media policy issues can provide the basis for incremental legal change. One of the biggest intellectual problems faced by those involved in media policy is building bridges between the definitional approaches necessary at different stages of the policy-making process. Doing so, however, is an important element of the definition of media policy. In order to be effective, theoretically and empirically based analysis of media policy issues must shift its definitional face so that its conclusions are translated into the language and genres of legacy law.

Exemplar media policy issues

Using this definitional approach, traditional mass media and the legal issues with which they are involved remain important. So, too, though, do the newer social media technologies and practices still under experimentation, and other types of technologies and uses with which the word 'media' has not typically been associated. A few examples may be helpful.

Internet service provider terms of service

Whether one is accessing the internet through a commercial internet service provider (ISP) or an entity serving an ISP-like function, such as a university or a library, one must agree to terms of service before being allowed online. These agreements are contracts that are the ultimate user interface with a flow-down contract system put in place by the Internet Corporation for Assigned Names and Numbers (ICANN), the global organization that manages the internet. Most of these agreements include provisions that sidestep, undermine, or counter altogether legal protections for freedom of speech and common expectations regarding intellectual property rights.[9] In the USA, one is free to sign away constitutional rights if one chooses, but historically this has been an option in situations in which there was also freedom to choose. If one did not want to give up one's right to be politically active, for example, one did not have to sign an employment contract requiring that abandonment of a constitutional right in order to work for AT&T. Today, however, there is no alternative mode of access to the internet. Terms of service agreements are becoming more and more like each other over time, so switching from one ISP to another is also not a meaningful option. Protections for free speech have long been considered essential to the public's ability to communicate with each other about shared matters of political concern. Should it be legal to require internet users to give up these rights?

Electronic voting machines

Laws and regulations related to election campaigns are recognized around the world as important elements of media policy. How the vote takes place has not in the past received attention from the media policy community. There is abundant evidence, however, that the types of electronic voting machines in use during the first decade of the 21st century are easily tampered with in ways that can significantly skew tallies – and the outcome of elections. There is also evidence that this potential has been actualized in election tallies that produced results that were not representative of the actual vote. Vote tallies are one way in which the nature of the public is defined. Falsification of these tallies inaccurately represents the public to itself – and has enduring political consequences. Under these conditions, laws and regulations dealing with electronic voting machines and practices should be considered a matter of media policy.

Data retention

Allegedly driven by antiterrorism concerns, data retention regulation has been put in place in the USA, the European Union and other places around the world which requires ISPs and other entities to retain data about e-mail and other use of the internet for extended periods of time in case it should be of governmental interest for surveillance purposes. People who are aware that they are under surveillance typically change their communication practices; in the contemporary antiterrorism environment the expectation that surveillance is possible and perhaps likely has caused many individuals to refrain from seeking out certain types of information or discussing particular issues online. Data retention regulation significantly deepens the potential danger to political speech from online communications and information seeking because the opportunity for surveillance changes from the ephemeral moment to, depending on the pertinent regulation, years. Given that communications within or between many countries will flow through servers in other countries, it is probably most wise to assume that the longest period required for data retention potentially is applicable everywhere. When data retention affects political knowledge and political speech, it is a matter of media policy.

Cell phone regulation

There are a number of ways in which regulations of cell phones can be understood as media policy, though historically telephony and the media were considered two very different legal subjects. Here we will just look at the legal impact of one type of cell phone use, mobilization of groups for participation in an event. This use of the cell phone in the political context has received a great deal of attention since its success – after weeks of training before the event – in the 'Battle of Seattle' demonstrations against the World Trade Organization. Legal treatment of demonstrators responding to this organizational tool falls in the category of traditional media policy, but in the past uses of telephones to organize a political demonstration was not the subject of media policy. The same functions of the cell phone have also increasingly been turned to the purposes of popular culture, generating swarms of individuals who convene at a specified spot to engage in play briefly and then disperse. Because these swarms can disrupt other activity, and because they can leave behind litter and possibly property damage, some governments are now considering regulations specific to such swarms. It is also possible that governments might choose to intervene in such activities by forbidding cell phone vendors and cell phone service providers from making it possible to communicate with more than one person at a time. From this perspective, regulation of cell phones is a media policy matter. It is impossible to know whether the political activities on their own would have led to these developments, but it is analytically interesting to note that the actual trigger has been cultural activities that then have political consequences.

Technical standards

The development of technical standards – the 'how many doo-hickies go on the whatie-what' question – has largely been treated as a matter of industrial policy or, perhaps, innovation policy, to be handled by engineers. In recent years, though, we have come to recognize that technology design and network architecture can have law-like structural effects that need attention from a media policy perspective because of their impact on the public sphere. Both specific standards and the nature of standard-setting processes should be subjected to analysis by media policy scholars. This is a difficult area for those in media policy, however, for it requires a level of technological expertise for which training is largely not offered in under-graduate and postgraduate media studies curricula.

Radio frequency identification (RFID) chips

The bar code scanners that were the first widely used digital application for tracking inventory came into the media world when codes and scanners became media or images for artists, but otherwise – like analogue inventory systems that preceded the use of bar codes – have not been the subject of media policy. The same cannot be said for RFID chips. Artists have also used these, but, more importantly, these miniscule chips are increasingly being implanted in retail goods for inventory tracking. While it is possible to have such chips 'turned off' at the checkout counter so that signals are no longer emitted after purchase points, this is largely not done. As a result, those who purchase items with RFID chips – say, from Walmart – carry with them identification information linked to the purchaser. This raises privacy issues that fall squarely within the realm of media policy, for the use of such chips can affect representations of the public in aggregated data and by presenting data about movements and activities that may be analyzed in order to derive inferences about political intention.

Conclusions

It is not the job of media policy to sustain either research or commercial industries. Redefining the domain helps us pursue the goals of protecting civil liberties and promoting effective participatory democracy under current political conditions. It is the public – our ability to act together politically – that is being mediated by media laws and regulations today. Bounding the domain of media law and policy in the 21st century in this way provides a valid foundation for thinking about laws and regulations in today's environment and keeps our focus on the constitutional and constitutive matters of the greatest importance. The approach to media policy analysis described here as a means of operationalizing this conceptualization of media policy offers a set of pragmatic steps that facilitate the effort to make incremental changes to the law as it applies to technological and social conditions that are undergoing radical change.

Notes

1. Much of this chapter was first published under the title, 'Where Has Media Policy Gone? Defining the Field in the Twenty-First Century', in *Communication Law and Policy* (Braman, 2004a). Here, that journal article has undergone some revision and updating, and the section that discusses specific policy exemplars is new. Thanks go to editor of the journal, Wat Hopkins, for his excellent editorial work during the first presentation of these ideas, and to Stylianos Papathanassopoulos and Ralph Negrine for the opportunity to take the argument one step further. The original journal article has a much more extensive citation apparatus for those who wish to deepen their knowledge of the long histories of the pertinent literatures.
2. The First Amendment protects assembly and the Postal Provision of the Constitution (Article 1, Section 8, Clause 7) established a postal service in order to provide universal access to the kind of distributed communication system considered critically necessary for the functioning of a democracy.
3. The principle of open government was established in a very general way in the Constitution in Article 1, Section 5, which mandates that Congress report to the public on its activities through a journal, and in Article 2, Section 3, which requires the President to provide Congress with information regarding the conditions of the country. The principle that individuals and groups have the right to form their own ideas and opinions is included in the First Amendment protection of opinion and indirectly in the 'mission statement' that introduces the Constitution.
4. The right to seek change in the governance system is protected via inclusion of the right to petition the government in the First Amendment, and via the vote.
5. These distinctions among types of constitutional spaces of importance to media law and policy receive extended treatment in the chapter on constitutional principles and the spaces they create in Braman, 2007.
6. Ithiel de Sola Pool's *Technologies of Freedom* (1983) remains essential reading for anyone who wants to understand the history of the three very different regulatory systems for the media that developed in the USA and its insights into

the inevitability and likely outcome of the problems to be faced in the course of the convergence of these regulatory systems. The details of this case study as handled by Pool also provide invaluable heuristics for those studying the same problematic history in other countries.

7. This definition of power in its virtual phase is in debt to the definition of virtual production processes offered by Italian economist Roberto Scazzieri (1993).

8. This is one of four elements required to deem speech of such danger that it is legitimate for the state to try to stop it. The other elements are that the content of the speech has the effect of incitement, that there be intention to incite and that there is a reasonable probability that the action being incited would actually take place.

9. For a study of the extent to which this was true half a dozen years ago, see Braman and Lynch (2003).

The Age of Access? Information Policy and Social Progress

Alistair Duff

Introduction

The 'postmodern' period has witnessed a growing appetite for information policy, both as a field of scholarship and a political preoccupation. It is not difficult to see why this should be the case. If we live in an information society, as many, although not all, believe, then information policy, it seems to follow, must be of paramount – or at least major – importance. Yet, in both theory and practice, information policy has not yet reached any kind of satisfying plateau. In the academy, it suffers from conceptual underdevelopment, disciplinary territorialism and even the absence of a widely shared definition. In the real world, too, measures promulgated as information policies have often lacked coherence, while, at the same time, many policies that are, arguably, information policies continue to be packaged with alternative labels. All of this reflects the chronic elasticity of the central concept, information, and consequent confusion regarding the objectives of an information society. The aim in the present chapter is to try to map the academic specialism of information policy with greater precision, building on useful previous work mainly from an information studies stable, and then also to suggest some paths down which the field could go in the future.

The discussion will begin with a brief history of information policy, highlighting Marc Porat's seminal contribution to the development of contemporary terminology and conventions. The current state of the information policy 'art' is then ascertained, with special emphasis both on the scoping of its subject matter – exactly how many issues are covered? – and on the specialism's location within the galaxy of academic disciplines. It will be argued that information policy must be understood as a multidisciplinary formation whose academic sources, while already diverse, will need to expand further, in directions such as political philosophy and (even) 'futurology'. Information policy thus needs to be more clearly positioned as a normative field, one which utilizes rigorous axiological argumentation to articulate goals for the future of society. The remainder of the chapter centres on a proposal that information policy fits inside the larger interdisciplinary specialism of *information society studies*, where its role is to prescribe conceptions of the good society. The chapter is offered primarily as a small contribution to conceptual groundwork, rather than as a vehicle for the author's opinions about the normative content of particular policies. However, such work, if sound, should facilitate practical progress towards what, presumably, we all desire: an 'age of access' (Cherry, 1985).

Marc Porat and the pioneering of information policy

In the beginning, it is said, there was information, and it seems clear, as suggested above, that the idea of information policy is anchored in bigger claims about the existence and nature of a so-called information society. While full-scale examinations of the information society thesis are available elsewhere (e.g., Duff, 2000; Webster, 2006), some introductory remarks will be germane to our present purposes. The first strongly recognizable argument to the effect that a modern nation was undergoing structural transformation towards an information society can be found in Fritz Machlup's *Production and Distribution of Knowledge in the United States* (1962). Machlup, an economist by trade, built his case on a fresh reading of occupational and national income statistics, concluding that the fastest-growing industries in the USA – higher education, information services, the mass media, etc. – were essentially engaged in various forms of knowledge production and dissemination. At much the same time in Japan, a *johoka shakai* (informationized society) tradition was getting off the ground, there drawing upon telecommunications research into the explosive growth of data flows (Ito, 1981). A third version of the information society thesis had also long been gestating: soon to become the best-known of the three, it stressed the role of technology, especially computers, in the 'informatization' of society (Nora and Minc, 1980). Much of this output, predictably enough, fell straight into the trap of technological determinism, but in its more sophisticated expressions (Fuchs, 2008; Slevin, 2000) it has helped to explain the social, economic and political significance of the 'information revolution'.

In addition to this trio of more or less *sui generis* schools of thought, there has been an elite cadre of information society theorists harbouring the more ambitious aim of working up a synthetic account of the information age in all of its dimensions. The classic statement was sociologist Daniel Bell's *Coming of Post-Industrial Society* (1999[1973]). It is difficult to exaggerate the impact of Bell's eloquent advocacy of post-industrialism, not only throughout academia, but also on policy-makers across the world. In his introduction to an anniversary edition, Bell notes with evident satisfaction that 'the term, the phrase, the idea, the concept of post-industrial society has passed into common currency and the academic lexicon' (Bell, 1999: ix). He reels off a list of public figures known to have cited his concept, including Margaret Thatcher, Bill Clinton, Tony Blair and even the Unabomber. These (in)famous persons are merely a fraction of the audience that has come into some kind of receptive contact with Bellian theses about 'new principles of innovation, new modes of social organization, and new classes in society' (Bell, 1999: xi). As Bell was writing his afterword, Manuel Castells (1996–8) was completing publication of *The Information Age* books. Castells also sought to fuse various sources of the information society thesis into a compendious macro-level synthesis, offering additionally – in these respects he goes appreciably beyond Bell – an explicitly global frame of reference and a focus on contemporary networked systems. It is only against this colourful backdrop that the emergence of information policy can be understood.

Given that people have only comparatively recently come to sharp consciousness of the importance of information in society, it is not surprising that the term 'information policy' does not enjoy a long pedigree. However, a standard point in historical sketches is that *de facto* information policy could be said to have existed ever since rulers started addressing informational issues, such as censorship, privacy and copyright. Thus, when John Locke, upon whose treatises the US Constitution is, of course, partly based, identified privacy as a natural right, he was in effect arguing for a policy to guarantee the protection of *personal* information. Similarly, the copyright clause of the Constitution can be interpreted as a recognition of the need for political regulation of innovative *scientific* information (Hernon and Relyea, 1991). Mairead Browne (1997a: 261) goes back further, observing wryly that 'Galileo was at the receiving end of Papal information policy when he sought an *imprimatur* to publish his exploration of Copernican theory.' One could equally suggest that Jesus was at the receiving end of Roman information policy when Caesar's population census caused the holy family to uproot from Nazareth to

Bethlehem (Luke 2: 1–5). However, such attributions are of limited utility. As Browne points out, information policies in that sense tended to be incidental to other policy preoccupations, and, in any case, to construe them as information policy is simply proleptic. Fascinating or not, such precursors are conceptually quite distinct from the later idea of information policy as a direct response to issues prompted by the growth of public consciousness of an information-centred society.

Is it possible, then, to assign a date for the inception of information policy proper? Browne herself mentions the Weinberg Committee, which advised the US government on ways to improve the flow of scientific, technical and medical (STM) information after the Soviet Union's space-race success with Sputnik. Its report, she relates, spurred self-conscious information policy activity all over the Western world. In a similar vein, it could be said that the launch-pad in Britain was the postwar Royal Society Scientific Information Conference, which led to the creation of the British Library. But such claims are arbitrary, and in any case STM is only one branch of information, albeit a particularly important one. Viewing information more comprehensively, one is drawn eastwards. Japan's political, academic and industrial leaderships were alive, at the very dawn of the information age, to the power of information and its nascent technologies, and had no qualms about pursuing intensive *johoka* policies. The Japan Computer Usage Development Institute made this abundantly clear:

> In the advanced countries, de-industrialization is now underway, and the world is generally and steadily shifting from the industrialized society to the information society. Therefore, this committee proposes the establishment of a new national target, 'Realization of the Information Society'. (Japan Computer Usage Development Institute, 1974: 175)

However, as regards English-language materials, Marc Porat's work is probably the firmest starting-point for real information policy. *The Information Economy* (Porat, 1977) crystallized matters in several crucial ways. First, it embraced the language of 'information economy' and 'information society', replacing Machlup's awkward phrase 'knowledge production and distribution' and Bell's never entirely co-extensive 'post-industrialism'. In addition, Porat approached information policy in the all-encompassing sense in which it tends now to be understood, and, as a result, was one of the first Westerners to vigorously promote the ideal of a national information policy. The latter, I will suggest, may be the stuff of illusions, but there can be little doubt that an understanding of Porat's text is a helpful place to begin an analysis of information policy.

'The foundation of the information economy,' Porat wrote, 'our *new* central fact, is the computer. Its ability to manipulate and process information represents a profound departure from our modest human abilities' (Porat, 1977, vol. 1: 205). Stripped to essentials, much of the voluminous theorizing which has gone forth under the rubric of information policy has been predicated on this 'new central fact' of computerized information processing. However, Porat was perceptive enough to recognize that stand-alone computers were only part of the picture. 'The computer', he continued, 'is one essential component of the *information infrastructure*. The other member of the infrastructure is the telecommunication network. The telephone lines, microwave stations, satellites and frequency spectrum are the analogs to the electrical and transportation grids of the industrial economy' (Porat, 1977, vol. 1: 205, emphasis in original). Policy, he believed, should be set against this socio-technical background of dynamic networks of information in a post-industrial society. 'The off-spring of that irresistible union', he foresaw, 'are the policy problems of the future, and the relevant policy agencies are now beginning to broaden their sights to include the computer *and* telecommunications' (Porat, 1977, vol. 1: 206).

Defining information policy as 'the issues raised by the combined effects of information technologies (computers and telecommunications) on market and nonmarket events' (Porat, 1977, vol. 1: 207), Porat argued that information technologies – or what we now call information and communication technologies (ICTs) – affect not just the industries which produce them but also the rest of the economy. *Ergo*, policy responses needed to be not just 'vertical' but also 'horizontal', and thus to be managed not by narrow technologists but by politically accountable bodies acting on behalf of society as a whole. As a way of framing a basic understanding of information policy, that is perfectly satisfactory. Yet when Porat came to spell out in an extensive typology the various branches of information policy, his list went well beyond concerns naturally associated with information and telecommunications and became, arguably, unreasonably large. For example, from the unexceptionable premise that education is among those 'horizontal' sectors penetrated by ICTs, he saw fit to deduce that information policy should incorporate education policy itself, and also literacy, job satisfaction, unemployment, quality of life, rehabilitation, recidivism reduction, copyright, school management, library efficiency and equality of opportunity (Porat, 1977, vol. 1: 215). Similarly, his information policy remit swallowed up most of the perennial challenges of journalism, including affordability of new technology, the impact of centralized editorial staffs on local diversity, alterations in the scope and content of news coverage, concentration of media ownership, survival of national dailies and broadband and satellite capacity for electronic distribution of news. As regards non-information sectors, the reach of information policy was even wider: everything from energy planning to tanker safety, to use of paramedics, to aesthetics of architecture, to regulation of the domestic airline industry, to national security (Porat 1977, vol. 1: 218–27).

Such scoping of information policy runs, unfortunately, on what the social philosopher R.H. Tawney once called a robust *non sequitur*. Health issues affect all persons in all sectors of the economy, but it does not follow that education policy, industrial policy and every other policy comes under health policy. Perhaps a form of technological determinism was responsible for Porat's profligacy. The rather sudden appearance of a seemingly all-purpose new technology – information machines – may have mesmerized him into thinking that the future belonged more or less entirely to the architects and executives of information policy. Perhaps Porat failed to fully appreciate the interactive nature of technology-policy relations, or what we now refer to as the 'social shaping' of technology. But in any case, to thus throw wide the boundaries of information policy is politically unrealistic, since it is hard to imagine a government minister for information convincing Cabinet colleagues that virtually everything should be part of his or her brief. Porat did to some extent draw in the reins by emphasizing a coordinating role. 'The essence of our recommendation', he proclaimed, 'is to develop an analytical capability (somewhere in the Executive Branch) whose charge is to establish a horizontal perspective' (Porat, 1977, vol. 1: 241). This proposed forum would coordinate and monitor interdepartmental policy-formation, rather than formulate or implement it. Yet Porat wanted his analytical capability to be located literally inside the White House, with budgetary influence and access to the President himself. Needless to say, his concrete recommendations were never taken up, and I suspect that even Al Gore – famous, of course, for championing information policy during the Clinton administrations – would have begged to differ.

Information policy: a state of the art

Now, in the third millennium, the information policy field continues to blossom. In a painstaking bibliometric survey, information scientist Ian Rowlands (1999b) identified the best part of a thousand articles on information policy in the period 1972–96, and calculated that the volume had been doubling every six years. Moreover, there have been full research monographs (e.g., Braman, 2007; Venturelli, 1998) and edited collections from top academic presses (e.g., Braman, 2004b; Kahin and Nesson, 1997; Loader 1998), in addition to innumerable actual policy documents. Here three areas are pinpointed where information policy thinking has been notably active, namely issue inventories, academic identity and national information policy. What, in these key respects, is the state of current thinking, and how might it be improved upon?

Issue inventories

Definitions lie, of course, at the heart of the matter. It will be assumed that the word 'policy' is relatively uncontentious: in the present context, it refers to formal governmental actions in pursuit of premeditated economic, social or political outcomes. The problem is rather with the word 'information', one of the 'godwords' (Roszak, 1994: 19) of the age, but also – perhaps rather like 'God' – one of the most misappropriated and misunderstood. The result of this long-standing semantic underdetermination has been, as Rowlands elsewhere (1996: 14) observes, a 'fuzzy set' of policy issues. This is evident if one compares the various inventories of information policy issues thrown up in the literature (e.g., Burger, 1993; Hernon and Relyea, 1991; Rowlands, 1999b). While no one today seems to be defending the full Poratian panorama, there remains a great deal of uncertainty over the remit of information policy, over whether, for example, it should include information technology industry policies or information resource management (IRM). Here a brief attempt will be made to normalize the situation: the production of a workable inventory is obviously essential to a rational information policy agenda.

If one sprang the question 'What is information policy?' on an innocent bystander, her reply would probably make some kind of reference to governmental attitudes to the dissemination of official information. What would be being identified is the popular availability of potentially useful or important documents, a world mediated by professional librarians, investigative journalists and pressure-group researchers, among others. Kirsti Nilsen's (2001) survey of the impact on the behaviour of social scientists of a Canadian government decision to privatize the nation's statistical materials is a good case study of this central information policy issue. More generally, it can with safety be said that freedom of information (FOI) issues are at the core of information policy. Theodore Roszak (1994: 3–6) is, therefore, correct to cast information firmly as the set of responses to the request for 'information, please'. Bell is more specific: 'Information is news, facts, statistics, reports, legislation, tax-codes, judicial decisions, resolutions and the like' (Bell, 1985: 17). Both authorities, I take it, are honouring, in a laudably Wittgensteinian manner, our underlying 'ordinary language' understanding of information as factual propositions and accurate, meaningful data. This is a far cry from the all-inclusive, non-semantic definition operationalized by physical scientists in their field of 'information theory' (Schiller, 2007).

Privacy, and also the now highly fashionable area of data protection (including policies aimed at those splendid hi-tech adventurers, the hackers), are, of course, the other side of the FOI coin, and must, therefore, feature on any list. Official secrecy issues too can be seen as a logical extension of FOI, albeit very much a specialism in their own right. But where should the list go next? Many inventories include freedom of speech, but that is surely far broader than FOI. It is not clear that all ethico-political questions of expression are relevant to information policy, because some kinds of expression, such as artistic freedom, seem to fall more naturally under cultural or educational policy. Much the same can certainly be said of literacy issues. However, the library community, unsurprisingly, has been concerned with national and public library and archives policy, and more widely with the development of efficient STM documentation networks. Both of these areas sit uncontroversially in any inventory of information policy. The economics of government information, especially the problem of the extent to which official publications should be treated as private or public goods, is also relevant to information policy. And, in this connection, copyright and intellectual property rights (IPR) are now absolutely central, not least since private corporations started slapping patents on the human genetic code (*Guardian*, 2000).

There can be no doubt too that national and international policies in the aforementioned areas, including what used to be called 'transborder data flows', are a proper object of information policy thinking. Information technology industry policy is beyond its remit, however. Computer scientists do indeed have an audible voice in information policy debates, but that voice speaks not technically but politically, on issues like regulation of the information superhighway or computer surveillance under democracy (Kizza, 1998; Sterling, 1986). By the same token, the technical details of government computer systems, IRM and the like, are not part of information policy proper. Broadcasting and associated matters, mentioned in some recent inventories as well as in Porat's blueprint, are a moot point. Traditionally assigned to the quite distinct field of media policy and regulation, and covering a much wider swathe of communications, they pose genuine problems for the conceptualization of information policy. The issue is addressed directly below. However, leaving that aside, we seem to have arrived at the following new, although still only provisional, inventory. It is hoped that this 'laundry list' (Table 3.1) makes the central issues of information policy more distinct – at any rate, it is designedly less overpopulated than the 'fuzzy set' resident in Porat's original typology.

Table 3.1 Laundry list of information policy issues

1	Freedom of Information (FOI)
2	Privacy and Surveillance
3	Data Protection and Security
4	Official Secrets
5	Libraries and Archives
6	Scientific, Technical and Medical (STM) Documentation
7	Economics of Government Publications
8	Copyright and Intellectual Property
9	National Information Infrastructure

Academic identity

A glance at the items above suffices to show that information policy issues touch on many disciplines, including library and information studies, economics, politics, computer science and sociology, as well as communication. Is it possible then to speak of information policy as having an academic identity? Thus far, most of the self-conscious studies of information policy have come from the library and information studies (aka information science) stable, often sponsored by the British Library (e.g., Grieves, 1998). Rowlands reveals that of the 771 information policy articles in his data set, no less than 540 were published in library and information studies journals; other fields fell massively below, with law claiming 92 papers, public administration 32, political science 31, communication studies 26, social sciences (*sic*) 24 and business and management 15 (Rowlands, 1999b: 60). Elsewhere, he has produced an intriguing scientometric portrait of the field, including a roster of significant authors; in most cases, these are from an information science background (Rowlands, 1999a). Even within Rowlands' venerable discipline, however, there is a recognition that interdisciplinarity is the way forward for information policy research. Thus, while allowing that it is 'an accepted part of the field of information studies', Browne (1997a: 263–4) argues that information policy needs to 'become truly interdisciplinary and develop entirely new frameworks of its own'. Such must indeed be the correct approach. Instead of trying to monopolize information policy in one or other academic territory, researchers ought to encourage as large a measure as possible of disciplinary and methodological pluralism. I pick up this issue below.

Before moving on, however, more must be said about media and communication studies. A curious feature of most of the academic work published so far under the information policy heading is the paucity of references to the mass media. Porat the pioneer was a communication scholar. On Rowlands' roster, however, only two names out of 21 have a communication affiliation. Browne (1997a: 263) mentions in passing 'anxieties about media ownership', but leaves it more or less at that. There is little doubt that this situation reflects the commentators' background in library and information studies, a field traditionally far apart from communication and one which, put bluntly, has been more comfortable with computers than with radio or television. Collaborative work has occasionally contemplated reconciliation. For example, Schement and Curtis (1995: 166) define information policy as 'all policies relating to the allocation of resources for purposes of institutionalizing information and for providing access to channels of communication'. However, while registering the affinity between information and communication policy, they too settle in the end for 'the modifier information' (Schement and Curtis, 1995: 167). From the other side of the disciplinary fence, communication scholars have begun to theorize the information age under the moving spotlight of technological convergence. For example, Minoru Sugaya (2000: 31), a media theorist in Japan, argues for 'a new philosophy of regulation for the age of convergence', and posits a dual structure comprising centralized regulation of broadcasting and local self-regulation of the internet. Similar kinds of messages about convergence have also emerged from media circles in Europe (e.g., Independent Television Commission, n.d.; Levy, 1999).

The present writer too has argued for fusion, even touting the neologism 'information media policy' (Duff, 2002). However, a strong case can still be made for keeping clear blue water between these specialisms. 'Information', in its ordinary language usage, still means something very different from 'media'. As argued above, 'information' to most people means factual statements and data; with 'media', on the other hand, we think of Hollywood, soap opera and entertainment. But, if this is the case, is an immediate conflation of the fields of information policy and media policy a feasible step? Moreover, to converge at the theoretical level could simply play into the hands of the private sector interests which stand to gain most from a further blurring of the lines between information and entertainment. One could make a case that information policy should work hard to maintain its niche in 'hard' information in contradistinction to 'soft' media flows. Such a stance might entail that news and other staples of objective information – by all accounts, the lifeblood of democracy – will earn more public respect and hence generate more state funding, at any rate in countries with a strong tradition of public sector involvement in the info sphere. However, this important cultural debate still needs to be played out (Mueller and Lentz, 2004; Negrine, 1989).

The holy grail of national and international information policies

The search for a national information policy has been perhaps the dominant theme in recent years, attaining almost totemic proportions in some quarters. This is another obvious bequest from Porat's pioneering formulations. It also reflects the premise with which my chapter started, that discussions of information policy are an aspect of the whole information society debate, that is, that 'national information policy discussions increasingly assume some concept of the information society as context and justification for considering specific policy directions' (Chang, 1995: 25). We are constantly subjected to deterministic-sounding statements, veritable ultimata, such as this from an oft-cited document known as the Rockefeller Report: 'To debate whether there should be a National Information Policy is pointless. There will be such a policy.' Apparently, there is only a stark choice of an 'articulated, coherent national information policy' or 'an assortment of inarticulate, incoherent, overlapping policies' (quoted in Hill, 1995: 273).

In a similar vein, Nick Moore has criticized the 'very British approach to [information] policy making'. 'We are far', he continues, 'from having a wide-ranging vision which sets the tone for the subsequent coordinated development of a coherent policy framework' (Moore, 1998: 343). Elsewhere, he speaks, to some extent approvingly, of alleged information policy successes by authoritarian regimes in East Asia (Moore, 1997). Charles Oppenheim, another enthusiast for a national information policy in the United Kingdom, argues Porat-style that the information policy agenda should be the responsibility of a single minister in charge of a national information infrastructure task-force; its brief would include privacy and data protection, copyright, public and national libraries, the internet, citizens' advice bureaus, FOI and e-democracy (Oppenheim, 1996). Yet, good idea though an information czar with such powers might seem from a theoretical standpoint, in the real world he or she would, I suspect, soon fall foul of interdepartmental politics. And democracy would get in the way.

Advocacy for an integrated information policy is not confined to the national stage. The logic of a coordinated approach leads its adherents to propound a regional response to the putative absurdity of policy fragmentation. Sillince, for example, maintains that European Commission information policy has been hampered by its subjection to a succession of competing paradigms, ranging from protectionism to an acceptance of globalization, from collaboration to deregulation. 'These paradigms', he notes, 'have been used in an unplanned way, so that methods in favour at one time have conflicted with the aims of information policy at another'

(Sillince, 1994: 234). Perhaps in response to such concerns, a powerful report by a 'High Level Group' under Herr Bangemann (1994) launched a no-nonsense action plan to turn the European Union into an information society. Eurosceptics would argue that the information society concept has since been used as an astute political device for pushing through far-reaching federalist policies, covering the whole societal range of economy, culture and polity.

Whether or not that is fair, Europeanism is in any case trumped by those clamouring for a fully international approach. Global information policy dates back to the New World Information and Communication Order (NWICO) era, when – hard though it is to believe – there was genuine political talk of the establishment of an international deontology and of rectification of imbalances in copyright and the distribution of the means of communication (MacBride, 1980). NWICO soon collapsed under right-wing pressure, but the United Nations is now again giving global information policy a major boost by its sponsorship of the World Summit on the Information Society. It remains to be seen whether this latest effort will translate into a more enlightened geopolitical information order (Mendina and Britz, 2004; Selian, 2004).

The future of information policy

In this final section, I suggest some of the directions in which information policy could go in the foreseeable future. One interface that must be explored is information policy's relationship with political philosophy. There is also much to be said for experimenting with futures studies, a field that some see as being at the opposite end of the spectrum from political philosophy in terms of academic calibre and pedigree. Finally, some details will be offered regarding the conception of information policy as a subset of the newish interdisciplinary specialism of information society studies.

Information policy and political philosophy

Axiology, the philosophy of value, and political philosophy in particular, is now a key area for cultivation. The British electorate, like many across Europe, has returned governments which have engineered a paradigm slide from information as inalienable public good to information as pure commodity. The USA, too, has long been witnessing a 'mounting tension' between information as 'value additive' and information as 'uniquely distributable public good' (Koenig, 1995). However, while this much is quite well understood in the various communities interested in information policy, there has been a widespread lack of rigour and sophistication in the axiological analysis. This state of affairs prompted Rowlands (1996) to call for the development of value-critical and paradigm-critical approaches, and Browne (1997a; 1997b) to follow up with an argument for a less positivistic, more prescriptive outlook. Both interventions were helpful. However, the axiological development of information policy must now go well beyond this – deep into the domain of political philosophy.

If there is a seminal text for the embedding of information policy in political philosophy, it is probably the coda of *Coming of Post-Industrial Society* (Bell, 1999[1973]), entitled 'Agenda for the Future'. This characteristically engaging discussion of major players like Rousseau, Mill and Rawls was a decent effort to work out the political philosophy most appropriate for the post-industrial societies to which the future allegedly belongs. However, Bell's start was not followed up, at least not within the *soi-disant* information policy literature. There have been occasional forays since (e.g., Bovens, 2002; Duff, 2004), yet most of the work at this interface is still to be done. Some of the big philosophical questions are not being considered, never mind solved. For example, everyone knows that individual privacy is under threat, but how, in a post-industrial epoch, should we conceive of the relationship between individualism and collectivism? How exactly might state interference in the 'info sphere' be defined and justified, in light of the tradition of Anglo-American analytical philosophy? At an even more profound level, what is the relationship between the right and the good (deontology and teleology) in the information society thesis? What, indeed, is the meaning of the words 'good' and 'right' in the emotive context of information policy? Much of this seems to be virgin territory, something that cannot be imputed to comparable fields in applied technology, such as environmental policy research.

Information policy and futures studies

Roszak (1994: 21) defines futurology, or futures studies (currently its preferred title), as 'an ungainly hybrid of potted social science, Sunday supplement journalism, and soothsaying ... featuring breezy scenarios of Things to Come pitched at about the intellectual level of advertising copy'. He is wrong, or at any rate he is wrong if he is trying to thus classify everything that emerges from the word-processors of authors in the field of futures studies. Bell, identified in sober rankings as one of the most influential thinkers of the 20th century (*The Times Literary Supplement*, 1995), and a former holder of arguably the top chair in social science in the world, at Harvard University, has long been an avid student of the future and characterized his post-industrialist *magnum opus* as a 'venture in social forecasting'. Forecasting is one of those comparatively precise modes of futurology which cannot be consigned to the lunatic fringe; nor can a reference work of the quality of *Encyclopedia of the Future* (Kurian and Molitor, 1996), or a journal such as *Futures*, be denied the status of scholarship. But if information is the new master key, if advanced nations are metamorphosing into information societies – a process facilitated by futuristic new technologies of information and communication – then information policy must have a special interest in futures studies. Allusions and tokenism are no longer enough: the nettle may need to be grasped and a systematic interface developed between these two fields.

Information policy as a branch of information society studies

Perhaps the most important attribute of information policy for the future will be open-endedness, an ability to evolve in its own way without being restricted by any of the traditional disciplines upon which it calls. But where then does it reside? Information policy must be positioned somewhere or other in the intellectual ether, and a proposal worth considering is that it belongs inside the specialism of *information society studies*. Defined as the macro-level study of the role of information flows and technologies in society (Duff, 2000; Saulauskas, 2005), information society studies is an appropriate interdisciplinary cluster to which information policy can be attached, as in the schema shown in Figure 3.1.

The scheme, which does not claim to be exhaustive, divides information society studies into two broad categories, the positive and the normative. Under the former fall sociological and economic studies of information, insofar as they remain empirically grounded. Under the latter falls information policy, as characterized in the present chapter, alongside information ethics, another prescriptive field which, while tending to focus on individual behaviour, also touches on social morality. Now, given that policy is

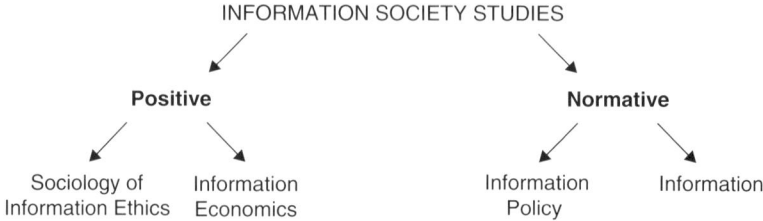

Figure 3.1   Information society studies

about social goals and the moral norms that they realize, the scheme allows us to say that information policy research seeks to determine the nature of the good or right information society. Information policy emerges, therefore, as the *normative theory of the information society*. Perhaps that can serve as a new definition for information policy, or at any rate as a basis for discussion about its future development.

A final qualification should be made. Believing that information policy should subsist in interdisciplinary space, as a subset of information society studies, does not make one blind to academic *realpolitik*. In the higher educational world as presently constructed, information policy, and information society studies generally, is comparatively secure in library and information science departments, and has a significant presence in schools of communication and media. Cultural studies has also been identified as a viable 'site' (Black, 2001: 245–6). Sociology and social policy would also be natural homes, if only they could overcome their insularity. However, these disciplines should act as lodging-houses, rather than as prisons to which information policy must be forever confined. What is really needed, as far as the academy is concerned, is the setting up of interdisciplinary research centres in information policy, functioning at university or faculty rather than departmental level. But the trouble with such outfits, as several now defunct information policy outfits discovered, is that they are much more vulnerable than conventional departments when the insidious call goes out for 'rationalization' or 'economization'. The institutional base of the specialism is likely, therefore, to remain indeterminate for the foreseeable future.

Conclusion: towards the age of access

The chapter began with an introduction to the idea of the information society and proceeded to calibrate a tradition of policy thinking which grew up alongside this putative information society. Now some of the claims associated with the information society thesis are undoubtedly technologically deterministic or even 'ideological' (Garnham, 2000), as a healthy body of left criticism insists. However, the information society thesis in its more reflective and restrained forms is not merely a manifestation of false consciousness. I think that we can still say that a central objective of civilized nations in the 21st century should be to realize the information society. The understanding of information policy which surfaces from this discussion is, therefore, a sympathetic one. While caution needs to be exercised regarding some of what the tradition has said on behalf of information policy, particularly with respect to its scope, we should recognize the basic value of the idea of public policies in and for information. Specific measures aiming at democratically selected social goals, such as FOI, privacy, or a just IPR regime, so long as they are not confused with the neo-Bonapartism of an all-enveloping 'national information plan', are often to be encouraged. By helping to clarify the nature of information policy, and by identifying some disciplinary directions in which it needs to travel (but not to terminate), this chapter hopes to have shown a few of the steps towards a normative theory of the information society. It seems certain that policy-makers will need to refer to some such theory if they are to pilot us safely into the age of access.

Media and Social Demand: Research at the Interface of Policy Studies and Audience Studies[1]

Marc Raboy, Bram Abramson, Serge Proulx and Roxanne Welters

For a period in the mid-1990s, academic journals and conferences were awash with polemical exchanges between proponents of two broad approaches to studying media: political economy and cultural studies (see for example, Gandy, 1995). These lively debates obscured what we characterized, a few years later, as a strategic dilemma facing scholars interested in policy-relevant research which tended to be located at the interface of these two broad currents: the dilemma of social demand.

In a suite of articles (Raboy and Abramson, 1998; Raboy *et al.*, 2001; Raboy and Proulx, 2003), and a thematic issue of the international journal *Gazette* (Raboy *et al.*, 2003), the idea of social demand was developed to refer to the range of expectations with respect to media that exceed economic (market) or political (state) considerations – that is to say, expectations as they can be extrapolated from what people say about their media use, as well as the efforts of organized social and cultural groups to influence the direction of media policy.

In the introduction to the *Gazette* issue, Raboy *et al.* (2003) wrote:

> The intersection of media policy and social demand may be approached starting from communication and cultural policy, whose role in framing citizenship lies at the heart of a broad and generous conception of public life ... Historically, the state has justified its attempts to influence the media by arguing that doing so is

in the public interest. Increasingly, however, public policy intervention requires a stronger base of legitimation.

We went on to say:

> Within the institutional order of the state, general reliance on a policy rhetoric of 'public interest' is insufficient for policymakers who seek empirical data with which to justify their action. Because the bulk of such data is currently produced as industrial audience research measuring a 'market demand', policy legitimation is skewed towards measures which conceptualize public interest as 'what the public is interested in', that is, what people are prepared to consume. An alternative form of audience research, based on a more sociocritical approach, would allow for the legitimation of types of cultural policy which incorporate a fuller conceptualization of the public interest and its ties to the exercise of citizenship. (Raboy *et al.*, 2003)

This alternative basis for policy legitimation is what we refer to as 'social demand', arguing that 'a clear understanding of social demand can allow media policymaking to be linked to a democratic cultural citizenship, in light of a whole range of emerging issues which policymakers as well as scholars have to consider in the double-edged context of technological convergence and media globalization' (Raboy *et al.*, 2003).

The theoretical foundation for a research agenda organized around the idea of social demand – situated at the interface of policy studies and audience studies – was proposed by the undersigned in a 2001 article in *Television and New Media*. The claims we made in that article are still valid today, and we present a version of them here.

Policy studies/audience studies: issues at the interface

At the intersection of ongoing geopolitical events and developments in social and political theory (see Thompson, 1995), debate about the media's role is tied in with new conceptions of citizenship and identity and a fundamental shift in notions of what is public and what is private (cf. Mouffe, 1992; van Steenbergen, 1994; etc.). Consider the following:

> The threshold separating the private sphere from the public is not marked by a fixed set of issues or relationships but by *different conditions of communication* [his emphasis]. Certainly these conditions lead to differences in the accessibility of the two spheres, safeguarding the intimacy of the one sphere and the publicity of the other. However, they do not seal off the private from the public but only channel the flow of topics from the one sphere into the other. *For the public*

sphere draws its impulses from the private handling of social problems that resonate in life histories [our emphasis]. (Habermas, 1996: 366)

This recent statement from a social philosopher who continues to influence a major current of media scholarship and to spark controversy is itself resonant. Use of Habermas's notion of the public sphere as a theoretical framework for research, and criticism of that framework, is too often based on a text first published in 1962 (Habermas, 1989). Yet Habermas's own thought has continued to evolve – although it is fair to say that his basic quest for societal rationality through communicative relations ('intersubjectivity') has remained constant. For 30 years he did not return to the subject of the public sphere at all. When he did take it up again in the early 1990s, it was with an entirely fresh approach, confounding those who would talk of discrete public and private spaces by reminding them that the public and private are in fact intertwined (Habermas, 1992).

Research that uses the public sphere as a theoretical and analytical category is inevitably preoccupied with democracy (Dahlgren, 1995; Price, 1995). Conversely, as more and more social science researchers are recognizing, talking about democracy should necessarily mean reflecting on the relationship between public and private spheres – and the media. As Morley points out, the media are fundamental 'in articulating the public and private spheres, and in the social organization of space, time and community' (1992: 1). Media use is never *either* public *or* private; it is always both. It always structures and is structured by both social and political institutions and the individuals who live them.

The equation becomes even more complex when we consider the multiple relationships of individuals to the media. Media users are variously constructed as viewers, consumers and citizens (Corner, 1991). Collectively, they are labelled the audience, the market, the public (Thomas, 1960). Are the various speakers referring to the same thing when they use these terms, or to different attributes of the same thing? Or are they referring to different things composed of the same people?

In the context of policy studies and audience studies, working through these oppositions means, first of all, thinking of the individual as traversed simultaneously by both the policy and media apparatuses. The communicative subject must be conceptualized as both media user and citizen. In this sense, agencies of the state intervene in the larger structures which organize media use, while public understanding of media use influences and structures state intervention. At the intersection of policy studies and audience studies, therefore, lie different approaches to a common problem, conceptualized as the media–audience relationship on the one hand, and as the media-public relationship on the other. The ground between them is both theoretical, working between two modes of analysis, and practical, testing and developing theory empirically.

Policy studies: one problem, two traditions

Communication policy studies stand at a double remove. In most countries, public policy in communication tends to be made independently of those who study it. And among academics, communication policy scholars have not engaged in extensive dialogue with the main schools to be found in departments of policy studies, public administration, or political science and their related journals. Communication policy studies as the site at which 'the academic research community can fulfil its own potential in participatory democracies' (Melody, 1990: 38) is therefore confronted with isolation both from its academic counterparts and the real-world objects of its study.

Clearly, the former is of significance only in as much as it may affect the latter. Communication policy studies are concerned with directing academic labour towards useful intervention into the institutions and industries which articulate the field of communications and culture – what Tony Bennett refers to as 'the need for intellectual work to be conducted in a manner such that, in both its substance and its style, it can be calculated to influence or service the conduct of identifiable agents within the region of culture concerned' (1992: 23; cf. *inter alia* Gomery, 1993; McQuail, 1994; Hagins, 1996; McQuail and Siune, 1998).

To what extent communication policy studies resemble or do not resemble mainstream policy studies, therefore – and they do not – is a question whose relevance is limited to the degree to which their isolation might hinder the real-world effectivity of communication policy studies (see introductory chapter).

Another approach to studying communication policy has been proposed by scholars emerging from the cultural studies trajectory. Ironically, while an important emphasis in cultural studies on texts and microprocesses has led to occasionally bitter polemics with political economy researchers who privilege institutional questions (cf. Gandy, 1995), policy proponents within cultural studies have in fact attempted to trace a route similar to that of political economists in privileging the institutional. This has been particularly true in the recent work of Australian specialists in cultural policy such as Tony Bennett, who writes that 'the programmatic, institutional and governmental conditions in which cultural practices are inscribed – in short, the networks of relations that fall under a properly theoretical understanding of policy – have a substantive priority over the semiotic properties of such practices' (1992: 28).

But whereas political economy tends to suspend the question of the cultural dimension in policy, the cultural studies approach to policy takes culture as its starting point, defines culture as a particular field of government, and suggests that policy is constitutive of different forms of culture. This is consistent with a continuing concern in cultural studies over how subjectivity is produced. Just as audience studies served as a key site for theorizing the formation of the self through media consumption (Allor, 1988), so policy studies serve as an entry point to examining how the state interpellates individuals as citizens, structuring the terrain upon which the individual is formed (Miller and Rose, 1992). Approaches from both cultural studies and political economy thus converge towards a concern with the complexity of the policy framework in which cultural practices evolve – what Stuart Cunningham calls the 'cultural infrastructure', which is 'the integration of policy, institutions and industrial practices as they together provide mechanisms for defining, justifying and delivering cultures to audiences' (1992: 4).

As we have emphasized, these are not the only two approaches to communication policy studies, and are certainly dwarfed by the range of approaches in the broad field of policy studies. But the common ground between the two bodes well, and explains our choice. Rather than moving away from local processes and the transformations that take place within them, however, we want to suggest that communication policy studies need to move back towards these and incorporate them into their modes of analysis. In particular, the area of audience studies – a favourite straw man for some, old baggage to be disposed of for others – has to be invited into, not excluded from, communication policy studies. The question is how to integrate what we can learn from each of these areas of scholarship into a workable model. Indeed, we would argue that policy cannot be studied without investigating how it is activated upon the population; conversely, intervention in policy-making should be connected with the ways in which citizens continue to live out the structures of government.

Audience studies: consumers and citizens

Communication policy is an ambiguous creature, in that it combines the logics of technological and political apparatuses – two competing logics which meet at the point of media use, co-habiting the individual who is constituted as, at once, consumer and citizen (Murdock, 1992). Communication policy thus functions as an intervention into two networks of relations: media-citizenry and media-audience. The role of audience studies in such a matrix is to do the work of investigating how the structures which policy set into play are lived out, not simply at the point of use or consumption, but as negotiated practices embedded in larger social and civic structures.

By making audience studies part of a programme for communication policy studies, in other words, the notion of an active citizenry[2] can replace the model of media users seen as the atomized objects of, alternately, government policy and cultural industries. Citizenries, like audiences, are located in partially determining structures which they negotiate and even resist: 'The subjects of policy – the communities that are in some sense brought into being by a policy programme – are not exhausted by the policy programme, and may reshape policy to their own ends' (O'Regan, 1992: 521). This is not the same as tracking down and then celebrating 'resistance' for its own sake. Rather, it is a taking account of the practices which continually recreate the structures which individual subjects negotiate – working across 'the difference between having power over a text and having power over the agenda within which that text is constructed and presented' (Morley, 1992: 31). And that means the retooling of reception and audience research for their reinvigoration in policy intervention. Audience studies cannot simply be injected into policy work wholesale; the trajectory from living room couch to policy chambers requires that the question of how the relationship between audience and text is negotiated be restated in rather different terms.

Empirical ethnographic research helpfully enables the mapping of different practices onto the social structures in which the subject is materialized, among which media consumption plays an important part. In policy terms, differing interpretations can be linked with the differentiated characteristics of the population, that is, of citizens. Media users are thus taken up as individuals with complex socio-economic positionings, rather than nothing-but-consumers who cease to exist the moment the television is turned off. Critical audience ethnography should therefore be an important part of the communication policy studies repertoire.[3]

On the other hand, media use is very much an act of consumption, engaged in precisely because it provides pleasure or enjoyment, fulfilment or distraction, as well as information and confirmation. Rather than elide the nature of media consumption by centring solely on its articulation with social structures, it is important that its place in the reproduction of the social be thought together with the transient practice of turning on or tuning in to communication technologies. The twin functions of 'connection with society, and gratification of self' (Katz *et al.*, 1973: 173) necessarily accompany each other, and the articulation of pleasure and social positioning through media consumption is a problematic central to the interface between audience studies and policy studies. Making audience research useful for policy intervention requires outfitting it for translation into active programmes of action, and this demands breathing new life into Katz *et al.*'s advice (1974: 31) that 'media researchers ought to be studying human needs to discover how much the media do or do not contribute to their creation and satisfaction'.

Let us be clear about this: to accept that the individual at the point of media use is traversed by needs and desires in no way implies that these are not the outcome of complex processes of social negotiation, already structured by social and class positions – just as looking back to uses and gratifications research in no way means adopting the model of the audience as an atomized mass of individuals (cf. Morley, 1992: 52–5). Rather, it is part of developing an approach to communication policy studies that is able to use earlier scholarship by reworking it in light of contemporary critiques (cf. Jensen and Rosengren, 1990).[4]

Reception and audience research can then play a key role in studying communication policy. They work across the endlessly cycling circuit between institutional structures and local negotiations, bringing together different research traditions in order to articulate social positioning and individual practices at the point of consumption. The social relationships between audience and text must be examined, but also conceptualized in terms of how policy seeks to influence those relationships, and how policy studies might understand and intervene in that influence.

Communication policy studies are thus confronted with two sets of questions. The first of these takes as its starting point the kind of mapping of the structures of domination at which political economists and other policy analysts have proven so adept: how can we understand how these institutional and industrial structures are lived out? How is policy activated upon and within the population? What are the precise connections between the structures which interpellate individual users as subjects, and the subjectivities which are reproduced inside and out of these interpellations? Here, structural concerns flow downstream into the difficult empirical and qualitative research of audience studies. The second set of questions, meanwhile, focuses on moving back upstream: how can the understanding of the effects of structural determinations contribute to adjustments of those structures? How can the patterns of individual and collective media use inform the organization of the field of culture as articulated through the state and other institutional actors who are at least partly under the state's domain? And what policies can be mobilized in order to influence the field's reorganization?

Thus, when Sonia Livingstone locates the crucial question at the interface of policy and audience studies as 'what are the implications for the construction of the public/audience by the media industries and to what extent are they right or wrong?' (1996: 51), she is only partly correct. The question is not simply to what extent media industries and institutions' constructions of the public are right or wrong, but more importantly, how they *become* right or wrong, through the process of actively constructing subject positions for the user to take up, resist, or otherwise negotiate. That is the crucial distinction for a policy intervention model which would operate 'through a process of consultation and evaluation involving those affected by [policy prescriptions]' (Miller, 1996: 146). Such a model would take as axiomatic the constantly changing nature of both structural conditions and social affiliations, and engage in a back-and-forth between policy prescriptions and the terrain upon which such policies, and the institutional conditions they regulate, are lived out.

It will have become obvious that while the points of entry for such analysis are infinitely varied – local conditions, an institutional intervention, modulations in state regulatory regimes, and so forth – the first step is always a mapping of the landscape. Researchers have put great effort into developing better theoretical and empirical understandings of how audiences are 'really' positioned by texts or by policies, and not enough effort into understanding how cultural and government institutions develop texts and policies to position audiences and citizens (cf. Hartley, 1988; Malo and Giroux, 1998). A gap exists between research models for understanding communication and audience processes, and the models informing industrial and institutional practices of communication (Ang, 1991). Asserting the superiority of the former over the latter is insufficient, for it leaves the real-world effects of the latter's deployment unexplored.

As Entman and Wildman (1992) have noted, new metaphors are needed to guide this type of research agenda.[5] Communication policy studies cannot focus simply on the relationship between state and citizens in the regulation of communication systems. They must position that relationship within the cluttered space of all of the industrial and institutional structures which make up those systems – and, indeed, confronted with an increasingly dispersed 'network state' it may no longer make much sense to think in such terms anyway (Braman, 1995). Bringing together different research traditions in confronting communication policy is only a first step. One must then wield these in fashioning the tools of the trade.

Regarding social demand

Media use is at once highly individual and part of the social positioning of the individual. It is polymorphic: a combination of taste and temperament, family situation, political interest and economic imperative. By situating media consumption within the constellation of activities through which the individual occupies a socio-political role, an appreciation of the individual's social complexity can correct the danger of reducing audience members to an undifferentiated group. As Proulx *et al.* concluded from a study of television use among Montreal families:

> The category of user obscures the other social identities of the individual; for
> example, his membership in a family, in various networks at work and at play,

in a socio-professional or ethnocultural group, and so on. It would no doubt be preferable to orient our research problem on the basis of a definition of the individual as parent, citizen, worker, etc.; this would allow for considering the individual at the level of his or her actual social practice. (Proulx *et al.*, 1993: 117–18. Our translation)

In considering the range of practices which locate the individual within social structures, social demand orbits around the field of citizenship as a space for intervention. Such a position depends on conceptualizing citizenship as the juncture between individual subjects and a democratic state, such that public policy is directed at ensuring a measure of control for the subject over the actualization of her or his own identity. Especially in rapidly evolving policy contexts, citizenship is the site at which the state directs the policy interventions that entail 'invent[ing] new mechanisms for the empowerment of social actors – who, for better or for worse, are still politically constituted primarily within national boundaries' (Raboy *et al.*, 1994: 296–7).

Now, citizenship is a contested concept. Charles Taylor, for example, has described two models of citizenship, the 'liberal' and the 'communitarian': 'One [model] focuses mainly on individual rights and equal treatment, as well as a government performance which takes account of the citizen's preferences. ... The other model, by contrast, defines participation in self-rule as of the essence of freedom' (1989: 178–9). We take a less categorical view of citizenship, as that which encompasses the individual's relationship to the state while intersecting with her or his self-image as an active member of society – 'a specific form of identity', to use Dahlgren's phrase (1995: 146).

Market demand

The notion of citizenship underscores both the legitimacy and the validity of state intervention: is it appropriate, and can it be significant? To begin to answer this question, we need to understand much more than we do at present about the nature of media use. To begin looking for that understanding, we need to reformulate the object of our search.

The democratic state has historically justified its intervention with respect to media in terms of their social and economic role. Public policy in this area has been implemented despite the counter-argument that only in an unfettered market environment can media be free of all obstacles and guarantee absolute freedom of expression. With the transformation in the role of media concurrent with the globalization of communications, these institutions are increasingly central to cultural development and the active participation of citizens in public life. Moreover, a vast literature attests to the weakness of the idealist model of 'free' media in an environment characterized for over a century by growing commercialization, and insertion of the media into the framework of cultural industries (see, e.g., Nerone, 1995).

These observations alone should suffice to justify the continuing effort to intervene in the evolution of media systems. But the combination of a severe fiscal crisis and changes in the nature of state power at the national level have brought about a general scepticism with respect to interventionist strategies. Until recently, for example, a key element of public policy in most of the industrialized countries was the support of public service broadcasting, supposedly insulated, in principle at least, from economic and political pressures. Public broadcasting was conceived as an alternative to market broadcasting, using public support but free of state control. Today, however, the need to renew the conventional public broadcasting model tends to be framed around market, rather than public, alternatives (Atkinson and Raboy, 1997).

If it is not to lose its *raison dêtre*, then, public policy in communication must seek a new basis for legitimation. Market logic rests on the conceptualization of media users as fully formed consumers whose social constitution is radically disconnected from their private selves. Market logic therefore emphasizes competition and the multiplication of choice as the path to fulfilling the needs of the consumer. This inscribes a radical disjuncture between private and public spheres, reproduced through industrial tools which measure private consumption habits such as television audience size at the point of viewing.

This logic of market demand clouds the possibility that the media user may have other media needs which the market does not, or cannot, address. In response, public policy aims, through formal policy texts, to articulate objectives with respect to media according to the national and other interests that traverse the network of state apparatuses (which vary significantly from one context to another depending on local circumstances). And to the extent that these interests coincide with democratic governance, communication policy attempts to serve as a corrective to the *a priori* split of public and private which drives most media programming, by reintroducing the public categories of citizenship into the sphere of private media practices.

Social demand

An important problem for the legitimacy of legislative and regulatory practices, however, is the difficulty in determining the ways in which media do or do not conform to the non-market objectives of policy. Legislators and policy-makers continue to articulate policy objectives in terms which extend beyond the market. Yet the bureaucratic need for quantifiable – and thus legitimized – information means that decision-makers are forced to return to market demand, which is more easily measurable when it comes time to evaluate policy's effectivity in meeting desired goals. Like the industrial logic for which it is a tool, the audience maximization model of market demand rests entirely on private consumption habits, that is, on a division of public and private realms. The logic of market demand positions this distinction as preceding the social activity of media use, rather than produced through it, and implies a sovereign self who comes to the media with fully formed identities, needs, interests, circumstances and aspirations. Faced with a lack of other modes of evaluation, policy-makers thus end up deploying the very market model of the media user that many stated policies purport to correct.

To suggest, on the other hand, that media use is a distinctly social activity and part of the ongoing production of self and society, is to suggest an alternative logic which rejects the public/private split as its starting point – and to highlight the need for a conceptual and evaluative tool produced within this alternative logic. Against market demand, therefore, we want to position what we call a model of 'social demand' which refuses an *a priori* division and recognizes the articulations between public and private in the various facets of every individual's life. Where market demand positions users as private creatures, social demand understands individuals, and the public–private structures which they inhabit, as socially constituted. This does not mean that corporate strategies which encourage consumption are based on unsophisticated research or on a poor understanding of potential customers social identities, only that, under strategies driven by market demand, the act of consumption *itself* is constituted as the process's endpoint. Nor does this mean that demand can be reduced to some expression of society's 'needs' – this would be another reification based on a faulty division of public and private – only that it is necessary to take account of the larger networks of power in society and the asymmetrical distribution of individuals along these networks.

Talking about social demand thus underscores the range of expectations with respect to media that are expressed independently of economic and political considerations. Expressions of social demand are situated at the interface of media use and the supply, or offer, on which media use is based. Media audiences, in this view, are composed of socially constituted citizens with multifaceted identities for whom media consumption is an activity among others – not simply as, say, viewers who come into existence (and thus under the jurisdiction of broadcasting legislation) when they turn on the television, and who cease to exist when they turn it off. The media public thus exists in society, aggregated differently than when the same individuals occupy the position of audience members. As citizens, individuals can have a critical relationship with media that is far more subtle and difficult to grasp than the catalogue of their use habits would seem to indicate.

If we take up citizenship and not simply consumership as the focus of policy intervention, therefore, it is less the function of some essential value in citizenship than the result of the differing forces at work within the two categories. While consumption emphasizes the relationship between the individual subject and the commercial market, citizenship emphasizes the individual subject's position with respect to the state. The state, meanwhile, generally conceptualizes both the citizen and the corporation as subjects (of the state) and its own role as one of applying constraints or incentives in the national interest. The idea of social demand seeks to refocus each of these roles on society, as the expression of the full range of individual, group and general interests. The figure of citizenship is thus recentred as the main mediating category between the state and the self. Within such a theoretical framework, the idea of social demand is at the heart of a public policy approach to media that is based on a set of evolving epistemological and political tools which link investigation with intervention.

Logically, public policy should provide the normative framework for legislation and regulation which seek to fulfil social demand. To achieve this, it is necessary to position media users as social actors rather than simply as consumers, as citizens as well as members of particular identity groups. The elaboration of social demand thus encompasses a strong normative aspect by intersecting with public policy, which is normative by definition. Or, to put it another way, public policy, in order to be legitimate, must take account of social demand. Research design with respect to social demand is therefore highly contextual. It makes more sense, in fact, to try to study *the ways in which social demand is expressed*, than to pretend to describe it as a material object. One can do this by bringing together socio-critical discourse analysis of policy texts and documents intended to influence policy, and qualitative individual and group interviewing that seeks to bring out self-descriptions of the finalities of media use. By bringing the active citizenry into its research design, policy-oriented critical research might be able to help formulate a closer approximation of appropriate public-policy objectives.

Translating demand into policy

For researchers interested in policy intervention, the idea of social demand provides a way to articulate a public interest with respect to media.

Epistemologically, its role is to provide a way to think through and to understand media use across a range of social categories that position the user. Politically, this task is intended to connect up with already-existing public policy that assigns specific social obligations to particular mass media operations. Article 3 of Canada's Broadcasting Act (1991), which is the centrepiece of Canadian media policy, provides an interesting example of what we are talking about. It states:

> The Canadian broadcasting system should...through its programming and the employment opportunities arising out of its operations, serve the needs and interests, and reflect the circumstances and aspirations, of Canadian men, women and children, including equal rights, the linguistic duality and multicultural and multiracial nature of Canadian society and the special place of aboriginal peoples within that society. (Canada, 1991: clause 3.1.d.iii)[6]

This formulation offers an interesting point of departure for our attempt to concretize social demand at conceptual and evaluative levels, in that it provides specific social categories – however imperfect – with which to decompose the interface of citizen and consumer. In our own research (Raboy and Proulx, 2003), those confronted with this text were, before all else, amazed to learn that the political-legal framework of their country provided them with such rights with respect to the media system at all. Depending on how they see themselves, they may agree or disagree with part or all of the legislator's way of breaking down Canadian society into so many serviceable categories. Yet they do express a range of expectations based on their real or desired media use, reflecting a particular view of the world and their own place in it.

How can this be translated into policy? Should it be? Is it possible? The Act does not enable one to determine with any precision what would be an adequate response to needs and interests, or an appropriate reflection of circumstances and aspirations – let alone how to speak to someone whose identity is not confined to the categories it mentions. It is precisely here that expressions of social demand can intervene, by working between policy objectives, the range of possibilities open to policy-makers, and the subjects of policy – that is, the citizenry. But the individuals who compose a given society vary enormously in how they exercise their citizenship. For some, it is a strictly personal expression of social concerns. Others seek to associate with their fellows in efforts to influence the course of events. For some, the material and emotional needs of daily life supersede all interest in social intervention. Others will integrate a measure of social intervention in their professional lives. Regardless, everyone has the right to expect that the media system will respond to their needs and interests, reflect their circumstances and aspirations.

How, then, can one grasp, describe, measure or qualify expressions of social demand, which can indicate whether such objectives are being met? This is a task infinitely messier and more difficult than attempting to quantify market demand, and beginning to answer this question would require an elaborate research programme. We can, for example, illustrate the nature of social demand by investigating media use. Similarly, we can explore which media people would desire if they could restructure supply according to their needs and interests, circumstances and aspirations. We can also evaluate public policy issues from a social demand perspective. We can verify the concordance between formal policy objectives and the lived experience of people targeted by policy. Obviously, just like media use itself, social demand is highly subjective and differentiated from one person to the next. One must avoid the pitfall of assuming that social demand can be described through the accumulation of individual expectations. The demand expressed through organized groups therefore remains an essential part of the policy formation process.

In collective terms, social demand is expressed through the public interventions of pressure groups, experts, editorialists, and so forth; it should normally be reflected in public policy. But in certain respects organized public expression of social demand is a mirror image of market-driven audience measurement, and raises similar questions of interest and representativeness. To be fully operational as a policy instrument, then, social demand must be shown to reflect both public and private expressions of media use. Alongside this organized expression of demand, policy must engage with the individual as an active citizen, living as a member of civil society in a complex relationship with the market, the state and other structuring institutions.

How should this be approached? First, research needs to reconceptualize the audience member as more than a media user, to give voice to the citizen within her or him, in whichever way he or she chooses to express that voice. This means more than the archetypical ethnographer's respect for the research subject. It means seeing audience members not for their relationship to the 'average', not as simple mimetic representations of larger populations, but as complex members of society. Along with Brunt, we would emphasize the 'typical' in this respect: 'Whether it is researching with groups or with individuals... "the typical" engages with often heightened circumstances, special conditions, exceptional cases, extreme positions, precisely in order to highlight tendencies that may in "normal circumstances" be merely incipient' (1992: 74).

Research which takes social demand as an evaluative tool must therefore be grounded in an understanding of the architecture of civil society, in the specific circumstances in which the research is being undertaken. Such understanding must be translated into a process of data gathering and analysis that combines consideration of actual policy texts with relevant collective expressions, submissions and commentaries regarding the issues addressed in those texts. This contextual articulation of policy data would inform the understanding of media use that can be gained through a programme of discussions and interviews with individuals that seek to sound out and draw in some of civil society's constituent elements.

The programme for researching social demand that we have outlined here is only a first step, particularly given its necessarily incomplete nature outside of specific political and social contexts. Its purpose is to generate useful research for policy-makers mandated to act and to intervene in the public interest by indicating an alternative to the market demand model for defining what that interest might be. As such, it can play an agenda-setting function by highlighting under-studied, unaccounted-for or unmet aspects of the public interest and necessitating, at least, larger-scale research or public debate, and at most, changes to the laws and regulations which intervene in the media environment.

Recent work in communication and cultural policy studies suggests concern for not only a specific set of research questions, but also a way of making the answers to those questions useful. An important consideration here is that useful answers cannot be found by analyzing the policy text alone, nor even by detailed study of the process by which a piece of policy is adopted and implemented. Only by confronting the imputed intentions of policy with the lived experience of the people within its purview can we begin to make such research meaningful.

Notes

1. This chapter is based on research funded by the Social Sciences and Humanities Research Council of Canada. The authors wish to thank Marcus Breen, Peter Dahlgren, Line Grenier, Tatsuro Hanada and Kevin Robins for their comments on earlier drafts. An earlier version of this chapter was published in *Television and New Media*, 2(2), May 2001: 95–115.
2. This is to be distinguished from the notion of an 'active audience', which, as a number of critics have underlined, is often falsely claimed to stand for the liberation of the individual through the act of consumption.
3. Here, we bear in mind the contested nature of the term 'ethnography' itself (Hammersley, 1992), as well as Lull's (1996) important caveat regarding the potential pitfalls of 'determined ethnographies' and Livingstone's (1996) well-placed scepticism towards the 'fad' of including an audience dimension in research designs of researchers who have little experience with audience research.
4. Cf., for example, McRobbie's (1996) suggestion that, after the critiques of empiricism, ethnography and the category of experience, researchers rehabilitate these practices critically rather than abandon them.

5. Thompson, for example, writes that only by developing 'regulated pluralism' can media institutions today 'occupy a space between the unbridled operation of market forces, on the one hand, and direct control by the state, on the other' (1990: 249).
6. This type of national media policy provision can be related to the increasing presence in international agreements of guarantees around the issue of cultural rights (cf. Niec, 1998; and Venturelli, 1998).

The Development of a European Civil Society through EU Public Service Communication

Jackie Harrison

Introduction

It is the case that one of the more intriguing things about Europe is that its history of wars and conflict is accompanied by its history of self-scrutiny and desire for cooperation; where the 'self critical appreciation of the wrongs committed by Europeans in their own history' (Offe, 2000: 8) has been and still is conducted. Or, as Habermas puts it, Europe has now a history increasingly based on the 'recognition of reasonable disagreement' (2001: 22). Correspondingly Moravcsik talks of the European Union (EU)[1] as being the 'most successful experiment in political institution building since the second world war' (2005: 2), one which has 'fundamentally altered the way Europeans think about national sovereignty and national identity' (2008b: 17). Currently in the EU the most important area where 'self-critical appreciation', the 'recognition of reasonable disagreement' and thinking about 'national sovereignty and national identity' is articulated is as a response to the question about the extent to which the EU must or must not accompany current negative economic integration with positive civil, social and political integration. It is in relation to this question that the agreed plaudits for the achievements of the EU thus far become differences of opinion, of a bewildering array, about its future. It is civil integration which interests me in this chapter, here expressed in the form of the question: how might the EU begin to develop a European civil society?[2]

To be precise, what follows is premised on the belief that the EU does need to and can do more to develop a European civil society. One which has attendant civil powers, where both public and popular versions of non-economic integration are able to challenge each other and subsequently to influence the extent of European integration desired by non-civil authority and institutions. Specifically, I am interested in the conditions under which the expression of European public opinions (inclusive of: those who favour the EU status quo; protagonists for incremental changes; advocates of extensive and greater civil, social and political integration; secessionists; and irredentists) can be communicatively facilitated in an audiovisual way which is both European-wide and which is independent from the various political and economic institutions that currently govern and regulate the EU. Given this, I argue that the EU once more needs to engage in some institution building. This time the EU should build a pan-European organization of public service communication (EU PSC) consisting of two distinct but related audiovisual institutions united in their concern for the facilitation of the EU's civil and social aims: one, an audiovisual institution of European public news journalism and, two, an institution of European social communication. I only deal with the former in this chapter, the purpose of which is to facilitate the development of a critically independent European civil society.[3]

I shall proceed by arguing as follows. The next section considers why such an audiovisual institution is needed, namely to contribute towards helping to overcome the EU's communication deficit, something which itself arises within the context of the EU's current democratic make up. The third section asks from what and where such an audiovisual institution derives its legitimacy, namely the common communicative assets of European-wide nationally based public service broadcasting systems, combined with some aspects of the Commission's plans for its own audiovisual communication services. And finally, in the fourth section, I offer some thoughts about the significance of such an audiovisual institution for a nascent EU civil society, a new set of public news journalism conditions for the EU, under which the expression of European public opinion(s) and civil contestation over the future of the EU in their diversity and differences could flourish.

The context of Europe's communication deficit

Any contemporary characterization of the EU, combined with a concern for the issue of European integration, is now faced (post the rejection of the Constitutional Treaty in 2005 and the Irish rejection in June 2008 of the 2007 Lisbon Treaty), as Moravcsik (2008a) rightly points out, with having to address the question of what European integration is. Moravcsik (2002, 2005, 2008a) provides the answer through what he consistently refers to as the 'European Constitutional Settlement' which represents 'a stable endpoint of European integration in the medium term' (2008a: 159). In other words, look beneath the rhetoric of citizenship and the rights of individuals in the Constitutional Treaty (2004) and the Treaties of Amsterdam (1997), Nice (2001) and Lisbon (2007) and you will still find Europe working within the purview of a perfectly reasonable democratic and constitutional settlement laid down as early as the Treaty of Rome (1957). Of the recent attempt to found a European constitution Moravcsik argues that it was ill-conceived and idealistic, and, worse, it was unnecessary. This, accompanied by the fact that 'the most fundamental source of the EU's legitimacy lies in the democratic accountability of national governments' (Moravcsik, 2002: 619; also see 2008b: 19–20), explains why Europe is such a success. Indeed, since the 1970s 'Constitutional checks and balances, indirect democratic control via national governments, and the increasing powers of the European Parliament are sufficient to ensure that EU policy-making is, in nearly all cases, clean, transparent, effective and politically responsive to the demands of European citizens' (Moravcsik, 2002: 605). The last point is the most important for this chapter and can be understood accordingly.[4]

The deliberative democratic critique of the EU rests on the curious premise that the creation of more opportunities for direct participation or public deliberation would automatically generate a deeper sense of political community in Europe. As a general claim, there is good reason to doubt that this is the case. Even if increased participation were desirable, it is unlikely to occur. European voters do not fully exploit their current opportunities to participate in existing European elections: the turnout across Europe in the 2009 election was a mere 43 per cent. In other words, when it comes to EU elections, citizens are non-responsive because, according to Moravcsik, they are apathetic in matters regarding the extent of EU competencies and integration. Also, for Moravcsik the inclusion of civil society into the workings of the EU is not salient to European voters' priorities, which remain nationally based and concentrate on domestic issues (2008a: 178).

By and large attempts to communicatively engage European citizens have been desultory and deracinated (Harrison, 2009) and the irony still remains that the voters most passionate about the EU are in fact its 'enemies'. EU ideals are judged to be either threatening and to be resisted, or at best irrelevant and, according to Moravcsik, their advocates, EU idealists, should be disowned (2005).

Much of what Moravcsik says is correct: the EU is largely an economic and political success, thus far, and intergovernmental cooperation is sufficiently liberal, flexible and transparent to ensure that the common market remains in relatively good working order and to show that democratic checks and balances work. While social policy is more difficult to assess than economic policy, most neutral Euro-watchers would say of it that it is in parts good and progressive and in other parts regressive, favouring national citizens and disadvantaging immigrants, the poor, the less well educated and women. Again the flexible market has its usual and customary array of victims, which European social policy, like social policy elsewhere, has done little to ameliorate in the face of neo-liberal economics. Nevertheless overall progress is being made in some areas of social policy. Alongside economic and social issues, it is also possible to begin to recognize a particularly European approach to international affairs, one where international conflict resolution is sought through the exercise of civilian power, or as it is also called 'EU normative power' (see Pace, 2007) – in diplomacy, trade and international law – rather than the threat or exercise of military force (though the EU does undertake policing activities).

At this point it would be prudent, given the wealth of evidence that supports Moravcsik's views above, to ask: why meddle with such success and advocate further institution building? Here one can only hold one's hand up and admit that it is a matter of principle (albeit a powerful one), which can be identified thus: 'a democratic polity requires contestation for political leadership and over policy. This aspect is an essential element of even the "thinnest" theories of democracy, yet it is conspicuously absent in the EU' (Follesdal and Hix, 2006: 533). Or to put the matter more bluntly, without an EU-wide deliberative communication ecology the EU cannot operate with democratic legitimacy. One means of achieving this legitimacy is via an appropriate and relevant communicative public and relational space, supported by appropriate civil institutions. Specifically, a space where civil contestation, by which I mean the expression of diverse public opinions and debate over Europe's future, can in part occur and where the obligation to be both part of this and to respond to such civil contestation by the EU's political and administrative apparatus is well understood and mainly observed. The relevant part for this chapter of Follesdal and Hix's critique of Moravcsik is as follows.

With regard to the non-saliency of the EU to European voters two arguments apply. First, current EU institutions acquire their legitimacy, not only because 'present outcomes are acceptable', but also because they can 'reliably be expected to secure more acceptable outcomes in the future'; however, without effective contestation over what constitutes 'more acceptable' and for whom it is the case, we are left with the problem of 'benevolent but non-accountable rulers' whose 'subjects have no institutionalized mechanisms that make them trustworthy' (Follesdal and Hix, 2006: 545). Second, it is incorrect to say that voters' preferences are fixed or purely exogenously determined. Rather, 'citizens form their views about which policy options they prefer through the processes of deliberation and party contestation'. In short, voters' preferences are shaped by the democratic process itself and this is based upon contestation and would almost definitely produce outcomes that are different to those produced by 'enlightened' technocrats. As a consequence, Follesdal and Hix (2006: 545–6) suggest that 'with no articulation of positions on several sides of a policy debate, it is no wonder that a debate over a particular policy area does not exist and that issues lack voter salience'.

For Habermas (2001: 15) the lack of an institutionalized mechanism of participation, trust and the non-salience of the EU for voters is due to the fact that: 'To date, the decisions of the Commission and Council of Ministers were largely legitimated through Member state channels.' And while this is entirely legitimate, and is regarded as a democratic strength by Moravcsik it belongs, according to Habermas (2001: 15), 'to a model of international treaty-based intergovernmental government that was appropriate only to the extent that market-creating policies were the sole object pursued'. Now that the EU is concerned with positive integration it can no longer confine itself 'to the negative coordination of operational constraints (freedoms) and must stray across the border into the positive coordination of distributive intervention'. However, 'the density of Europeans decisions, the opacity of the decision making process and the lack of opportunities for European citizens to participate in those processes provoke grass roots mistrust'. As a consequence of this, the EU lacks any meaningful form of civil contestation and European citizenship-based solidarity.

Others like Offe take a wider view; citizen involvement in Europe is premised upon the need to build a 'European Society' because the

> uncertain outcomes of the European integration of markets and countries do call for some kind of organizing capacity that is able to impose rules (voluntarily adopted rules, that is!) ... Such rules are the means for alleviating fear, generating certainties, and engendering mutual trust. Again the task of organizing civility is put on the agenda. (Offe, 2000: 15)

In short, the current institutional design of Europe is insufficient to meet the basic necessities of both civil contestation and effective civil expression. To redress this institutional insufficiency, Follesdal and Hix (2006) propose electoral reform and the adoption of 'limited democratic politics' in the EU (spelled out more fully in Hix, 2008). Habermas (2006) advocates the adoption of mechanisms that enjoin territorial consciousness with political citizenship to produce a civic citizenship-based solidarity, of which the most important mechanism is the adoption of a European constitution which protects the separation of the civil and political and enshrines within it a European patriotism, or less inspiringly, normative integration based upon a common value orientation from which the two separate spheres can deliberate and agree a future Europe. Offe (2000 and 2002) ultimately wants to see substantive arrangements made on behalf of a European-wide 'organized civility', while I advocate a new pan-European communication ecology.

None of this is to suggest that EU institutions have not been success-ful – clearly they have; nor is it to suggest they are secretive – they are more transparent than those of many corresponding member states' institutions.[5] However, past successes and current transparency do not in any logical sense entail or provide for a future of European civil contestation (or for that matter a future of public accountability or social welfare, other than that which is filtered through the mechanism of nation state representation). While transparency is certainly a necessary convenience for the already engaged (and those who understand the arcane language of such things as EU comitology) and is always an essential aid to voter deliberation, it does not in and of itself require or encourage participation in the European civil, social and political processes and it most certainly should not be confused with publicness. As Kant (1999: 347) noted: 'All actions relating to the right of other human beings are wrong if their maxim is incompatible with publicity.' While this is a negative injunction, relating only to what is 'not right', it nevertheless points, albeit indirectly and by analogy, to the same institutional insufficiency noted above; namely that there is no European-wide guarantee of publicity. In other words, the European political process is not justified in calling itself public, even though institutional transpar-ency and democratic nation state involvement through comity, nationally based commissioner appointments and ministerial sponsorship and MEP direct elections exist.

My point is that this institutional insufficiency can be redressed, in part, by creating an independent audiovisual institution that enables the public scrutiny of both the formation and application of EU policy and from which independent European-wide civil contestation can be based. Today, public scrutiny of EU political policy means and requires European-wide media scrutiny. The creation of this can only occur through the development of insti-tutional arrangements of European-wide, independent and publicly inspired journalistic scrutiny of EU policy that itself facilitates civil contestation.

The significance of Europe's communication deficit

If a journalistically inspired form of democratically motivated civil con-testation is dislocated from influencing the formation of EU policy and its application, then one aspect of this is down to the fact that nationally based media still play relatively little attention to the civil structure of Europe.

What follows is an attempt to explain the civil requirement for building an EU PSC audiovisual institution, from what particular European communicative legacy or contemporary state of affairs it can be derived and, hence, from where it acquires its legitimacy.

Alexander (2006: 31) argues the normative integration of citizens or civic solidarity is to be found in civil society, best understood as 'a sphere that can be analytically independent, empirically differentiated, and morally more universalistic vis-à-vis the state and the market and from other social spheres as well'. The civil sphere is, according to Alexander, 'a new topic for sociological analysis, a concept that can illuminate social solidarity as an independent topic in its own right and throw new light on its often tense boundary relations with other domains' (2006: 213). At the base of the civil sphere are symbolic binary codes (2006: 53–67) which divide, Durkheimian fashion, into the pure and the impure, or more specifically from our point of view, the civil and the uncivil. Importantly, these codes operate in the civil sphere at three discursive levels: motives, social relations and institutions. Motives refer to the question, 'What kinds of people are necessary for viable democracies to form?' Social relations refer to the question, 'How do civil and uncivil people get along?' Institutions refer to the question, 'What kind of organizations would be formed by these kinds of persons, with these kinds of relations?' (2006: 57). The answers to these questions provide the civil narratives of civil society. It is the publicly contested nature of these narratives that provide us with what we regard as civic virtue and civic vice and with whom we identify as fellow citizens and non-citizens. In short, these narratives depict whom we regard with trust and solidarity and whom we do not. As members of a civil society we operate within both a cultural environment and an institutional one, with the former providing the symbols and discourse of civil society and the latter its social organization. Of the latter, Alexander (2006: 69–70) writes: 'Social organizations operate inside a cultural milieu: An institution can think only inside of the categories that culture provides. At the same time, organizations are as strongly orientated by pragmatic as by ideal concerns... The institutions of civil society crystallize ideals about solidarity with and against others in specific terms.' For Alexander the institutions of civil society are of two types: communicative and regulative. The former consist of the mass media, public opinion polls and civil associations. The latter consist of law, office, party organization and free and fair elections. It is only the former that concern us here.

Communicative institutions are anchored in the life world of public opinion and they articulate, 'the inclusive and exclusive relationships established by civil society... [the] structures of feeling, the diffusely sensed obligations and rights that represent, and are at the same time evoked by, contrasting solidary ties' (Alexander, 2006: 70).

These evaluations and descriptions of the civil sphere are provided by both the fictional and the factual mass media. Of the latter it is publicly inspired news journalism, located in and serving intelligent public discourse and the formation of public opinion that contribute to a participatory political way of life whilst being (ideally) independent of the political and economic spheres. It is also ultimately and symbolically the civil news journalism of people who demand that political authorities, public bodies and organizations are subject to the basic principle of public scrutiny which is regarded as foundational and essential to the legitimacy of all forms of political and economic arrangements. Indeed, for Calhoun (2007) this is the too frequently overlooked positive side to the nation state; the way national identity is fostered in a civil and un-coerced way (or corrupted by power, money, administrative abuses or violence). Conversely, Calhoun (2003: 233) has also noted elsewhere that: 'If Europe is not merely a place but a space in which distinctively European relations are forged and European visions of the future enacted, then it depends on communication in public, as much as on distinctly European culture, or political institutions, or economic, or social networks.' In other words, the challenge for the EU is to identify and build a European-wide public communication space to replicate the great communicative achievements of the nation state. To understand this last point properly we must look at the way nationally based public service broadcasters (and broadcasters with public service obligations) and EU communications policy share overlapping civil aspirations and aims, and it is towards understanding these aspirations and aims that we must now turn.

National public service broadcasting across Europe is, admittedly, a patchwork quilt of success, failings and failures, with the aspirations of some services at variance with what actually happens currently.[6] To be clear, I focus here only on stated civil aspirations and aims and not on their particular adherence or subversion locally.[7] Across Europe, PSB policy-makers talk of PSB being variously: a 'medium and factor in the process and free formation of individual and public opinion...to provide a comprehensive overview of international, European, national and regional affairs in all essential areas of life in order to promote international understanding, European integration and social cohesion' (Germany); a service of 'quality diversity and plurality' (Denmark); to 'encourage knowledge of constitutional values (such as liberty justice and pluralism) and of civic values, such as peace...provide objective and truthful information...actively promote democratic debate and the right of relevant social and political groups to have access to public service programming...foster the exchange of information among citizens of the European Union' (Spain); to 'support democracy...support tolerance and multiculturalism...promote cultural interaction and provide programming directed abroad' (Finland); a medium for 'sustaining citizenship and civil society, a vehicle for promoting education and learning, stimulating creativity and cultural excellence' (United Kingdom); and a service which has 'an appropriate number of hours...devoted to education, information, cultural promotion...access to programmes for political parties, trade unions, religious groups and other associations of social interest...long distance teaching...realization of interactive digital services' (Italy). With regard to France the following description suffices; the *sociétés nationales de programmes* (SNPs) are 'under the retrospective supervision of the regulatory authority' responsible for interpreting the requirements of the public sector broadcasters to represent cultural, linguistic, information (including 'currents of thinking'), opinion and genre pluralism, maintain programme quality and introduce innovation.

In its recent Communication the European Commission (Commission, 2008b: 3) described the aspiration and aims of EU's communication policy thus: 'better use of the audiovisual media should aim at supplying information in a form that is attractive to users, promotes active European citizenship and contributes to the development of the European public sphere'. The means to do this is by supporting future European-wide networks of EU content broadcasters, as well as maintaining current support for EuroNews, Europe by Satellite (EbS) and EUTube, all of which is seen as a logical extension of the Commission's communications policy. The Commission's rationale for the audiovisual element of the EU communications policy is simple; 64 per cent of Europeans are interested in EU news and would prefer this news on 'their favourite TV and radio channel' (Commission, 2008b: 4). However, 'the EU-related information provided by national audiovisual media takes up less than 10% of the time allocated to national news' (Commission, 2008b: 4). The solution, it is suggested, is threefold: one, to make available to media professionals a greater quantity of information about EU affairs; two, to develop and improve the EU's communication policy of creating networks of TV channels while respecting full editorial independence; and, three, to increase the production and dissemination (on EU platforms) of high-quality edited audiovisual reports and explanatory video news releases (VNRs). The first solution is supported by Europe by Satellite (EbS), the EU Audiovisual Library and the EU Events Calendar. The second solution is supported by the European Radio Network (EURANET), a proposed European TV Network (2009–10) and EuroNews. The third solution is supported by greater video production, improved video and audio on demand, improved guidelines of EU audiovisual products and the use of promotional activities (which includes attendance at media fairs, distributing updated material, seminars for journalists and enabling commission staff to engage in open debate). All in all, this represents a comprehensive audiovisual package serving an explicitly civil and public purpose of developing a deliberative European public sphere.

What the selective citations from the constitutional missions of diverse European public service broadcasters and the stated aim of current EU communications policy point to is an apparent consensus and similarity of purpose with regard to the plausibility of public service communication initiatives achieving net democratic and civil benefits. This is clearly understood by the EU Commission: 'The Commission's overall objective, in the very fragmented, multifaceted and evolving audiovisual market, is to increase coverage of EU affairs and thus help people to engage in a properly informed and democratic debate on EU policies' (Commission, 2008b: 11). Overall it seems as if both nationally based EU public service broadcasters and EU communication policy share the same aspirations and aims which can be summarized as: (a) to provide the opportunity for deliberation and to aid the settlement of political contests; and (b) to be part of that that which is specifically concerned with civil identity, civil power, 'civil repair' (the phrase is Alexander's) and the capacity of peoples to independently respond to political and economic policy formation and application. The former (a) attempts to underwrite political legitimacy, while the latter (b) ties political legitimacy to specific issues of the nature, extent and effectiveness of civil cooperation, or more ambitiously civil society. It is PSB understood this way that provides the EU with a form of legitimacy from which to engage in public communication. But once past these laudable aims, the EU's own audiovisual services are much more narrowly practised.

Regrettably the EU's own audiovisual services are more concerned with matters of explanation; by providing media professionals with justificatory audiovisual reports and explanatory VNRs; enhancing the availability of EU-produced information and information about the EU through networks of TV channels; and promoting administrative transparency, which in part are commendable and correct, but only go some little way to meeting the requirements of democratic deliberation and debate and the development of a European civil society. The example of EuroNews shows how quickly the rhetoric surrounding EU audiovisual policy turns into something much more limited.

The civil legitimacy set by nationally based public service broadcasters is emulated only in the rhetoric of EU communications policy and not in the application of that policy, which is disappointingly thin. Current EU communications policy is not wrong in principle, but in application it lacks the facility to enable civil contestation. And that is, I contend, because it has no institution of public news journalism contained within it. Because of this it cannot redress the situation summarized by Schlesinger, as

> The mediated public sphere in the EU remains first, overwhelmingly national; second, where it is not national it is transnational and Anglophone but elitist in

class terms; third, where it is ostensibly transnational but not Anglophone, it still decants principally into national modes of address. (2004: 17)

A European audiovisual communication institution of public news journalism

What I have described above is a circle, which can be summarized thus: the thin application of the EU's own communications policy has the effect of reinforcing the political and civil deficit, and the continuing political and civil deficit ensure the continuing application of a thin EU communications policy. In effect the civil deficit across Europe is such that EU communications policy can only provide rhetorical support for the development of a European public sphere(s) simply because it has not created the communicative conditions or the opportunities for European-wide civil contestation and therefore the opportunity for the development of a wider European civil society. The trick is to break out of the circle. And this can only be done by an act of political will. What needs to be done is to copy the way nationally based public service broadcasters have, following best practice, been so successful in helping to develop and protect their respective public spheres by using a repertoire of cultural categories, principles and values that circumscribe their public news journalism effort and which links to the stated aims of developing and protecting civil contestation. And while nationally based public service broadcasters do not differ from country to country in their idealization, it is quite easy to separate out best PSB practices from the diversity of achievements represented by European PSB providers. Countries like Austria, Belgium, the Czech Republic after digital switchover, Denmark, Germany, Netherlands, the UK *et al.* have much to teach the EU with regard to independent public news journalism, the promotion of civil identity, pluralism, openness, diversity, quality and the promotion of education and learning, the point being that from a variety of backgrounds strong nationally based public service broadcasters can and do deploy their public news journalism efforts independently of the political and economic systems and the type of broadcasting regime they operate under.[8] They do this to support and apply the principle of public scrutiny (or publicity). And ideally this is what EU communications policy needs to replicate, particularly at a time when national public service broadcasters are themselves at the mercy of EU competition policy (Harrison and Woods, 2007). It is through the public news journalism of PSB that the idealistic cultural categories of civil society are applied. In Alexander's (2006: 214) terms, it is the institutions of civil society (of which PSB is one) which 'crystallize ideals about solidarity with and against others in specific terms' and which feed the debate about openness and closure and ultimately constitute progressive social change. And yet, where EU communications policy is concerned, an understanding of the necessity to have an audio-visual institution which houses an institution of pan-European public news journalism, which resides alongside initiatives like the pan-European channels such as EURANET, the proposed European TV Network (2009–10) and EuroNews, is missing.

What I am proposing as the way out of the circle described above is that if the EU wishes to move forward with regard to developing a European civil society that conducts itself at the level of deliberation, debate and civil contestation it needs to build an independent pan-European audiovisual communications institution of public news journalism which is anchored in the idealistic aspirations and aims of European PSB and its best practices, and remains loyal to the idea of reporting European public opinions, thereby facilitating the development of a European civil society:

> For most members of civil society, and even for institutional elites, the news is the only source of firsthand experience they will ever have about their fellow citizens, about their motives for acting the way they do, the kind of relationships they form, and the nature of the institutions they might potentially create. (Alexander, 2006: 80)

I do not want to exaggerate the role of public news journalism, nor do I wish to diminish its influence either. What I am suggesting is that public news journalism is an institution of civil society that helps to protect and develop the boundaries of civil society and stands for the principle (and one form) of the application of public scrutiny. In this regard it is an important way of independently informing public opinion. An illustration of this is the way the American Civil Rights movement was shaped by the news media. Alexander (2007: 650–1) notes:

> In contrast with its southern counterpart, the leading northern media was sympathetic to demand for expanding civil solidarity, and they performed their communicative role in a more professional manner, giving more play to independent norms of universalism and less to the particularistic primordialities of race. Whether the journalists who carried out these institutional mandates were of northern or southern origin, black or white, or Jewish or Christian was beside the point. It was the independence of their institutions of civil power that allowed them to succeed.

The point here is that independence and influence combined with a form of purposive public news journalism and came together to shape the development of American civil society and, in this case, to advocate and to help institute a form of civil repair (on this see Alexander, 2006: 307–17, 359–95). Using this as just one empirical example of the civil power of public news journalism (albeit a wide-ranging example, consisting as it does of both press and audiovisual news services) to show how it can influence a social movement and effect a variety of forms of legal and civil repair, it seems reasonable to suggest that there is a capacity for public news journalism to be a mode of influence and sentiment which can help bring about civil society, or engender change within civil society.

Current media scholarship supports the broad-based view that public news services are a vitally important element of democratic communication only where they are trusted – that is, judged to be accurate, balanced and independent of vested interests. Where these conditions apply then public news journalism does have civil influence and is subsequently used as a trusted source to inform and debate civil actions. From this (and here I am arguing by extension) I would say that there is no very good reason why an independent pan-European audiovisual institution of public news journalism cannot translate the idealistic aspirations and aims of EU communications policy into a pragmatic and critical assessment of their civil significance and their application independently of the political and economic spheres. Such an audiovisual institution should be able to facilitate debate over whom or what constitute the core groups of European civil society and what they stand for. Equally, justificatory narratives used to depict who are core and who are not, who are civil and who are uncivil would also be brought out into the open. In short, an independent pan-European audiovisual communications institution of public news journalism could instantiate genuine European-wide debate about the EU's future form and scope. If this is so then it seems to me that any risks inherent[9] in the EU supporting the development of an independent EU-wide institution[10] of public news journalism seems worth taking if current EU communication aims, with regard to the establishment of a European public sphere(s), are serious and authentic and are to stand any chance of being fulfilled.

Notes

1. I use the term EU and Europe synonymously.
2. I shall leave aside discussing the place of the ECJ and its civil role and how far the ECJ is itself a civil force for the development of a European civil society.
3. Importantly an EU PSC strategy is also a social necessity and should provide for a new set of EU welfare conditions through the utilization of interactive services in areas like health, education and other elements of social policy.
4. I am only interested in Moravcsik's response to the deliberative democracy critique of his notion of 'The European Constitutional Settlement' here and not his respective responses to the libertarian and the pluralist and social democratic critique which can be found (2008a: 173–7).

5. And will be even more so if the Treaty of Lisbon 2007 is ratified.
6. See Harrison 2009 and Harrison and Woods (2007).
7. On this see Open Society Institute (2008).
8. For an assessment of different types of European public broadcasting regimes see Hallin and Mancini (2004) and Jakubowicz (2007b).
9. The inherent risk to which I refer is that all too frequently relationships between journalists and politicians and administrators break down with unpalatable results – evasion and spin on the one side and attack journalism, invasion of privacy and abuses of free speech on the other, with equal amounts of piety on both sides. But it has always been like this since the inception of the political press and in all likelihood will always remain part of the journalism, political and civil landscape, see Runciman (2008: 145–50, 197–202), although ultimately it will also remain the least important and least significant part.
10. As it did with the very independent European Central Bank.

PART TWO

Issues

The Escalating War against Corporate Media

Robert W. McChesney

A recurring issue for the Left historically has been how to address the capitalist media. In recent years the problem has grown ever more severe, and no small amount of attention has been given to examining the problems of the commercial media and how closely they reinforce and accentuate problems within the broader social order. The logic of this criticism has become clear: progressives need to work on challenging the corporate domination of media as part of the broader struggle for social justice. If changing media is left until 'after the revolution', there will be no revolution, not to mention fewer chances for social reform. But politicizing control over media has proven to be extraordinarily difficult for activists. That is why the massive and largely unanticipated 2003 campaign in the USA to stop further media concentration, which almost overnight reached a scale not seen in media reform struggles since the 1930s, is so important and instructive. This chapter chronicles that revolt.

The media reform movement comes to life

Today we can see that hidden from public view in the 1990s had been a mounting concern over media. The changes wrought by neo-liberal measures such as the 1996 Telecommunications Act only fanned the flames of this burgeoning movement. Magazines such as *The Nation*, *The Progressive* and *In These Times* began to feature stories not only criticizing mainstream media but also reporting on nascent efforts to change media policies. The progressive media watch group Fairness and Accuracy In Reporting (FAIR) flourished, as did the Media Education Foundation, the premier producer of critical videos on media. Across the nation local media watch groups, reform organizations and independent media outlets began to sprout. Critical books on media and journalism began selling better than they had in the past. National 'media and democracy' conferences were held in San Francisco and New York in 1996 and 1997, respectively, drawing many hundreds of activists.

Media activism was enjoying a distinct dynamism. The emergence of Independent Media Centers in the wake of the Seattle protests against the World Trade Organization (WTO) in 1999 galvanized opposition to corporate media among a generation of young activists. Already media reform activism had reached a level not seen in many decades, but it still had not reached the levels of the Progressive Era and the 1930s. Despite all the activity and despite evidence that the American people were concerned about this issue, the media reform movement was almost entirely outside the mainstream political culture and invisible within the commercial news media. It did not exist in the minds of the overwhelming majority of the American people.

At the dawn of the 21st century, the media reform movement had its first notable skirmish in the battle for low-power FM radio (LPFM). The technology began in the late 1980s, when it became possible to transmit radio signals easily and inexpensively, and soon several people began conducting low-power broadcasting on the open FM frequencies in their communities. The pioneer was an African-American activist, Mbanna Kantako, who began broadcasting to his neighbourhood in Springfield, Illinois. By the 1990s, scores of people were engaging in low-power broadcasting, and they were doing so without licences from the Federal Communications Commission (FCC). Commercial broadcasters demanded that the FCC stop the 'pirates', and the FCC obliged – taking legal action against several micro-broadcasters. But it soon became apparent that the low cost and ease of use of the technology made it virtually impossible to police. That these broadcasters were able easily to locate open slots in the FM band – and therefore not interfere with existing stations – made LPFM seem benign, and it roused no public concern.

FCC chairman William Kennard recognized the difficulty in policing LPFM and decided to implement a widespread but cautious programme to legalize LPFM stations across the nation. He was especially concerned with how the lifting of the radio ownership caps in 1996 had led to a sharp decline in the number of African-American station owners. Because most minority station owners generally held only a small number of stations, they found it impossible to compete with emerging giants like Clear Channel and were forced to sell out. Kennard wanted a plan that would get LPFM licences into the hands of community groups representing people underserved by the commercial radio system.

After months of study the FCC released its plan – generally regarded by LPFM advocates as being more cautious than necessary – for the establishment of more than 1,000 LPFM stations in 2000. These non-commercial stations would be licensed to locally based non-profit organizations. On the surface this looked like a clear victory for the American people: more stations, more choice, no commercialism and more local content. Only one very small group of individuals disliked the plan: owners and managers of commercial broadcasting companies. These broadcasters did not want more competition for 'their' listeners, especially not of a non-commercial and local variety. Such competition might require them to reduce advertising and increase local content to keep listeners from defecting, and those changes would come directly out of their profit margins.

The National Association of Broadcasters (NAB) put a full court press on Congress to overturn Kennard's LPFM plan. The lobby could not, for PR purposes, admit to greed as a motive; instead it argued that 1,000 new LPFM stations would create interference with the signals transmitted by existing broadcasters. The House, led by the commercial broadcasters' chief advocate in that body, Representative Billy Tauzin, voted to overturn Kennard's plan and reduce the number of LPFM stations to around 200–300, mostly in small cities and rural areas. The Senate was less willing to oblige corporate broadcasters, significantly because the ranking Republican on the relevant Senate Commerce Committee, Arizona's John McCain, refused to comply with the NAB's wishes.

Media reform activists learned crucial lessons from the LPFM fight: organizing around tangible reform proposals could actually generate popular support and sustained attention on Capitol Hill. For the first time in memory, organized people were challenging organized money on media policy issues. The industry had been forced to resort to a middle-of-the-night manoeuvre to get its way. Momentum for media reform continued to grow. The issue that finally put the media reform movement on the map was media ownership regulations. The 1996 Telecommunications Act required the five-member FCC to review its media ownership rules every two years to see if they needed to be revised in view of changing circumstances.

The FCC announced its next biennial review of media ownership rules in September 2002. As a result of this review, ownership restrictions would have to be defended or else the rules would be tossed and media ownership would be subject only to antitrust enforcement, like other industries. Six rules were under review, including the prohibition against newspaper–broadcast cross-ownership and the rules regulating the number of TV stations a single firm could own locally and nationally. At that point, firms were permitted to own only one TV station in a market, except in the very largest cities, where they could own two. Firms were also prohibited from owning TV stations that, in total, reached more than 35 per cent of the population, though both Viacom and News Corporation had been granted waivers by the FCC to exceed that figure. These were the rules that the industry was most eager to see relaxed or eliminated.

Powell and Copps take the stage

It was ironic that FCC chairman Michael Powell would be the official responsible for demonstrating to the courts that media ownership rules could be justified as serving the public interest. The son of Colin Powell, Michael Powell was being groomed for a career as a major player in the Republican Party. Long before the autumn of 2002, Powell had emerged as an enthusiastic, almost religious, proponent of neo-liberal ideology and called for extending 'full First Amendment rights' to commercial broadcasters. In theory that meant unvarnished praise for free markets; in practice it meant giving the corporate media lobbies whatever they wanted. Powell had never been especially concerned about media concentration. 'Monopoly is not illegal by itself in the United States,' Powell commented in early 2002. 'People tend to forget this. There is something healthy about letting innovators try to capture markets' (Rose, 2002). While he acknowledged that a complete monopoly was problematic legally, he characterized the duopoly of satellite television – with two firms controlling the entire market – as 'a vibrant competitive market' (*Broadcasting & Cable*, 2001). Powell conceded that he found the very notion of public interest regulation dubious: 'The public interest works with letting the market work its magic' (Rose, 2002). In Powell's view, he was 'working himself out of a job' at the FCC by having public interest regulation eliminated, and the sooner he did it, the better (Roberts, 2001).

Having this corporate media enthusiast in charge of defending the FCC's right to regulate media ownership in the public interest was like putting Florida's Republican then-secretary of state Katherine Harris in charge of Al Gore's Florida recount team in November 2000. The other two Republican members of the FCC, Kathleen Q. Abernathy and Kevin Martin were, if anything, even more devoted to advancing commercial media interests. Because the commission had a vacancy for a Democratic member in the autumn of 2002, the one dissenting voice to a thorough relaxation of media ownership rules was Michael Copps, a Democrat with a doctoral degree in history, who had been appointed to the commission in 2001. A self-described New Dealer, Copps was the one vote against approving Comcast's takeover of AT&T's cable systems in 2002: 'The sheer economic power created by this mega-combination, and the opportunities for abuse that would accompany it, outweigh the very limited public interest benefits that either the Applicants or the majority find here.' Copps rejected the Powell–Abernathy–Martin formulation that if a merger generated increased efficiencies (generally measured by profits) it meant the deal would be beneficial to the public: 'It strikes me as bedrock that our review of proposed consolidations must venture beyond economic efficiencies if we are to ensure that combinations serve the public interest' (Copps, 2002).

At the end of 2002 all indications were that the Republican majority would get their way and ownership limits would be greatly relaxed, if not eliminated. The courts were on board. The FCC majority was on board. Only three votes were required; the deck was stacked against Copps. But in January 2003 the tide slowly but perceptibly began to change. Jonathan Adelstein, an aide to then-Senator Tom Daschle, joined the FCC as the second Democrat and immediately demonstrated that he shared Copps's concerns.

Here the work of the Consumers Union and other activist organizations to educate members of Congress on media ownership issues paid dividends.

Beltway opposition stiffens

By the end of January 2003, any hope that Michael Powell and the FCC majority were going to breeze through relaxation of media ownership rules was dashed. Powell's refusal to join Copps and Adelstein in a series of public hearings around the nation to solicit public input was becoming more and more of a PR problem. Finally, 'clearly feeling the pressure', as one broadcasting trade publication observed, Powell made an 'unusual turnaround' (McClintock, 2003) and agreed to hold one official hearing in Richmond, Virginia, in February.

In a sense, Powell deserves some sympathy. His career had been built upon lavishing praise on the market and unbridled contempt for ownership rules or regulation in the public interest – but, as the response from Congress and the public made clear by January, that tack would be counterproductive in 2003. Powell began to present himself as an earnest pragmatist repelled by extremism and incendiary rhetoric. 'I am absolutely a good middle-of-the-road moderate' (Fine, 2003) he told an audience at Harvard in April. His moderation, however, was not based on any moderation of his extreme views on regulation, but, rather, upon his willingness to proceed at a slower pace to get what he wanted.

Powell spent much of the first half of 2003 painting himself as the reluctant deregulator. The court of appeals in Washington DC had based its 2002 ruling on the belief that Congress's intent in the 1996 Telecommunications Act was to eliminate media ownership rules unless incontrovertible and overwhelming evidence justified their continuation in the public interest. Powell accepted this view and elected not to appeal the court's interpretation. Had Powell elected to appeal the court's interpretation of the Telecommunications Act, he would have had a powerful legal case. Although the spirit of the law pushed towards relaxation of the rules, since competition was presumed to be increasing, Senator John McCain, chairman of the Senate Commerce Committee, argued that the law permitted the FCC to *tighten* media ownership rules if it found market conditions warranted doing so in the public interest. At any rate, conditions had not changed much since 1996 when the law was passed. If Congress had wanted to throw out the ownership rules in 1996, it could have done so itself. Indeed, the evidence from Congress was clear: many who voted for the Telecommunications Act intended ownership rules to remain unless striking, unforeseeable developments occurred. The FCC's job was to monitor these developments.

Few in Congress bought Powell's line that 'the courts are making me do this'. Literally scores of members of Congress wrote to Powell in 2003 making explicit their conviction that the appeals court interpretation of congressional intent was wrong.

Powell's three arguments

In general, as Powell made his case for relaxing the media ownership rules, he seemed to be channelling Rupert Murdoch or Sumner Redstone as he spoke. This hardly helped his image as a moderate pragmatist determined to salvage what he could of public interest regulation in a hostile world, or at least, in the face of a hostile Appeals Court. Powell made three points over and over during the course of 2003. First, he argued that with the radical increase in media channels due to cable TV and the internet, concerns over media concentration were quickly becoming 'a moot issue'. 'Today choices abound,' Powell wrote in *USA Today*. 'This abundance means more programming, more choice, and more control in the hands of citizens' (Powell, 2003). In addition to hundreds of TV channels, 'Americans now have access to a bottomless well of information called the Internet.' Powell maintained that this 'democratization of technology' (Powell, 2003) undermined traditional concerns about media concentration and any rationale for ownership regulation. Here Powell echoed NBC CEO Robert Wright, who termed media ownership rules 'ridiculous' (Bishop, 2003). Indeed, Powell proclaimed that the problem with the media system was not too much concentration but 'hyper-competitiveness' that led desperate firms to present vulgar fare they might not produce otherwise.

Although Powell was correct about the emergence of new channels, the argument that this undermined the need for ownership regulation was far from convincing. Chris Murray of the Consumers Union pointed out, 'Yes, there are 500 channels on cable television, but five companies control the same market share that the three networks did in the 1970s' (Glasner, 2003). The degree to which the same large media corporations owned the TV networks, the cable TV channels and the Hollywood film studios was a subject that Powell, with his purported obsession with quantitative data, never acknowledged. If the FCC relaxed the ownership rules further, those five companies would only increase their hold. Although there were a gazillion websites, that hardly qualified as genuine commercial competition.

But there was an even more fundamental problem with Powell's argument that the multitude of new media undermines concerns about media concentration. There *was* and *is* an empirical measure of the truth behind this statement, a way to determine whether conditions had changed sufficiently to justify relaxing media ownership limits on broadcasters. The traditional justification for having media ownership rules was based on the idea that the government was granting firms beachfront property in the media system when they were given monopoly licences to broadcast channels. Therefore the public had an interest in preventing firms from monopolizing these scarce licences and dominating the media system. If the existence of so many new media channels through cable TV and the internet had undermined the market power of the broadcast licences, then having a TV or radio channel was no longer owning beachfront property but rather holding a mere grain of sand on the digital beach, as Michael Powell suggested.

In that scenario, one would rationally expect the value of radio and TV licences to stagnate and eventually fall. After all, what rational capitalist would spend hundreds of millions of dollars to purchase a TV station if someone else could effectively compete with him by spending a pittance to produce 100 websites? In fact, the value of radio and TV licences had increased since 1996, and at a much greater rate than the rate of inflation. These licences do indeed continue to confer tremendous market power or, as economists would say, monopolistic power. That is why large media companies lobby incessantly to relax the ownership rules: they want to purchase more stations. That is why media ownership rules continue to be necessary. When News Corporation and Viacom and Disney and General Electric are dumping their TV stations and the price of a licence is going into the toilet, Powell will have a more convincing case.

Powell's second argument on behalf of relaxing media ownership rules was related to the first; he claimed that unless big media companies could own more and more TV stations they would not be able to make a profit and 'free TV' would end. The current media ownership rules were going to drive the major TV networks out of business. In making this argument, Powell presented himself as a populist crusader focused on the needs of those who could not afford cable TV, satellite TV, or pay-per-view channels. (This, of course, seemed to contradict his first argument about everyone having access to limitless choice on the internet.) The hardship claim was straight out of the TV networks' playbook. Viacom president Mel Karmazin told the Senate Commerce Committee in May that network television is 'not a very good business'. Viacom's lobbyists argued that media ownership rules had to be relaxed 'to help ensure that free, over-the-air broadcasting continues to be available across America'. Rupert Murdoch told Congress that allowing broadcast companies to own more stations was necessary for over-the-air television to survive: 'It's about impossible to run an entertainment network at a profit' (Boliek, 2003a).

There were two problems with this argument. First, even if true, is it rational public policy to protect firms in a dying industry? Shouldn't there be a broader debate about how best to deploy public resources, if the network TV structure had become outdated? Also, even if the networks were struggling, the parent companies were almost all doing very well and also owned most of the cable TV channels. What guarantee was there that these firms would maintain free television in the future? Perhaps these companies would get to own all the stations and then determine that there was a more profitable use of the public airwaves. Was Powell prepared to require these companies to broadcast free television in exchange for receiving more TV channels? In short, Powell's 'policy' with regard to saving network TV seemed half-baked.

The second problem with Powell's campaign to 'save free TV' was that it was premised on a bogus claim – in fact, an outright lie. Media mogul Barry Diller, who built the Fox TV network, scoffed at Powell's concerns about the networks' financial health. Ironically, exactly at the moment Powell was pressing this case, in May 2003, the same TV networks that claimed to be on their deathbed recorded the greatest wave of advance advertising sales in US history. Market research suggested that broadcast advertising was expected to continue to climb at a healthy clip through 2007. Their economic future was bright indeed.

Powell's third argument contradicted the logic of his second argument, in which he suggested that media mergers might save free TV. He now claimed that the relaxation of media ownership rules that the FCC proposed would not amount to a big deal. Powell wrote, 'our nation's media landscape will not become significantly more concentrated as a result of changes to the FCC rules' Powell, 2003). Therefore, Powell suggested, his opponents were making much ado about nothing.

Powell provided no evidence for this argument. Indeed, there was considerable evidence that the largest media firms and Wall Street investment banking houses anticipated a major wave of media mergers once the rules were relaxed. 'Everyone is waiting for the new rules; then they'll pounce,' one banker predicted. The trade press teemed with articles throughout the first half of 2003 in which industry insiders discussed the impending merger mania. The tone was often giddy. 'Major media companies are drawn and cocked,' the *Denver Post* publisher and MediaNews Group CEO William Dean Singleton announced. Singleton was especially pleased because the FCC rule changes would make it possible for firms like his to grow so large as to assure their dominance of the internet: 'We are in the news and information business. In fact, we own it' (Young and Weber, 2003: 96).

The greatest wave of mergers was expected at the local level, where the profit potential of owning the daily newspaper, two or three TV stations and eight radio stations was the stuff of media owner fantasies. After all, look at what Clear Channel had accomplished with radio since 1996. Imagine if you could toss in the daily newspaper and a few TV stations, too. As one investment analyst put it, 'The media companies' top priority is more concentrated power in local markets.' 'The big guys will get bigger,' a leading media financial analyst concluded, sounding a bit like Don Corleone, 'and the little guys will have to decide whether they want to exist anymore' (Klein and Vise, 2003). Of course, no one knew for certain what would happen. Perhaps time would prove Powell's third argument correct and there would not be all that many deals as a result of rules relaxation.

Opposition grows beyond the beltway

Michael Powell's campaign to advance the case for loosening media ownership rules in the spring of 2003 was based upon contradictory arguments constructed with dubious evidence. In the battle for public opinion, this put him at a decided disadvantage. His arguments did not appear to convince people who were not invested in the system and did not share his euphoric attitude towards the US commercial media system. In years past, that wouldn't have mattered because Americans would have been clueless about the FCC's proceedings. But in 2003 many things had changed, not the least of which was that FCC member Michael Copps had taken it upon himself to rouse public interest and involvement in the issue.

The official FCC hearing in Richmond on 27 February was an omen. Four of the five hours were devoted to panelists, and most of the 21 experts were from out of town, including a large contingent of industry representatives. The public then had an hour to make statements – and every speaker opposed relaxing the media ownership rules. Over the next three months 12 more public hearings were held across the nation. The events were always non-partisan, organized by a local university or civic group and featured representatives of the broadcasting industry. Numerous activists groups, like Jeff Chester's Center for Digital Democracy and the Benton Foundation, helped organize the events. There were also a number of smaller events, sometimes attended by Copps or Adelstein separately. In most cases, members of Congress from the area participated. Some events were attended by fewer than 200 people, as in Detroit, Chicago and Phoenix, but most of the rest became standing-room-only affairs with 400–1,000 attendees, as in Seattle, Philadelphia, Burlington, Atlanta and San Francisco. Even more than the turnout, it was the public's comment that caught the attention of Copps and Adelstein and energized them as they squared off with Powell and the Republicans back at FCC headquarters. 'Of the hundreds of citizens I heard from, many extremely articulate, not one of them stood up to say, "I want to see even more concentration in our media ownership." Not one,' Adelstein observed. 'The public knows instinctively what the FCC is supposed to do – protect them from large entities gaining too much control over critical channels of communication' (Federal Communications Commission, 'Statement of Commissioner Jonathan S. Adelstein, Dissenting').

This attendance was all the more incredible because the local press gave little or no advance coverage and in most cases no follow-up coverage either – especially curious since local media often had executives on hearing panels. 'That people even found out about these meetings,' Copps (2003) acknowledged, 'is a miracle.' This pointed to a problem that faced the activists throughout 2003: the paucity of mainstream news coverage. As a study conducted for the *American Journalism Review* concluded, in the first five months of 2003, commercial TV and the cable networks offered 'virtually no coverage' of the FCC deliberations on media ownership. Even the handful of newspapers that covered the story on occasion throughout the year, like the *Chicago Tribune*, 'seemed to lose interest in the consumer and democracy angles, treating the story mainly as a business and investment issue' (Lee, 2003; Ostrow, 2003).

Despite the mainstream news blackout, the movement grew rapidly. What happened to radio following the relaxation of radio ownership rules in the 1996 Telecommunications Act spurred Americans' concern about media policies. Radio was often invoked as the 'canary in the coal mine' that would predict what would happen when ownership rules for television, cable and newspapers were relaxed. And the consensus about radio was almost universally negative. Local news had disappeared, musical variety had diminished and commercialism had increased.

'If you really like what happened in radio,' Copps argued, 'you'll love what's barreling down the FCC track toward you' (Linder, 2003). Or, as he told his colleagues, 'this experience should *terrify* us'. As one reporter put it, 'The sorry state of the radio industry is sabotaging FCC chairman Michael Powell's plans to let media conglomerates run wild' (Curry, 2003; Black Commentator, 2003). Much opposition to ownership relaxation in the African-American and minority communities could be attributed to the bad experience with radio, an industry that saw minority ownership collapse since 1996 and journalism for minority groups shrivel. Indeed, Powell acknowledged that radio was in crisis, but he refused to let its condition influence his evaluation of ownership rules changes for other media.

Another issue that mobilized citizens was the fate of journalism under media concentration. The FCC had ignored or mangled this topic in its study with its 12 reports; indeed, if one looked at who actually wrote or produced news in local markets, the effects of concentrated ownership on journalism would be apparent, as would the likely impact of further relaxation of ownership. A study released by the Project for Excellence in Journalism in February 2003 concluded that larger TV station-owning companies used their market power to reduce their commitment to local journalism. Powell not only defended the status quo but also argued that increased media concentration would improve journalism: 'Scale and efficiency are becoming more vital to delivering quality news and public affairs' (Media Institute, 2003). Not many shared Powell's enthusiasm. Common Cause, the public interest citizens group, received so many expressions of concern from its several hundred thousand members about how concentrated media ownership would affect journalism and public life that it made fighting Powell its main organizing issue in 2003. Even more striking was the opposition to the relaxation of media ownership rules that came from working journalists. Their ire certainly undercut Powell's effort to wrap his media ownership plan in the guise of protecting the First Amendment. Those on the front lines saw what concentration had done to journalism and they did not want to see more of it.

For what may have been the first time in its history, the International Federation of Journalists, representing 500,000 journalists in more than 100 countries, weighed in on a US media ownership policy matter, calling Powell's plan 'a dangerous shift of power at the expense of democracy'.[1]

Journalists were not the only ones closely connected to the media industries who spoke out. All the Hollywood unions worked to oppose Powell and the FCC, in combination with most of the independent producers. 'This is really unprecedented,' the president of the west coast branch of the Writers Guild of America noted. 'It's remarkable how this one issue seems to have captured the entire community' (Sanders, 2003). Driven by the media unions, the AFL-CIO Executive Council formally opposed the relaxation of media ownership rules in March 2003. Even the Public Relations Society of America condemned Powell, and leading advertisers criticized media concentration. Numerous independent media owners such as Frank Blethen, publisher of the *Seattle Times*, stepped forward to fight against rule relaxation. Even the huge conglomerate Sony expressed concerns about concentration in the TV industry. The arguments invariably were that concentration produces lousier media content.

Powell and his supporters could rightly claim that much of this opposition within the media industries came from self-interested parties who had much to lose. But Powell's entire base of support also came from self-interested parties with much to gain. And it hardly helped Powell's cause that those on the inside of these industries, such as journalists, stated emphatically that concentration was bad for quality media content.

Left and right join the fight

As impressive as this opposition to Powell looked, two additional developments generated what would be the lion's share of the more than 3 million Americans who would formally oppose the relaxation of media ownership rules in 2003. First was the US invasion and subsequent occupation of Iraq. During the build-up to the war, in the first three months of 2003, the burgeoning antiwar movement spent considerable time castigating what it regarded as the uncritical and propagandistic nature of TV news coverage of the Bush administration's war rationale. Phil Donahue's programme was terminated by MSNBC in February; its cancellation came in the wake of an internal NBC report claiming that Donahue projected a 'difficult public face' for NBC in time of war. Cable giant Comcast refused to air an antiwar ad during Bush's State of the Union address.

The concentrated world of radio was seen as being particularly hostile to all who did not support the Bush administration. Clear Channel's DJs led pro-war rallies, fired the South Carolina 2002 'Radio Personality of the Year', allegedly for her antiwar politics, and, along with fellow radio giant Cumulus, dropped the Dixie Chicks from its playlists after a member of the band criticized Bush at a concert in England. When activists learned that the same companies that seemed most aggressively pro-war – for example, Clear Channel and Rupert Murdoch's News Corporation – were leading the lobbying fight to acquire even more media, activists started publicizing the FCC issue. Around this time, Murdoch announced his intention to purchase DirecTV, the firm that dominated US satellite television delivery.

When Powell praised the outstanding and 'thrilling' TV news coverage of the Iraq war as justifying his contention that media concentration actually promotes better journalism, it was like waving a red flag in front of a bull. The second striking development was the emergence of conservative opposition to the relaxation of media ownership rules. Some of it grew from public distaste with the vulgarity of radio and television – what conservative media activist Brent Bozell termed 'the raw sewage, the ultraviolence, the graphic sex, the raunchy language that is flooding their living rooms day and night'.[2] This persistent lewdness was exacerbated by media concentration, because huge firms provided the cheapest fare possible and were unaccountable to local communities. Conservatives also disliked the decline of local ownership and localism in commercial media. The National Rifle Association (NRA) shared these concerns – it regarded the big media conglomerates as unsympathetic to gun owners – and, at the urging of its membership, became an aggressive force against the FCC in the spring of 2003. The NRA generated several hundred thousand postcards in opposition to relaxing media ownership rules. People were astounded by the emerging alliance, with Jesse Helms in tandem with Jesse Jackson. 'When all of us are united on an issue, then one of two things has happened,' Bozell observed. 'Either the earth has spun off its axis and we have all lost our minds or there is universal support for a concept.'[3]

As popular opposition grew, increased attention turned to what, exactly, the FCC was doing. Although Powell claimed he was too busy to attend any of the public hearings in the spring, he apparently was able to carve out time to attend major conferences of media owners.

In May, a revealing report from the non-partisan Center for Public Integrity (CPI) disclosed what Powell and FCC staffers had been doing most of the spring. Since the formal review of media rules had been announced in September 2002, FCC officials had held 71 closed-door, off-the-record meetings with corporate media CEOs and their lobbyists, but only five such meetings with public interest groups. Rupert Murdoch and Viacom's Mel Karmazin had each had a series of meetings with commissioners and staffers in late January and early February, precisely when the FCC was crafting its new ownership rules. On 11 March, a group of Disney executives met with 18 different FCC officials in six different closed-door meetings. That was probably more contact than most consumer groups had had with the FCC in a decade.

The CPI also reported that corporate interests had lavished $2.8 million on FCC members for junkets over the previous eight years and that much of the data the FCC used to make its determinations of policy was provided by industry. Finally, on 2 June, a *Wall Street Journal* investigative report disclosed that Bear Stearns media analyst Victor Miller, whose job is to advise large investors concerning media stocks, played a central role in helping the FCC draft the new ownership regulations. In February

Powell had encouraged Americans to use the internet to let the FCC know their thoughts on media ownership. With interest picking up speed like a hurricane crossing the open sea, the number of e-mail messages, letters and petition signatures reaching the FCC had climbed to an extraordinary 750,000 by the end of May. There was almost no indication that anyone in the country, aside from big media owners, strongly favoured relaxing the rules.

From the FCC to Congress

Throughout the spring, as public attention was being drawn to the issue of media ownership, a sense of impending doom hung over the opposition since it was obvious that Powell was determined to ram the changes through. The counsel Powell was getting from the Bush administration fortified his resolve. In April, Commerce Secretary Don Evans informed Powell in no uncertain terms that the White House expected the ownership rules to be relaxed as planned and without delay. The Bush administration's interest in delivering relaxed media ownership rules to the media giants could be explained by its ideological commitment to 'deregulation'. It was possibly influenced as well by media corporations' large political donations, especially toward Republicans. Certainly the Bush administration's stance did nothing to discourage such donations.

In addition, the Bush administration counted some close political friends in the corporate media community. Some of the media firms most aggressively lobbying against the ownership rules were strong ideological allies. Clear Channel had a close relationship with Bush going back to his stint as Texas governor, and its stations were notorious for their pro-Republican slant. Rupert Murdoch's Fox News Channel was similarly well known as a bastion of Republican support; in October 2003, Charles Reina, who worked as a producer and writer at Fox News Channel from 1997 until he resigned in 2003, revealed that the station's management gave daily directives on issues and angles to cover that tended to correlate with White House spin. Indeed, Roger Ailes, head of Fox News Channel, had offered advice to President Bush about how to react to the 9/11 attacks.

There were even suggestions in the trade press that the administration's FCC stance was payback to the media for its treatment of Bush during the 2000 election and after, with an eye towards encouraging continued favourable coverage in the future. Generally soft media coverage extended beyond news reporting. In September 2003, Viacom's Showtime aired a docudrama, *DC 9/11: Time of Crisis*, which portrayed George W. Bush as a cross between Winston Churchill and Abraham Lincoln. Only two months later,

Viacom's CBS cancelled a miniseries on Ronald Reagan when Republican critics charged it was unsympathetic; the station then passed a watered-down version to Showtime to fend off critics charging censorship. The *Financial Times* noted that News Corporation's Fox News Channel hammered CBS on this issue and Viacom caved in exactly as the media ownership rules were in jeopardy on Capitol Hill. Even the rabidly anti-regulation trade publication *Broadcasting & Cable* was appalled by CBS's cave-in, paraphrasing Viacom's position as 'we'd better do what we're told by the DC powers that be – in this case, the Republican National Committee – if we want to be able to buy more stations' (*Broadcasting & Cable*, 2003: 40).

While we may never know the Bush administration's precise motives, it was clear that relaxation of media ownership rules had become a high priority. From its vantage point, supporting the media giants seemed to be a no-lose proposition.

On the opposing side, in the spring of 2003, activists intensified their pressure on Powell to disclose the proposed rules changes so that the public could provide input before the FCC vote. Even the trade publication *Television Week* urged Powell to 'bring the public into the process'. 'We don't know what we're going to be working on,' a frustrated Copps said in early May. 'It's like a state secret' (*Television Week*, 2003: 8). The new rules were finally turned over to Copps and Adelstein on 12 May, exactly three weeks before the planned 2 June vote, the legal minimum notice. As expected, the rules called for eliminating the ban on cross-ownership, permitting companies to purchase two TV stations in most markets and three TV stations in the largest markets, and letting the biggest TV station-owning companies increase their market coverage from 35 per cent to 45 per cent of the population. Copps and Adelstein immediately asked for a delay of the vote, a 'traditional right of commissioners', which had never been denied in anyone's memory. Powell rejected the request, citing counsel by Abernathy and Martin. Over Memorial Day weekend, for yet another first in US media history, demonstrations protesting the FCC's impending relaxation of media ownership rules took place in 14 cities.

The outcome of the 2 June FCC meeting was a foregone conclusion, but the debate was far from anticlimactic. Copps and Adelstein each delivered long and meticulous dissenting statements that exposed the majority's arguments to be baseless and the FCC's review to be nothing short of fraudulent. Adelstein was more accurate than he may have realized. In all the commotion surrounding Powell and the FCC during the first half of 2003, Congress's role had received little attention. In fact, the FCC is not a body like the Supreme Court, established to be independent of the legislative branch. To the contrary, the FCC was created by Congress, funded by Congress and expected to fulfil the interests of the American people as specified by Congress. The court decision shifting the burden of proof to the FCC to justify the continuation of media ownership rules was predicated on that being the will of Congress. Powell acknowledged at all times that if Congress was dissatisfied with the FCC's actions, all it had to do was pass legislation instructing him to do something else.

Under normal circumstances, Congress would be unlikely to pester the FCC to act against powerful media interests, due to the media industry's massive lobbies, control over the news and hefty campaign contributions. But these were not normal circumstances. Even if Bush's FCC appointees Powell, Abernathy, and Martin could afford to ignore the input of 750,000 Americans, members of Congress had to pay closer attention to their constituents. And Congress was getting the message. Two days after the FCC vote, the Senate Commerce Committee called all five FCC commissioners to the Hill to explain the vote and spewed unbridled contempt. 'We are moving to roll back one of the most complete cave-ins to corporate interests I've ever seen by what is supposed to be a federal regulatory agency,' Senator Byron Dorgan of North Dakota declared (Sevastopulo, 2003). Then Democrat Ernest Hollings of South Carolina accused Powell of 'spin and fraud' and slammed the FCC as an 'instrument of corporate greed'(Timms, 2003). A few days later, Republican committee chairman John McCain remarked that the media ownership issue had 'sparked more interest than any issue I've ever seen that wasn't organized by a huge lobby' (Safire, 2003). A handful of conservative Republicans such as Trent Lott and Representative Frank Wolf of Virginia came out strongly against the FCC changes, despite pressure from on high. 'I did not get elected to be a potted plant,' Wolf asserted, 'and I don't care what the White House thinks' (Boliek, 2003b). 'In all the years I've been here,' California senator Barbara Boxer observed, 'I've not seen such deeply held feelings across ideologies' (Shiver *et al.*, 2003). 'It's an issue that has huge momentum,' McCain concurred. 'It's a classic populist issue' (Simon and Hook, 2003). The politicians with their fingers firmly on the national pulse, the nine candidates campaigning for the Democratic presidential nomination, all came out strongly against Powell and the FCC. By the end of June the Senate Commerce Committee, with significant Republican support, voted to overturn key elements of the FCC rule changes. The vote shocked the political establishment and demonstrated that the issue was in play on the Hill.

Public opinion research confirmed what members of Congress were sensing. A Pew Research Center poll conducted in summer 2003 found that the number of Americans who had heard 'a lot' or 'a little' about the FCC's review of media ownership rules had doubled to nearly 50 per cent since February. Most striking, the figures showed dramatically that the more people knew about what the FCC was doing, the less likely they were to support it. Of those 12 per cent of Americans who had 'heard a lot', seven in ten believed that the effects of relaxing media ownership rules would be negative, while only 6 per cent thought they would be positive.

By now Powell and the commercial media had quit suggesting that rule relaxation had popular support. To the contrary, they started arguing that most Americans were apathetic and that apathy should be interpreted as support for the status quo. Powell asserted that he represented the 'silent majority' of Americans. More or less, he presented a contradictory stance: he announced that support for his ownership plan was minuscule only because the public debate had been 'lopsided' against him – yet he had done everything possible to avoid public debate because, as surveys showed, the more people knew, the more ground he lost. His strategy, as he tacitly acknowledged, was to keep people ignorant – the FCC's modus operandi – so he could then claim their support for whatever he did.

The poll energized activists, who knew that the more people learned about the issue and the more members of Congress heard from their constituents, the more likely Congress could be persuaded to overturn what the FCC had done. Russ Feingold related that on a trip home to Wisconsin, the popular opposition to the FCC overwhelmed him. 'When they heard that these rules came out,' Feingold recalled, 'they were angry' (Rimlinger, 2003). For the balance of the summer and autumn, activist attention went towards generating more public pressure upon members of Congress. On Capitol Hill, a wide range of public interest groups conducted the lobbying effort, led by Consumers Union, Free Press, Common Cause, MoveOn.org and organized labour. On numerous occasions MoveOn.org used its vast subscriber list to generate petition signatures and telephone calls by constituents to Congress. In one afternoon alone, House members received an estimated 40,000 dissenting telephone calls from constituents. As Democratic Representative David Price of North Carolina put it, his colleagues were saying, 'Call off the dogs, my office is being flooded with constituent calls on this issue.'[4] By the calculation of FCC commissioner Jonathan Adelstein, over 2.3 million comments registering opposition to media concentration were made to either the FCC or Congress by the end of the summer.

The problem facing opponents of the FCC ownership plan was getting legislation through Congress. Despite having a clear majority of members of Congress opposing the FCC, White House pressure and the Republican leadership were able to keep the measure from coming to the floor of Congress for a vote. For media activists across the nation it seemed like the fix was in. Big money rigged the system to foil the will of the people.

But all was not lost, not at all. The activist group, Media Access Project, filed a petition with the Third Circuit Court of Appeals in Philadelphia, on behalf of the Philadelphia-based Prometheus Radio Project, arguing that the media ownership rule changes violated federal statutes and were generated improperly. To get the case out of the dreaded Washington DC court of appeals, activists had filed lawsuits in federal courts around the country. When all the cases were consolidated, a lottery was used to pick a federal appeals court to adjudicate. The DC court had three-to-one odds stacked against it, and Philadelphia won. Even so, winning the case was regarded as a long shot, but on 3 September the court agreed to hear the case. More important, the court issued an immediate stay so that the rule changes would not be put into effect. 'The harm to petitioners absent a stay would be the likely loss of an adequate remedy should the new ownership rules be declared invalid in whole or in part,' the court wrote. 'In contrast to this irreparable harm, there is little indication that a stay pending appeal will result in substantial harm to the commission or to other interested parties' (McConnell, 2003: 3).

Copps was satisfied by the turn of events: 'The court has done what the commission should have done in the first place.' As the *New York Times* noted, 'The court raised tough questions for the commission and its industry supporters' (Labaton, 2003). that suggested the future could not be predicted. It constituted an enormous victory for opponents of media concentration; and it bought time to work the halls of Congress to get the FCC's rules overturned before they could go into effect. By the beginning of 2004, the meagre mainstream news coverage had disappeared, and there were considerable pressures to have the issue return to backrooms with a billion dollar ante for admission. But there was no reason to think public opinion had shifted back. In December, CNN's *Lou Dobbs Tonight* ran another informal poll on the question 'Do you agree big media companies should be broken up?' Over 96 per cent of the 5,000 plus respondents said yes.

The media ownership fight of 2003–4 was a remarkable and unprecedented moment in US media history. For the first time in generations, media policy issues were taken from behind closed doors and made the stuff of democratic discourse and political engagement. The change in climate since 1996 – when the corrupt Telecommunications Act had been drafted, debated and passed in almost total silence – could not have been more dramatic. Most incredible of all, in January 2003 nobody anticipated this transformation.

In June 2004, victory came when the Third Circuit Court of Appeals in Philadelphia ruled for Prometheus and threw out the FCC's media ownership rules changes. In its decision, the court cited the FCC's shoddy procedures and dismissal of the enormous amount of public input on the matter. The organizing paid off, and the movement could grow and develop for when the FCC returned to media ownership rules in 2006 and for a wide range of other media policy issues. In the subsequent four years the media reform movement enjoyed tremendous growth to become one of the great success stories of American grassroots politics of recent decades.

Notes

1. 'IFJ Criticizes Proposed Changes in Media Ownership Rules', news release, May 2003.
2. Federal Communications Commission, 'Statement of Commissioner Michael J. Copps'.
3. Ibid.
4. Rep. David Price in discussion with the author, 25 September 2003.

The Role of the European Institutions in National Media Regulation

Alison Harcourt

Introduction

Each European Union (EU) member state has developed a specific regulatory regime to govern its media industry. From the mid-1980s, a gradual convergence in national regulation can be observed due to processes of Europeanization. This chapter investigates the processes through which the EU has become a salient actor in national regulation. Under observation are the actions of the European Commission (EC), the Merger Task Force and the European Court of Justice (ECJ). The chapter shows how these institutions have pursued Europeanization with intersecting but different agendas. The ensuing pattern is one of policy convergence – a result which is surprising in a policy area which is considered to be deeply seated at the national level.

Authors writing on media policy within Europe (Levy, 1997, 1999; Williams, 2005) have argued that media policy represents a limitation to policy convergence within the EU. This argument is based upon the academic literature on policy style, which considers national cultural considerations (beliefs, values, historical experience, etc.) to diffuse the influence of European policy. This observation is important as media policy has traditionally been influenced by cultural variables and is a policy of high salience at the national level. However, over time these obstacles to policy convergence have been overcome by the EU institutions resulting in rather a high occurrence of convergence in the policy field.

Börzel (2001) and Bulmer and Burch (2001) argued that Europeanization is a two-way process. On the one hand, member states seek to export policy models and ideas to the EU. On the other, they have to adapt to Europe when they 'download' (Börzel, 2001) EU public policy – for example, when transposing a directive into domestic law. By contrast, Radaelli, although acknowledging that real-world processes of EU policy formation and adaptation to Europe are intertwined, argues that analytically one should distinguish between the formation of EU policy and the reverberation of policy in national policy arenas (Radaelli, 2000). Europeanization thus becomes a typical case of the 'second-image reversed' research design as defined by Gourevitch (1978). This chapter sticks more closely to this (latter) more restrictive definition of Europeanization. The reason for this is not theoretical, but empirical. Although it is recognized that more complex research designs consider the whole interactive process of Europeanization described by Börzel (2001) and Bulmer and Burch (2001), the empirical focus of the analysis presented in this article is restricted to processes wherein national regulatory frameworks are brought into line with EU policy goals.

The chapter concentrates on two mechanisms of Europeanization. The first mechanism is a 'top-down' process wherein the European institutions mandate the form national policy choices should take. This mechanism can occur in two ways, either directly, whereby national governments comply with EU mandates, or indirectly, whereby domestic policy-makers – once their frameworks are Europeanized – bring national policy in line with EU options even in the absence of a direct compulsion from Brussels. This latter indirect mechanism has already been observed by scholars of EU policy (see *inter alia* Knill and Lehmkuhl, 1999; Radaelli, 1997). The second 'bottom-up' mechanism is one in which member states transfer debates on domestic policy to the European level. Again, this mechanism can occur in two ways: either formally, whereby a national court refers decision-making to the ECJ; or informally, whereby domestic policy-makers attempt to influence debates at the EU level in order to steer domestic policy choices at home. The mechanisms do not work in isolation from one another; rather they work in tandem. The mechanisms reflect combined, complementary and even multiplier-type effects of EU institution actions effectively heading towards a single direction – in this case, policy convergence at the national level.

Convergence in national media policies

The beginnings of convergence took place in the mid-1980s and accelerated after 1990 when EU member states implemented the Television Without

Frontiers (TWF) directive. The degree to which the directive was implemented in the member states was dependent upon how well the directive fitted with the widely varying national regulatory structures (Levy, 1999). However, dissatisfaction of the EU institutions with the mode of implementation led to pressure for revision to national laws. The pressure exerted by the European institutions was substantial. In particular, when faced with efforts by member states to bypass TWF requirements (De Witte, 1995), the diligence of the European Court of Justice enforced implementation throughout EU member states and in turn led to a greater capacity for regulation at the European level. In parallel to the actions of the Court, the Commission's Merger Task Force (MTF) was active in moulding Europe's commercial broadcasting markets through the application of competition law. In some cases, the dual actions of these EU institutions ran roughshod over cultural considerations of the member states despite cries of subsidiarity (even from national ministers and heads of state).

To complement actions of the ECJ and the MTF, the European Commission simultaneously practised an indirect approach to furthering Europeanization through the suggestion of best practices, models and solutions to the problem of regulating media markets. This was done specifically through the promotion of regulatory instruments in Commission reports, green papers and draft directives. Consultation with national administrations and interest groups enabled the dissemination of suggested policy instruments to national levels. Since the regulatory framework for communications was introduced in 2002, this influence has increased due to the greater use of 'soft' forms of governance.

From the mid-1980s, a gradual pattern of market liberalization, regulation and deregulation can be observed at the national level. Key waves of deregulation can distinctly be marked as occurring during the mid-1980s and mid-1990s. Much of the driving force behind national policy during this period is EU industrial policy. Central to this policy is the fact that the communications sector was identified during the 1980s and 1990s as a key growth industry by the European Commission. Indeed, predicted growth in the communications sector came to be seen as an antidote to the very serious problem of growing unemployment within Europe. This prediction was outlined in two White Papers submitted by the European Commission to the European Council: the 1993 Delors paper on *Growth, Competitiveness and Employment* and the 1994 Bangemann paper on *Europe and the Global Information Society*. The Delors paper identified the media industry as representing 5 per cent of EU GDP and one of only three sectors predicted to produce future job growth. The Bangemann paper restated the importance of the sector's growth and strongly attacked national media regulation as preventing sector growth. Section 17 of the paper stated that national media laws are 'a patchwork of inconsistency which tends to distort and fragment the market'. Following a similar line of argument, at a 1998 conference in Birmingham, Jacques Santer predicted a 70 per cent global growth rate in the industry was to take place within the next decade.[1]

During the mid-1980s, many European countries liberalized their media markets. This resulted in the appearance of commercial broadcasters which began to stress the need for deregulation to attract investment for new technologies. National liberalization and the 1986 Single European Act paved the way for the Television Without Frontiers directive, which was passed in 1989. The Directive permitted broadcast of audiovisual services (television and radio signals) from one state to another. The implementation of the directive mandated changes to national media laws. During revisions to laws, governments were faced with strong pressure for greater liberalization from new commercial broadcasters and the growing advertising industry. The result was a key overhaul of media regulation in the mid-1990s in most EU member states. During this period, the following acts were implemented: the French 1994 Broadcasting Law,[2] the German 1991 Interstate Broadcasting Agreement,[3] the Italian 1990 Broadcasting Act,[4] the Spanish 1994 Televisión Sin Fronteraş Law[5] and the UK 1990 Broadcasting Act. Deregulation occurred again at the end of the 1990s with: the French 1996 Information Superhighway Law,[6] the German 1996 Interstate Agreement on the regulation of broadcasting, the Italian 1997 New Media Act,[7] the Spanish 1998 Law on digital television and the British 1996 Broadcasting Act. The content of these national laws was greatly shaped both formally by decisions of the ECJ and the EC and informally by EC policy proposals. A full understanding of how this has occurred and in particular how formal decisions of the ECJ and MTF have mandated revisions to national laws requires an analysis of each national case.

Since the Lisbon Summit, informal influence has been more prominent. This is due to an increase in the use of soft governance since this time. Soft governance instruments were inserted into the 2002 Regulatory Framework for Electronic Communications and Services. The framework, which consisted of five directives and one Decision, contains provisions for the establishment of a number of committees and co-regulatory fora. DG Info Soc was operating over 80 committees by 2008. The EC also embedded financial provision for the establishment of European level NRA platforms into legislative packages. In line with this, 'co-regulation' has been introduced at the European level wherein rules agreed upon by self-regulatory bodies are formalized through (soft or hard) legal instruments and overseen by co-regulatory fora. A great number of decisions are being made within such fora which have direct effect upon policy-making at the national level since 2002.

Germany

The European Commission has had a significant say in the governance of the German media market. This has occurred 'top-down', both directly, through decisions of the MTF, and indirectly, through Commission influence upon the formation of Länder broadcasting policy. MTF decisions on mergers and joint ventures involving German media groups are numerous. Between 1994 and 1999, the MTF dealt with no less than 14 cases involving German groups. Four highly controversial national cases resulted in negative decisions by the MTF wherein concentrations were prevented.[8] During the last case (the proposed acquisition and joint control of the German pay-TV operator Premiere and BetaResearch by Bertelsmann and Kirch), the Commission, first, put informal pressure upon the German government and the Cartel Office to block the agreement at the national level. Only when the German government decided to approve the joint venture, did the MTF open an investigation. Under Kohl's leadership, the German government at the time responded angrily to this decision. Despite this political resistance, the Commission prevented the joint venture under the EU Merger Regulation.

However, in the cases above, the Commission justified referral based upon linguistic market considerations rather than financial thresholds, hence Kohl's protest. The Commission had justified intervention based upon the fact that the German channels were broadcasting across more than two member states (Germany, Austria and the German-speaking populations of the Benelux countries). Since this time, most MTF cases have dealt with the German company Bertelsmann, with 11 cases handled between 2000 and 2008 as Bertelsmann became involved with other large European players external to the German market, such as Vodafone, Springer, Mondadori, Pearson, Havas and others. All were approved.

After Kohl left office, Germany set up its its Kommission zur Ermittlung der Konzentration im Medienbereich (KEK) (German Commission on Concentration in the Media) under the Schröeder government. The Kommission is responsible for monitoring media markets along with the Bundeskartellamt (Federal Cartel Office). KEK presents a report on the state of media concentration in Germany every three years or upon request of individual Länder. In the 2006 report, both horizontal and vertical concentration were considered, as well as international concentration in the media sector. Since the establishment of the KEK, media concentration has been much more closely monitored and in some cases prevented within Germany, which has negated the need for European intervention. For example in 2006, Axel Springer's bid for Germany's largest broadcasters, ProSiebenSat1, was blocked by the Federal Cartel Office upon advice from the KEK.

To complement decisions of the MTF, the EC was able to indirectly influence policy formation at the Länder level. In the 1990s, it was able to influence the German regulatory authorities in the choice of a policy instrument used to regulate media ownership: audience share. Audience share, whereby broadcasting companies are limited to a 30 per cent share of national audience, was introduced in the German 1996 Interstate Treaty on Broadcasting. The idea for this policy instrument came from a DG XV study sent out to national authorities in 1993. Diffusion of the idea was enabled by the organization of meetings with German state-level policy-makers by an EC head of unit. Since this time, a number of decisions have been made on the German market under the 2002 Regulatory Framework for communications.

United Kingdom

As in Germany, the EU institutions have had a substantial influence upon British media markets and regulation. In contrast to its light-touch regulation of press markets, the UK has regulated ownership in broadcasting markets to a greater extent than other EU member states for a long period. Relatively few television channels were permitted to broadcast at the domestic level, and ownership therein was tightly regulated. The 1989 Television Without Frontiers directive changed all of this, mainly because it permitted satellite broadcasts from abroad. In the UK case, this meant chiefly allowing the Rupert Murdoch-owned BSkyB satellite service full access to the UK market via broadcast from Luxembourg. When Television Without Frontiers was enacted the 1990 UK Broadcasting Act, Section 43 of the Act applied a separate regulatory regime to non-domestic satellite services. Companies broadcasting from abroad, even if headquartered in the UK, were only required to obtain a *non-domestic* satellite licence. Non-domestic satellite licences were exempt from rules on domestic broadcasters, including those on ownership and content.

The European Commission was dissatisfied with UK implementation of TWF and informed the UK that it had failed to correctly transpose several articles. As the dispute could not be settled informally, the Commission eventually took the UK to the European Court of Justice in 1994. The Commission challenged the UK on two accounts: first, it objected to the criteria set out in Section 43 of the 1990 Broadcasting Act which applied a different regulatory regime to non-domestic satellite services as that applicable to domestic satellite services. Second, it claimed that the UK had failed to fulfil its obligations under Articles 2(1), (2) and Article 3(2) of TWF by exercising control over broadcasts transmitted by a broadcaster that falls under the jurisdiction of another member state. This meant that the UK was not permitted under EU law to authorize a non-domestic satellite licence to BSkyB as it was broadcasting from Luxembourg and should therefore be licensed in Luxembourg. The ECJ ruled in favour of the Commission and suggested a rewording of the 1990 Broadcasting Act.[9]

This ruling led the UK government to lobby for a revision in the 1997 Television Without Frontiers directive. Since 1998, there have no longer been 'non-domestic satellite licences' in the UK, as such, merely 'satellite licences'. However, the UK continues to apply different regulatory regimes to satellite broadcasters than to terrestrial broadcasters. Hence, only terrestrial broadcasters are subject to stricter content and ownership requirements.

As in Germany, the UK's media market has come under scrutiny from the MTF and it investigated many cases in the British media market. In two cases, British Telecom/MCI (1993) and BSkyB/British Digital Broadcasting (BDB) (1997), the Commission prevented market concentrations. The Independent Television Commission – the then regulatory body – had asked the MTF to intervene to exclude BSkyB from British Digital Broadcasting (BDB) in 1997 (Snoddy, 1997). In a third case, *Microsoft/Liberty Media/Telewest*[10] (2000) the MTF expressed concern that the proposed joint control of the UK cable group would affect the choice of set-top box technology. The proposal was withdrawn before a formal decision was taken.

In the 2000s, the MTF has been less active within UK markets. However, DG competition has become more involved in setting guidelines for public service broadcasting. In the 1990s, the Commission faced a number of complaints from private broadcasters against the national financing of PSBs (Levy, 1999: 95–6). Complaints surfaced in France, Spain and Portugal in the early 1990s. In 1997 and 1998, additional complaints came from Germany, the UK and Italy and, later, Portugal. The German association of commercial broadcasters (Verband Privater Rundfunk und Telekommunikation (VPRT)) complained about competition from the digital PSB channels Kinderkanal and Phoenix. BSkyB accused the UK government of an illegal application of state aid with the creation of the BBC News 24. In Italy, Fininvest denounced the underwriting of RAI's debts by the Italian government. DG Competition made some attempts to define rules governing PSB funding in a 1998 document. As Hills and Michalis explain, it proposed 'to apply the "net cost" text developed for financing universal service in telecommunications' (2000: 458). This meant that advertising would not be permitted to PSBs receiving a licence fee if 'it exceeded the "net cost" of fulfilling their public service mission' (Hills and Michalis, 2000: 458). At that time, DG Competition proposed that PSBs would be prevented from producing content that went beyond what it considered to be its public service remit, in particular that they would not broadcast major sporting events and entertainment programmes. The proposal naturally came under grave opposition from PSBs and some members of the European Parliament and was withdrawn.

The Commission eventually decided on the three pending PSB cases. In the VPRT complaint, the Commission ruled in 1999 that state funding of digital channels was justified under state aid rules (NN-70/98). In the News 24 case, the Commission decided in September 1999 that PSB funding from licence fees was admissible under Article 87 of the Treaty (Case NN-88/98 and CEC 1999e). The Commission ruled in this case that the channel was fulfilling a clearly defined public service remit and therefore the aid was proportionate. It stated in the same ruling that PSB funding could also be granted without prior notification and approval (Competition Policy Newsletter, 2000: 43).

Private groups then challenged the European Commission in three European Court of Justice cases.[11] Rather than making a definitive statement on state aid, the ECJ instead called for DG Competition to clarify its position on PSB financing. Following this, the Commission published its 2001 *Communication on the Application of State Aid Rules to Public Service Broadcasting*[12] in which it recognizes PSB importance for maintaining pluralism (Craufurd Smith, 2001; Ward, 2003). The Communication, quotes the 'public service' Protocol of the 1997 Treaty of Amsterdam and the 2001 EC *Communication on Services of General Interest in Europe* as its basis. The Communication states that

> the choice of the financing scheme falls within the competence of the Member State, and there can be no objection in principle to the choice of a dual financing scheme (combining public funds and advertising revenues) rather than a single funding scheme (solely public funds) as long as competition in the relevant markets (e.g., advertising, acquisition and/or sale of programmes) is not affected to an extent which is contrary to the Community interest.

This recognizes member states' right to maintain PSB funding, but at the same time it enables the Commission to continue to decide on a case by case basis.

The Communication also enabled the European Commission to mandate a number of requirements from member states relating to their PSBs (for a discussion of this point, see Chapter 8).

As in Germany, the European Commission was able to indirectly influence the choice of policy instruments. The UK chose the instrument of audience share in its 1996 Broadcasting Act. However, the measurement limited audience share to half that permitted in Germany – broadcasters were limited to only 15 per cent of total audience share (for both television and radio stations). Civil servants within the Department for Culture, Media and Sport (DCMS) adopted this idea directly from proposals outlined in the EC studies (GAH, 1993; European Institute for the Media, 1994) and the 1994 Green Paper on media ownership (European Commission, 1994).[13]

From 2002 onwards, informal decision-making has taken place under the regulatory framework for communications. For example, in 2004, the eCCTF disagreed with Ofcom's proposal to impose differential regulatory obligations on 2G and 3G mobile operators. The European Commission also proposed that spectrum should be subject to market tradability (the buying or selling of frequency bandwidth). In 2006, it proposed that one-third of spectrum below 3GHz (that suited for terrestrial communication) should be privatized and managed by the market. Operators would be given the right to trade frequency rights in a given spectrum band for terrestrial services and to use those frequencies in a flexible manner. This policy initiative provides a stark contrast between the ways in which committee governance and democratic governance operate. Although the EU's policy proposal is based upon the developing UK policy model of a spectrum trading system, the decision was made within a committee. By comparison, the UK policy was enacted in Parliament, namely, under the 2003 Communications Act, following extensive public consultation built upon an independent review.

Italy

Italy has long suffered from a high level of concentration in broadcasting markets with the private company Mediaset and the public broadcaster RAI dominating terrestrial and digital broadcasting markets. Satellite and cable remain embryonic, although there is growing competition from the satellite operator Sky Italia. Italy has often looked to Europe to solve difficult domestic disputes. Many cases originating in Italy were referred to the European institutions by national courts and regulatory authorities.

The failure of Italian regulation to control excessive concentration in its broadcasting market led domestic Italian politicians and Italian Members of the European Parliament to lobby the Commission to introduce European rules on media ownership from very early on. In particular, CULT's rapporteur, the Italian MEP Luciana Castellina, of the Italian Rifondazione Comunista party, spoke out against European trends in media concentration. This in-depth treatment of the issue led the European Commission to embark on a policy initiative for media ownership; this, however, never came to fruition.

At the national level, the Italian parliament met with many hurdles in producing statutory legislation (a great deal of policy is established by decrees in Italy, which only last five years (Della Sala and Kreppel, 1998)). It could not come to agreement on a media law until 1990. Meanwhile the market was developing in a regulatory vacuum. The Broadcasting Act of 6

August 1990 implemented the 1989 Television Without Frontiers directive. It also implemented a Constitutional Court ruling mandating that private broadcasters need to apply for national broadcasting licences.

The 1990 Act lays down rules relating to media ownership and transparency. Importantly, it introduced advertising rules, which had not been present in Italy up until that point. The advertising rules contained in TWF are incorporated into the Act.

In line with the Television Without Frontiers, the 1990 Act mandated that 51 per cent of programming be of European origin. It further required that half of this quota should be Italian. This held after the first three years of a company's licence. For the first three years of broadcasting, a new company needed only guarantee that 4 per cent of its transmission time be of European origin. This was meant to encourage new entrants to the market. Even though Italy had been, along with France, instrumental in inserting the 'European quota' rule into TWF, Italy itself was successful in 'exempting from the quota clauses "local television broadcasts not forming part of a national network" – known as the "the Berlusconi article"' (Hirsch and Petersen, 1992: 49). For that reason the regionally owned (but nationally networked) Fininvest channels were exempt from the quota rule.

Italy has fundamentally provided ample opportunity for the ECJ to expand EU competence for media policy. Specifically, the willingness of Italian courts to refer media cases to the ECJ has enabled the Court to further its own competence in the field. Three of Italy's regional courts, Biella, Lazio and Ragusa, have referred media cases to the European Court of Justice.

In 1974, a case was brought by the cable operator, Giuseppe Sacchi, to the tribunal court of the Italian town of Biella. Sacchi challenged the national Italian PSB RAI's monopoly over advertising. He argued that it prevented obstacles to the sale of goods from other member states. The Biella Court refereed the case to the Italian Constitutional Court in 1974. The national court upheld RAI's national monopoly on advertising. The Biella Court then referred the case directly to the ECJ. It asked specifically whether the movement of *goods* within the common market applied to television signals. The Court did not find that RAI's monopoly restricted the trade of *goods* within the EC. Neither did it object to the fact that RAI was acting in the capacity of a monopoly. However, the case gave it the opportunity to redefine broadcasting signals as an economic activity, thereby coming under the jurisdiction of the Treaty of Rome. The ECJ ruled that 'in the absence of express provision to the contrary in the treaty, a television signal must, by reason of its nature, be regarded *a provision of services*'. Related to this, it added that 'trade in material, sound recordings, films, apparatus and other products used for the diffusion of television signals are subject to the rules relating to freedom of movement for *goods*' (European Court of

Justice, 1974). This is interesting, as GATT at that time had not yet liberalized services. By delineating broadcast signals as services, the Court took broadcasting out of the realm of GATT with this decision. The decision for EU media policy was also highly significant as the ruling gave a foundation to the EU's TWF Directive.

The second Italian case concerned *Maria Salonia* v. *Giorgio Poidomani and Franca Baglieri, née Giglio* in 1980.[14] Again, an Italian regional court looked to the Luxembourg Court to solve a tricky domestic dispute. This was the regional court of Ragusa in Sicily (Tribunale civile di Ragusa, Sezione civile, Ordinanzadel). This was the third media case to be brought before the ECJ (after *Sacchi* and *Debauve*). At this point in time, the ECJ maintained a hands-off approach to the case, which involved the 'National Agreement' between the Federazione Italiana Editori Giornali (Italian Federation of Newspaper Publishers) and the Federazione Sindacale Unitaria Giornalai (the United Federation of Trade Unions of Newsagents) made on 23 October 1974. The legality of the exclusive distribution agreement for national newspapers and periodicals was assessed in terms of its compatibility with the articles of the Treaty of Rome.[15] The agreement was looked at only to determine whether it would affect the market for publications from other member states. The Court ruled that there was no conflict with the Treaty as the agreement did not affect member states other than Italy.

In 1994, the Italian regional court of Lazio referred the case to the European Court of Justice. The RTI decision,[16] dealt with the use of *telepromozione by* Italian broadcasters. The case was brought by the Italian Ministry for the Post and Telecommunications against the Italian broadcasters Reti Televisive Italiane SpA (RTI) (C-320/94), Radio Torre, Rete A Srl, Vallau Italiana Promomarket Srl (C-337/94), Radio Italia Solo Musica Srl and Others (C-338/94) and GETE Srl (C-339/94). The Italian Ministry argued that domestic broadcasters were violating not only national law, but also European law on advertising as set out in the TWF Directive. Incredibly, the Court intervened in national policy siding with the broadcasters, stating there was provision in Community law for an increase in the maximum transmission time for direct offers to the public as this 'type of sales promotion requires more transmission time than spot advertisements'. This had consequences for the 1997 revision of the TWF Directive, which loosened advertising rules.

Like Spain, Italy embraced the EU's convergence initiative in 1997. In July 1996, the Prodi government drew up proposals for a new Media Act which would allow telecommunications companies to compete with broadcasters. In July 1997, the Italian parliament replaced the 1990 Act with the 'Maccanico Law' (New Media Act No. 249) .[17] The Act established an Authority for Communications (Autorita per le garanzie nelle comunicazioni), replacing the Press and Broadcasting Authority, located in a new Ministry for Communications located in Naples. It established a Register for Communications Operators. The authority registered not just companies with television and radio interests but all companies offering communications services. The Authority also monitors media mergers and acquisitions (across all media, including telecommunications and new services) and draws the attention of the competition authority to any undesired market concentration.

The old rules on ownership remain in place under the new Act. The only innovative measure was that no company can own more than one pay television service. This prevented Berlusconi from moving into satellite and cable markets. With the Act, Italy adopted the European Commission 'convergence' recommendation that no one could control 30 per cent of the financial resources of the *entire* communications market. The definition is so wide and vague that it cannot possibly decide on market concentrations below what competition law could account for. Nevertheless, liberalization was expected in the widening of existing market definitions on media markets.

In 2002, a further Constitutional Court ruling mandated that Mediaset's Rete 4 be moved to satellite by the end of 2003. In January 2004, the Berlusconi government passed a decree actually overturning the Constitutional Court's decision. President Carlo Azeglio Ciampi ordered the decree to be reconsidered by parliament. But then the Berlusconi government passed its 'Gasparri Law' in 2004. It aimed to lower ownership requirements to meet with the 30 per cent rule (on communications markets) as introduced under the Prodi government. However, a provision, added to the law in April 2003, kept cross-media ownership restrictions in place with Berlusconi's government voting against him (!). The Gasparri Law restricts a single legal entity from owning licences that allow broadcasting of more than 20 per cent of television programmes or more than 20 per cent of radio programmes that can be transmitted on terrestrial frequencies over the national area. This is basically very similar to the previous rules, which set limits to 20 per cent of national channels. There is an additional limit restricting companies to 20 per cent of total revenues collected in the entire communications market ('Integrated Communications System'). The 'Integrated Communication System' includes broadcasting; press (newspapers, magazines, books, electronic publishing); cinema, television and music production and distribution; and any form of advertising. This limit is reduced to 10 per cent for a legal entity who has more than 40 per cent of revenues in telecommunications services (i.e., Telecom Italia). RAI is not exempt from these rules. The following resources can be taken into account in calculation of total revenue: public revenue allocated to the RAI by the government; national and local revenues from television advertising, sponsorship and teleshopping; revenue from pay-TV services;

and contractual agreements with public administrations and other public institutions. The enforcement of the new ownership limits was postponed until the national digital frequency plan is fully implemented.

The law also restricts a legal entity owning more than one television network from owning shares in publishers of daily newspapers until December 2008 (i.e., Berlusconi). Cross-media ownership provisions as laid down in the 1997 Act are still in place. The law also allows for the partial privatization of RAI by releasing 20 per cent of stock. It would be transformed into a public company with a retained state stockholding. No single entity would be allowed to hold more than 1 per cent of the share capital.

France

Like Germany, France has taken a relatively hands-off approach to regulating media markets. However, unlike with Germany, the French case shows European intervention to be negligible. Despite a high degree of market concentration and joint ventures between large French media groups, the European Court of Justice and the EC Merger Task Force have taken little interest in the French market. This is quite surprising given the sheer size of French groups and the fact that they are active in so many other EU member states. France's largest media groups are Lagardère and Havas in publishing and Bouygues and Vivendi in broadcasting. Vivendi ranks among the top ten global communications companies, with a turnover of €21.6 billion in 2007. Lagardère is also among the top ten, with a turnover over of €14 billion in 2006. Havas had a turnover of €14.6 billion in 2006. In advertising, the French group Publicis is a leading European player but also fourth-largest advertising group in the world.

The Merger Task Force has not prevented any concentrations with the French media market. The MTF did prevent Canal Plus from forming an alliance with the Spanish telecommunications company, Telefónica. This was during the Spanish race to introduce digital television (as detailed above). However, this MTF decision allowed Canal Plus to singularly launch Spain's first digital satellite television in January 1997 (under its subsidiary, Canal Satéllite Digital), defying the political pressure of the incumbent Spanish government (Llorens-Maluquer, 1998: 582). Without the support of the European Commission, this would not have been possible. The justifications for non-intervention by the Commission cannot be easily defended based on economic considerations if a comparison with German decisions is made. However, the 'European' behaviour of French groups seems to be looked upon favourably by the European Commission. The French broadcasting group, Canal Plus, was once considered the most 'European' of European groups, having cooperative subsidiary holdings in most member states and allocating importance to the production of European content.

The indirect influence of the EU institutions upon French media laws is also negligible. In its 1994 law, France introduced a new policy instrument: audience reach,[18] but audience share was not considered. The 1996 Information Superhighway Law (No. 96-299) is not revolutionary. Although often discussed, no new broadcasting law has been yet introduced.

Despite this apparent reluctance by the EU institutions to intervene in French media policy, 'bottom-up' mechanisms can be observed. In contrast to the lack of formal intervention by the EU institutions, informal feedback from the French to the European level is lively. Relations between the French Ministry for Culture and the European Commission are reportedly cosy (Collins, 1994; Trautmann, 1998). Proponents of French cultural policy have been successful at influencing European policies, particularly regarding the promotion of European production. Content laws, as governed by the CSA, are relatively stringent in France, particularly regarding requirements for French content.[19] The CSA requires a minimum of 60 per cent European works and a minimum of 40 per cent French productions. French music radio stations must broadcast a minimum of 40 per cent French music (50 per cent of which must be dedicated to 'new' French artists). This fact has been relatively significant for Europe. The 'French lobby' (Belluzzi, 1994) was successful in requiring a minimum of 49 per cent European content requirement in both the 1989 and 1997 Television Without Frontiers directives.

Conclusion

This chapter has shown that there is clear convergence in member state media policies. The European institutions (the EC, MTF and ECJ) have been shown to be influential in Europeanizing national policies. The individual actions of these institutions have played a decisive role in shaping both the present state of national media markets and the direction of national media policies. This has occurred through two mechanisms of Europeanization. The first (top-down) mechanism has acted, first, as a direct constraint upon national policies. This occurred with the introduction of legislation directive and MTF decisions which exacted Europeanization through direct implementation by EU member states. Decisions of the European Court of Justice also shaped national regulation.

This 'top-down' mechanism has also worked indirectly. The European Commission acted as a policy entrepreneur, by suggesting policy models and solutions to the national administrations. Suggestion and discussion of policy instruments formulated at the European level (the example was given of audience share) undoubtedly had indirect influence upon policy formation at national levels. In this way, the Commission can be seen to have steered the course of debate over the deregulation at the national level. With the Lisbon agenda, DG Info Soc was able to greatly expand its use of soft governance. This was evident with the 2002 regulatory framework for communications. This is expected with the implementation of the 2007 Audiovisual Media Service Directive, which will set up a number of soft fora and committees for implementation.

The 'bottom-up' mechanism was also seen to work in two ways: formally and informally. In the first (formal) case, national courts gave the ECJ opportunity to determine the direction of national policies through their referral of media cases to the European level. In the second (informal) case, the mechanism involved a more subtle process which involved communication, dialogue and learning. An example given of this was the 'French lobby' having influenced the direction of EU media policy. This example is consistent with the emphasis on socialization mechanisms as one of the two main factors producing Europeanization (Börzel and Risse, 2000). Through this mechanism, changes have been induced in preferences that go beyond the idea that Europeanization is merely superimposed on static preferences.

It is clear that there is a definitive pattern of policy convergence emerging within Europe. Key overhauls of national media policies can be distinctly marked as occurring around the mid-1980s, the early 1990s and the mid-1990s. Liberalizing acts in the mid-1980s required the regulation of media markets. As detailed, these acts were the French 1986 Press and Freedom of Communication laws; the German 1987 Inter-State Agreement on the Regulation of Broadcasting, the Italian 1987 Publishing Law and the Spanish 1988 Law on Commercial Television. Deregulation of privatized markets occurred when national laws were revised to implement the 1989 Television Without Frontiers directive: with the French 1994 Broadcasting Law, the German 1991 Interstate Agreement on the Regulation of Broadcasting, the Italian 1990 Broadcasting Act, the Spanish 1994 Television Without Frontiers Law and the British 1990 Broadcasting Act.

The end of the 1990s saw the French 1996 Information Superhighway Law, the German 1996 Interstate Agreement on the regulation of broadcasting, the Italian 1997 New Media Act, the Spanish 1998 Law on digital television and the British 1996 Broadcasting Act. By suggesting the adoption of certain policy instruments for national legislation, the Commission created the preconditions for diffusion and legitimized its policy suggestions through dialogue with national administrations. Both the British 1996 Broadcasting Act and the German 1996 Länder Broadcasting Treaty contained a new policy instrument suggested in two Commission studies (1993 and 1994) and a 1994 Green Paper. Ireland later adopted audience share in 2001. Italy's 1997 New Media Act created a new joint authority for both media and telecommunications as recommended by the Commission's 1997 convergence Green Paper. The 'convergence' initiative has since been embraced by Spain, Switzerland, Slovenia and the UK.

The 1990s laws were shown to be affected through formal decisions of the ECJ and MTF. The UK Act had to include revisions as directly stipulated by the ECJ. Spain had to allow for greater market choice than desired by its national government. Apart from the five countries under examination in this chapter, media acts were introduced in Austria, Denmark, France, Greece, Holland, Luxembourg, Portugal and Sweden solely during the years 1996 and 1997. These acts show similar effects of Europeanization. The last stage of regulatory convergence embraces soft governance initiatives of the European institutions. Lisbon introduced the EU's i2010 agenda. i2010 created a number of initiatives to be executed through committee governance, which is having great effect at national levels such as the intro-duction of spectrum trading. There is little doubt that policy convergence, promoted by the actions of the European institutions, is under way.

Notes

1. European Audio-visual Conference: Challenges and Opportunities of the Digi-tal Age, 6–8 April 1998, Birmingham.
2. LOI no 94–88 du 1 février 1994. Modifiant la loi no 88–1067 du 30 septembre 1986 relative à la liberté de communication.
3. 1991 Staatsvertrag über den Rundfunk im vereinten Deutschland.
4. Legge 6 agosto 1990, n. 223. Disciplina del sistema radiotelevisivo pubblico e privato.
5. Ley 25/1994 Televisión Sin Fronteraş de 12 de Julio, amended by 22/1999 de 7 de Junio.
6. Loi no 96–299 du 10 avril 1996 relative aux expérimentations dans le domaine des technologies et services de l'information (1) J.O. Numero 86 du 11 Avril 1996 : 5569.
7. New Media Act No. 249. Legge 01.07.97, n. 249.
8. MSG Media Service (Case No. IV/M.469, OJL 364, 09.11.94), Deutsche Telekom/Betaresearch (Case No. IV/M.1027, 27.95.98) and DF1/Premiere (Case No. IV/M.993, 01.06.98.), Betaresearch/Bertelsmann/Kirch (1998).
9. Case C-222/94: *Commission of the European Communities* v. *United King-dom of Great Britain and Northern Ireland* 1996 [30.04.96, ECR I-4025] failure to implement Directive 89/552/EEC.
10. JV.27, 22 March 2000.
11. *Télévision Française* v. *European Commission* (1999), *SIC* v. *Commission* (2000), *Commission* v. *TF1* (2001).
12. Communication from the Commission on the application of state aid rules to public service broadcasting. (Annex 2) and Commission clarifies application

of state aid rules to Public Service Broadcasting Press Release – IP/01/1429 – 17.10.2001.

13. The NERA study (assessing audience share), commissioned for the UK Department of National Heritage, came after the Commission studies (NERA, 1995).

14. Case 126/80 *Maria Salonia v. Giorgio Poidomani and Franca Baglieri, née Giglio*, 16.96.81, ECR 1584.

15. In this case, the Agreement was alleged to have produced a dominant position in terms of vertical integration.

16. Joined cases Radio Torre, Rete A Srl, Vallau Italiana Promomarket Srl, Radio Italia Solo Musica Srl and Others, and GETE Srl (Appendix 3).

17. Law No. 249 of 31 July 1997.

18. See Article 15 of Law No. 94–88.

19. Along with the requirements in broadcasting law, France enacted 'la loi Toubon' in 1994. The 1994 law forbids public bodies and companies engaged in public activities from using an English expression where there is a French equivalent. It was passed as a direct reaction to the flood of US popular culture into France. The law requires all advertising to be in French.

Public Broadcasters in the Digital Age

Stylianos Papathanassopoulos and Ralph Negrine

In the last decades, European public service broadcasters have faced the erosion of both their viewing share and their revenues. Although they have responded to the challenge from commercial broadcasters, technological convergence and the digitalization of the communication landscape present public broadcasters with new challenges. Public broadcasters may have entered the most difficult phase in their long history since their survival in the new digital and convergent media environment is uncertain. This chapter describes the challenges public broadcasting faces in an increasingly competitive digital television market. It provides an account of the current state of public broadcasters in Europe. It then explores the two major challenges they are going to face, the fiscal crisis and the threats posed by convergence and digitalization. Finally, it discusses the role of public broadcasters in the new European television landscape.

The position of the public service broadcasters in Europe

Public broadcasters in Europe have a long history. They were the founders of the radio and later television industries in Europe, with the single exception of Luxembourg, where a private company developed the market. In the early days of broadcasting, public broadcasters operated as monopolies under strict national regulation and in most cases tight governmental control. In the main, these organizations were funded through some form of licence fee and, to a much lesser extent, if any, through advertising revenue. In those early years, broadcasting services were defined as public services run by public entities, which were, in turn, subject to public regulations.

The European public service broadcasting model had always faced challenges that were at once conceptual and contextual (Jakubowicz, 2007), but it was justified on political, economic, social and cultural grounds. The *de jure* monopoly status of European public broadcasters was regarded as necessary in order to cope with the scarcity of radio frequencies and the fear that broadcasting could lead to the dissemination of subversive ideas, and to preserve free access to opinions rather than a free marketplace for advertisers (Papathanassopoulos, 1990). Although public service broadcasting (PSB) always meant different things to different people (Syvertsen, 1999; Jakubowicz, 2003), it was broadly regarded as 'a particular model of media governance, a set of political interventions into the media market with the purpose of ensuring that broadcasters produce programs that are valuable to society' (Syvertsen, 2003: 154). This was established through various laws, which were used as the basis on which the state could legally and legitimately extend its powers, initially over radio and later over television (Papathanassopoulos, 2002).

The broadcasting models that consequently developed in each state reflected individual political, economic and cultural considerations. Within Europe, broadcasting was considered as a public service (PS) and was either run by public bodies or was subject to government licensing, programming and organizational requirements (see also Syvertsen 1999, 2003; Iosifidis, 2007b; Jakubowicz, 2007). Regardless of the differences, one can summarize three kinds of duties that public broadcasting organizations were entreated to fulfil:

- *universal coverage*: services should be accessible to the whole population;
- *programming diversity*: a set of content requirements, most typically that programming should be diverse and of high quality, that minorities and smaller 'taste groups' should also be served, and that news and political issues should be covered in an impartial manner;
- the obligation to protect and strengthen national culture and identity. (Syvertsen, 2003: 157)

With the deregulation of broadcasting systems in Europe in the 1980s, public broadcasters were faced with major challenges in respect of their share of the audience, but also in respect of their share of available revenues

Table 8.1   European public channels' combined audience share (%) in their home markets 1992–2006

Country	1992	1998	2006
Austria	72.7	50.0	48.0
North Belgium	34.3	32.4	38.3
South Belgium	18.2	18.0	17.1
Denmark	75.0	66.5	72.4
Finland	49.0	46.0	43.8
France	32.6	43.0	38.6
Germany	51.1	41.3	44.7
Greece	17.7	10.0	16.6
Ireland	63.0	52.0	41.5
Italy	46.3	48.1	42.6
Netherlands	47.7	36.6	32.8
Norway	57.0	41.0	43.4
Portugal	91.5	37.7	29.9
Spain	45.7	34.3	38.8
Sweden	67.0	48.0	38.3
Switzerland	28.0	34.0	33.8
United Kingdom	44.4	40.8	46.2

Sources: based on Mediametrie/Eurodata TV reports, 1995–8; Molsky, 1999; *IRIS Special Series*, 2007.

(Traquina, 1998; Picard, 2003; Iosifidis, 2007b). Although public channels have been severely affected by process of deregulation, they still retain, with a few exceptions, a sizeable share of the viewing audience and of public and advertising revenues (see Table 8.1).

Whilst some Western European public broadcasters are mainly funded by special taxes and grants from the government, the majority of public broadcasters still rely on licence fees as their main source of income. Public broadcasters in Europe, with a few exceptions, used to have two main sources of revenue: the licence fee and advertising. A few public broadcasters, such as in the case of Portugal, are mainly funded by advertising and to a lesser extent by public subsidies (see Table 8.2). A recent trend is the replacement of the licence fee by public funding, as in the Netherlands and the Flemish community of Belgium and in Hungary. By and large, a general trend is that European public broadcasters that carry advertising have experienced a decrease in their share of advertising revenue. This has been compounded by the fact that, even for the most successful public channels, the arrival of competition has reduced revenues.

Table 8.2 The funding of public broadcasters in selected European countries*

WAY OF FUNDING	PUBLIC BROADCASTERS
LICENCE FEE	BBC (United Kingdom)
	DR (Denmark)
	YLE (Finland)
	STV (Sweden)
	NRK (Norway)
	FRANCE TELEVISION (France)
PUBLIC FUNDS	VTR (Belgium–Flanders)
	NOS (Netherlands)
	RTVE (Spain)
LICENCE FEE AND ADVERTISING	ARD + ZDF (Germany)
	Advertising is allowed only from 8 pm and for 20 minutes per day
	RTE (Ireland)
	ORF (Austria)
	No advertising in primetime since January 2009
	RAI (Italy)
	RTBF (Belgium)
	ERT (Greece)
	Licence fee is charged on the electricity bills
PUBLIC SUBSIDIES AND ADVERTISING	RTP (Portugal)
	MTV (Hungary)

*Broadcasters funded from advertising also derive revenue from sponsorship. In some cases, organizations funded solely by the licence fee, such as NRK, may also get some sponsoring funding. All PSB broadcasters, in addition, obtain funds from sales of programmes, services, etc., and, in some cases (like the BBC), from involvement in commercial activities and channels.

Source: Papathanassopoulos, 2007.

Given the dual nature of these funding systems, it is hardly surprising that private interests, discussed below, have accused public broadcasters of unfair competition. In one way or another, it could be that the traditional way of funding public broadcasters (mainly) through the traditional licence fee system has entered a new phase as it becomes a more problematic source of revenue, with consequences for the public service broadcasting system, at least as we have known it. For the time being, the licence fee system still plays a pivotal role in the financing of public broadcasting in Western Europe. The level of that fee, though, can have important consequences on the work of broadcasters: set too low at a time of rising production costs, quality and diversity may suffer; set too high – an unlikely scenario – private broadcasters are likely to cry 'foul' and put forward a case of 'unfair' and 'uncompetitive practices'. Inevitably, then, the problem of how – and how much – funding should be devoted to public broadcasters moves into the political policy arenas.

Old challenges, new challenges

The changes which overtook broadcasting systems in the 1980s were generally described as the deregulation of the European audiovisual landscape, that is, the relaxation of the rules that governed the state-controlled broadcasting monopoly and a more general response to the imperatives of globalization, to developments in technology, going hand-in-hand with a particular set of ideological preferences.

In many ways, the situation today is not dissimilar from the situation that public broadcasters faced in the recent past. As in the 1980s, they have to contend with the challenges of the new technologies, especially processes of convergence and digitalization, since neither can be ignored and they challenge the status quo in significant ways. Furthermore, public broadcasters have to face not only the neo-liberal strategies in their own countries, but also the scrutiny of the European Commission and the European Court of Justice.

Convergence and digitalization

If the break-up of the public monopoly was the first major transition for the identity of the European public broadcasters, convergence and digitalization of the communication environment probably represent their second major transition (Prado and Fernández, 2006). The new digitalized television universe 'continues to decimate the array of privileges that governments have at their disposal to grant to selected broadcasters' (Syvertsen, 2003: 160) and it goes without saying that as these privileges become less valuable, broadcasters will feel the need to challenge traditional attitudes to the principles of public broadcasting.

The digital age poses further threats and challenges to public broadcasters in the form of a greater fragmentation of audiences, increased costs of programme production and threats to advertising revenue streams (Molsky, 1999; Iosifidis, 2007b; 2007c; Papathanassopoulos, 2002; 2007). Almost all Western European public broadcasters have responded to these challenges in various ways, such as by adopting digital strategies and entering into the internet ventures (Moe, 2008). Individual responses, however, vary. Some public broadcasters like the BBC (UK), NOS (the Netherlands) and TVE (Spain) have introduced a range of free- and/or pay-per-view digital television channels; some are active on the internet. Some, like the BBC and the NRK (Norway), have regarded the internet as a true content provider; others, like France Télévisions, use the web as their public relations vehicle and a support for its traditional programming (Van den Bulck, 2007; Aslama and Syvertsen, 2007). Aslama and Syvertsen (2007: 169) also point out that this uneven development

> is partly caused by variations in financial resources and strategic capacity. Many of the smaller European broadcasters, particularly in Eastern and Central Europe, have only small staff and no standard organization structures for their new media and multimedia activities. There is much uncertainty about how important the internet will become as a supplement (or as a threat) to broadcasting, and this creates insecurity about whether the business models developed for the internet and on-line media will make them profitable investments.

Not surprisingly, the involvement of public broadcasters in the internet world has made commercial and private online publishers concerned that the growing use of internet by 'traditional' broadcasters will further strengthen their position and underpin their status.

That said, it is clear that public broadcasters can rely on a certain number of significant assets, such as:

- their legacy and 'brand' loyalty
- their offering of a wide choice of quality programming to the widest possible audience, and
- their generally popular and a comprehensive service at a very reasonable cost to viewers. (Molsky, 1999: 21–2)

In this respect, public broadcasters have a significant role to play in shaping the future convergent and digital communication universe. Their past and their legacy, as well as their continued importance in all European countries, suggests that their role will not diminish. If anything, it will continue to be pivotal in the new communication environment.

Neo-liberal strategies and challenges to funding systems

Although some of the developments noted above may have positive outcomes for public broadcasters (and society), it is unclear whether they will be able to benefit from them greatly, since the main factor that will affect the future of public broadcasters is the level of financial support (Papathanassopoulos, 2007). That, in turn, will depend on whether the system of dual funding of public broadcasters (licence fee and advertising) can survive. This has been the subject of heated debate for a considerable time now and commercial broadcasters continue to press their point that advertising should be the sole domain of private broadcasters (or that public service obligations placed on private broadcasters, e.g., news provision, should be paid for though licence funding).

This issue goes back to 1988 when leading private broadcasters such as the French TF1 and Italian Fininvest were asking for breathing space to enable them to establish themselves in the increasingly fierce competition between private and public broadcasters. They argued that public broadcasters should not be allowed to carry advertising and that they enjoyed an unfair competitive advantage because they were/are financed both from public funds and advertising revenues (White Paper, 2004). In March 2004, leading private media associations – the Association of Commercial Television, European Publishers Council and Association Européenne des Radios – issued a White Paper (2004) pointing out that years of over-funding and under-regulation of public broadcasters have undermined the competitiveness of the television industry, as well as adversely affecting multi-channel television, television production, radio broadcasting, internet content and the press.

They also accused the European Commission of delays in dealing with these issues since it had taken over ten years to deal with some of the complaints against the system of funding public service broadcasters. This delay was compounded by inadequate financial transparency in publicly funded broadcasting and the failure of EU member states to properly define their remit. The private media associations contend that public broadcasters have benefited and will benefit from the growth in state aid and the fact that over half of Europe's publicly funded broadcasters do not fully comply with the independent regulation requirement set out by the European Commission on the application of state aid rules to public service broadcasting. Therefore, they called on the EU member states to initiate the process of migration to a single funded model for public broadcasters and to implement correctly and in an impartial manner the existing competition as provisioned by the EU Treaty, as it has been applied to other areas with a significant public sector element.

Alongside these discussions, there is one other noticeable trend that is having an impact on public broadcasters. Many governments across Europe have either abolished the licence fee (Portugal) or abolished the use of advertising revenue for public broadcasters (France and Spain). Both moves have been made to appease private interests. Countries which have abolished or replaced the licence fee merit some attention, though it is important to distinguish between those countries that abolished the licence fee and replaced it with public grants (the Netherlands, Flemish

Belgium), and those countries that have replaced it with direct public funding. Irrespective of the approaches taken by states, it looks as if public broadcasters will continue to face challenges to their funding regimes and to their independence in this increasingly converging environment (Jakubowicz, 2007a).

The role of the European Union

Originally, the European Commission had found it quite difficult to deal with complaints from private broadcasters. Although it refused to consider PSB as an exception to rules on state aid enshrined in Article 87 of the Treaty, it was also under pressure from member states to recognize the special case of PSB. Its first effort to create a legal framework for dealing with this issue was the adoption of the Amsterdam Protocol in 1997, which was annexed to the EU Treaty of Amsterdam. Under this framework, state aid would be prohibited when subsidies, coupled with advertising revenues, exceed the costs of meeting public service obligations. This was intended to address, for example, newspaper publishers and other private content providers' fear that state aid may be used exclusively to fund the online activities of the public broadcasters.

However, the Amsterdam Protocol only formulates some general principles and does so in an ambiguous way. Further development of the EU's policy on this matter was needed. Various efforts were prepared by the Competition Directorate and, in May 2000, the Commission adopted a decision that granted an exemption from normal antitrust law to the rules of the European Broadcasting Union (EBU) governing the joint acquisition and sharing of broadcasting rights for sports events in the framework of the Eurovision system. However, some complaints were left pending and private channels sued the Commission before the European Court of First Instance (CFI) for failure to act in accordance with its obligations.

In November 2001, the Commission released a broadcasting *Communication of the Commission on the Application of the State Aid rules to Public Service Broadcasters* to public service broadcasting (European Commission, 2001). It was, for the time being, a definitive stand on the issue, stating the need for a clear definition of the remit (while stating that a 'wide' definition, practically encompassing everything that a PSB broadcaster puts on the air, could be acceptable), for formal entrustment of the public service mission to a particular broadcaster or broadcasters, the need for transparency (including dual accounting, so that public funding cannot be used to finance or cross-subsidize commercial activities) and independent supervision. It also noted that while member states are free to define the public service remit, subject only to checks for 'manifest errors', they are nevertheless required to lay down the public service obligations in a clear and precise manner (European Commission, 2008), and the *state aid should not exceed the net cost of the public service mission*, taking into account other direct or indirect revenues derived from the public service mission. Also, the broadcasting *Communication* states that the existence of state aid for public broadcasters in a particular country cannot be assumed automatically, but must be established on a case-by-case basis, and the Commission examines possible disproportionate effects on competition through overcompensation and cross-subsidization into commercial activities, as well as anticompetitive behaviour.

In fact, since the adoption of the 2001 broadcasting *Communication*, the Commission has taken almost 20 relevant decisions in this field (European Commission, 2008). In 2005–6, it closed the procedures involving Spanish, Italian, Portuguese and French public broadcasters. In the following years the Commission continued its scrutiny of the financing of their operations. In most of the cases the basic premise for the EU policy was that the public funding of public broadcasters could be maintained, but only to finance the type of services that were strictly within the public service remit (Storsul and Syvertsen, 2007). In January 2008, the Commission published a consultation paper on the future framework which will apply to state funding of public service broadcasting and called for a review of the broadcasting *Communication* marking the new policy of the EU with respect to the public service remit in the new media environment (European Commission, 2008). By and large, the Commission seeks to 'modernize' the broadcasting *Communication* and, according to Commissioner Neelie Kroes (European Commission, 2008): (a) to give full value to the Amsterdam Protocol, (b) to strengthen the principle of subsidiary, (c) to enhance the flexibility of the regulatory framework and (d) to have more effective control at the national level. In effect, as Karen Donders and Caroline Pauwels have commented: 'Whereas Member States fear too much Commission intervention, the European Commission, on the contrary, fears that Member States abuse the margins of the European Treaty in order to expand the digital public service remit in unauthorized ways, such as financing commercial digital activities' (2008: 295).

In February 2008, the Commission decided to deal with some other cases relating to state aid for public funding, including in Irish public broadcasters RTÉ (Radio Teilifís Éireann) and TG4 (Teilifís na Gaeilge), in Flemish broadcaster VRT (Vlaamse Radio- en Televisieomroep), as well as to close another investigation concerning the financing regime for German public service broadcasters in the light of formal commitments from the German government to amend the current regime (April 2007). The amendments included a more precise definition of the public service mission in particular as regards new media activities. But in April 2008, the Commission launched an investigation concerning state aid for the British Channel 4 in order for it to meet the capital costs of digital switchover. The Commission sought to investigate whether this subsidy threatened to distort competition in the Single Market, especially in those cases where broadcasters also operated websites and broadcast via mobile phones.

It seems that the European Commission wants to have the upper hand, even a 'light touch', on developments concerning the role of the public broadcasters in the digital age (see also Humphreys, 2007). As it sets out in the review of the broadcasting *Communication*, its overall objective 'is to design an appropriate legal framework for the future financing of public service broadcasting in a new media environment' (European Commission, 2008). In July 2009, following extensive public consultations in the previous two years, the Commission adopted a revised *Communication* on state aid for the funding of public broadcasters. The main changes in the revised *Communication* (European Commission, 2009) concern the following:

- the *ex ante* control of significant new services launched by public service broadcasters (balancing the market impact of such new services with their public value);
- the need for clarifications relating to the inclusion of pay services in the public service remit;
- the need for more effective control of overcompensation and supervision of the public service mission on the national level;
- and the need for increased financial flexibility for public service broadcasters.

The revised *Communication*, according to the Commission, is designed to safeguard healthy competition in the rapidly evolving media environment. Public broadcasters will be able to take advantage of digital technology and internet-based services so as to offer high-quality services on all platforms, without unduly distorting competition at the expense of other media operators. Moreover, European citizens and stakeholders will be able to give their views in public consultations before any new services are put on the market by public service broadcasters (European Commission, 2009).

Although the Commission does not wish to hinder public broadcasters entering the new media field, it does seem that it does not wish them to do so using public money to distort competition. As it noted in the *Communication* of 2009, the 'Commission considers that it is in the first place up to the national authorities to ensure that public service broadcasters respect market principles. To this end, Member States shall have appropriate mechanisms in place which allow assessing any potential complaint in an effective way at the national level' (European Commission, 2009: 22).

The role of the larger European countries

As in other cases, the fate of the public broadcasters in Europe will be associated, sooner or later, with the developments that take place in the larger countries. This is because, in the age of globalization and EU 'Europeanization', the smaller countries have to act and react to new developments taking place in the larger states. In other words, the fate of public broadcasters in Europe will be connected to the fate of the public broadcasters in the larger European countries (Papathanassopoulos, 2007; Iosifidis, 2007c). By and large, as history has tended to show, the direction public broadcasters will follow in the larger countries will be significant for the future of the entire public broadcasting sector in Europe (Tunstall, 2008). But, the fate of large public broadcasters is not entirely secure. In the UK, for example, the British media regulator, Ofcom, on 10 April 2008, announced that it would consider requiring the BBC to share its annual licence fees with commercial broadcasters that offer public service programmes. The proposal was one of several under consideration as Ofcom began its second major review of the sector. Ofcom is looking for a 'new sustainable model' for public service broadcasting in the era of digital television and a model that does not disadvantage commercial broadcasters that seek to fulfil some public service broadcasting obligations, however minor. Furthermore, whilst the BBC's funding remains secure, private broadcasters are struggling under pressure from convergent technologies and a decline in advertising revenue, a situation that they often see as grossly unfair.

In this new technological and economic environment, it is unlikely that the BBC will succeed in retaining full access to the licence fee; it may do so in the short term but there are increasing pressures on it, in part because its commercial rivals are finding it increasingly difficult to pursue public service obligations at a time of intense commercial competition and economic turmoil. Nevertheless, nothing has been ruled out but, then again, nothing has been ruled in.

In France, regulations drawn up in 2000 decreased the amount of advertising time allowed on public channels. France 2 and France 3 used to carry up to 12 minutes of commercial breaks per hour. President Sarkozy's new reform plan for public broadcasting is the eventual elimination of advertising from these channels. This will be completed in two phases. The first one started in January 2009 when advertising was prohibited after 8pm. In the second phase, which will start in January 2012, advertising will be banned from public television. The lost revenue will be covered by a 3 per cent tax on private broadcasting revenues, as much as €80 million. In addition, telephone operators and internet service providers will be charged 0.9 per cent of their revenue for the support of public broadcasting. And that bill – certainly passed on to consumers – would add as much as €380 million annually. President Sarkozy adopted this stance as he considered that indirect taxes are easier than raising the licence fee (tax) on households. Needless to say, the reorganization of the public broadcaster – on a BBC model – provoked and upset the employees. Some commented that the tax would be 'counter-productive and illegal' under EC state-aid frameworks, but the European Commission approved, in July 2008, a €150 million capital injection for France Télévisions. The Commission considered the capital injection was justified given the net costs that these specific policies involve and the French authorities' commitments regarding control of the funds. But it stated that the decision was unrelated to discussions on possible new types of public financing for the public broadcaster.

Several other European countries have made efforts to reduce the amount of advertising on public television and for similar reasons. Inspired by the French reform, the press and politicians have asked for the transfer of this model to Spain. In January 2010 Spain banned any TV advertising on the public broadcaster TVE. In Germany, leading politicians want Germany to follow the lead of France and eliminate advertising on ZDF and the other major public broadcaster, ARD, both of which rely on licence fees to finance most of their budgets.

As a result of the economic downturn, we may be entering a period when the British duopoly model triumphs: a strong public sector and a strong(ish) commercial sector. In such circumstances, it may be the economy rather than technology that changes the fate of public broadcasters. Interestingly, though, the ban of advertising on French public television has not had the expected effects for private broadcasters: the advertising revenue of the two major private channels has gone down and not increased (Dutheil and Psenny, 2009). This suggests that the future for broadcasters – both public service and commercial – is anything but clear. Technology has created new circumstances; the economy, however, has created a crisis of major proportions.

Concluding remarks for policy considerations

The above trends have created a new situation: the public service broadcasters will need to justify their legitimacy in a new climate that may or may not favour them (see also Padovani and Tracey, 2003; Syvertsen, 2003). Media legislation in individual countries, especially the larger ones, and to lesser extent EU policies, seem to be having a major impact on the future of public broadcasting in Europe. But technology has also intervened. For instance, private broadcasters, facing the same technological changes but more dependent on the vagaries of the advertising market, are now forcefully restating their claim that public broadcasters have an unfair advantage in developing new media ventures. Thus they are putting pressure on politicians and policy-makers to implement policies of fair competition.

A number of studies, reports and papers on the future of public broadcasters, have often suggested that if public broadcasters wished to survive, they would need to redefine their role (Raboy, 1998; Collins, 1998, Syversten, 2003). For these authors, the principles justifying the role of the public service broadcasting are already passé or 'designed for another age' (Biggam, 2000: 21). If this is so – and it is not entirely clear that the fundamental principles have become outmoded – public broadcasters certainly need to think about their future role in the new media and political ideological environments.

By and large, public broadcasters were established to cater for the mass public. The digital era, on the other hand, is characterized by fragmentation and the end of the mass audience, so public broadcasters face the most severe challenge in their long and distinguished history. A solution for public broadcasters may be for them to pay more attention to catering for neglected minority interests. In this case, however, a major redefinition of their remit is necessary which, in the long run, does not guarantee the universality of the licence fee. Moreover, most of the new channels are expected to cover niche markets or segments of the audience. In other words, new (or existing) private niche channels will obviously compete with any new 'approach' developed on behalf of public broadcasters.

On the whole, European and national political actors support, in principle and rhetorically, public broadcasting principles and the financial status of the public broadcasters (Hultén, 2007). But often their policies indicate quite the opposite. As a result, public broadcasters have faced increased scrutiny regarding the financing of their operations. In effect, since the mid-1980s, the mainstream policy in Western Europe has been a gradual withdrawal of the public sector from the communication and broadcasting field. It becomes clear that in the era of cost-effectiveness and the abandonment of the welfare state in which public broadcasting is regarded as an integral part, the future of public broadcasters seems uncertain. Perhaps the survival of public broadcasters will be associated, as in the past, with the future of West European societies.

In terms of future policy, it seems that it will be focused less on the harmonization of the public service remit and more on the structure and financing of the public broadcasters. In the age of convergence and digitalization of the communications universe, it is possible, if not reasonable, to discuss the prospects for public media rather than for public service broadcasting. If this is so, the whole policy approach should change. This may mean that if public broadcasters produce new content for new digital/online media, they can demand payment. But if this is so, it is questionable whether one can support the argument for the continuation of their compulsory licence fee. The licence fee, in this case, could also be directed to those media, either public or private, which produce relevant content.

In the digital and internet era, public broadcasters face the need to define their futures. Lars Nord (2009) has suggested some possible futures. One is to adopt an 'expansive strategy' allowing public service broadcasters to use public funds and licence fees for web operations and also by accepting additional commercial/private sources such as sponsoring or advertising to secure online activities. A second option is for public broadcasters to use their 'existing revenues freely on different media, but without receiving any extra money for Internet operations.' A third option is that policy makers might 'adopt a restricting strategy, accepting public service presence on the Internet, but only with special kinds of content.' The fourth option is to adopt a free-market approach 'where public service on the Net is allowed as long as all its operations are financed by commercial revenues from the Internet activities'.

It is clear that we have entered a transitional period of communications policy regarding public broadcasting or media. In this phase, the concern is not whether public TV channels will carry advertising, but rather whether public money (licence fee) will fund broadcasters or media content providers. In this new era, policy-makers have to decide:

- whether 'public service broadcasting' is synonymous with the 'public sector';

- whether they will continue the financing of the public audiovisual media or public media in general;
- whether the EU will continue to search for transparency in the financing of the public broadcasters, leaving aside the issue of media concentration and cross ownership of private media; and
- whether public broadcasters deliver public value and to what extent this public value needs to be guaranteed.

Transformations of the State in Telecommunications

Johannes M. Bauer

Introduction

Since it became involved in telecommunications during the 19th century, the state has played overlapping and complementary – but sometimes also conflicting – roles in telecommunications: owner-operator, regulator, facilitator and stopgap for private sector deficiencies. The state became involved in telecommunications for different reasons, in several ways and in a variety of forms. In some nations military control of communication facilities dominated. In others it seemed obvious to extend the postal service monopoly to electronic communications. Starved for tax revenues, other nations saw telecommunications as a promising revenue-generating activity. Frequently, the state intervened to overcome the unsatisfactory performance of private telephone service providers (e.g., Noam, 1992; Millward, 2005). In North America the state became involved as a reluctant regulator to prevent the abuse of market power by private firms (Phillips, 1993). During the early 20th century, the view that telecommunications was a 'natural' monopoly – implying that it would be most economical to entrust the provision of services to exclusive franchisees – was gradually accepted.

Institutional responses to this policy challenge varied in Europe and North America, the two regions to which this chapter is confined. In the USA and Canada, a system of privately owned utilities, subject during the late 19th century to oversight by municipalities and beginning in the 20th to be regulated by specialized state and federal agencies, was established. In contrast, in Europe, with few exceptions such as Spain and Italy, state ownership was the dominant model. Government oversight was executed through parliament and ministerial departments but no specialized regulatory agencies were established. Throughout most of the 20th century, state ownership and government regulation were considered as alternative, workable forms of public control, means of achieving public values in sectors deemed of critical importance to economy and society. This situation started to change, beginning in the 1970s, as weaknesses of the state-owned postal, telephone and telegraph companies (PTTs) to provide efficient information and communication infrastructure became visible. At the same time, trust in the ability of government agencies to successfully regulate monopolies started to fade and made room for a stronger belief in deregulation and the superiority of market organization and competition.

Despite these qualms with regulation by specialized agencies, it was considered a superior arrangement than state monopoly (or at least a second-best necessity during the transition from monopoly to competition). Therefore, as PTTs were gradually privatized, countries that historically had opted for state ownership established independent regulatory agencies to oversee the reorganized incumbent service providers. In many countries, the reduction of state ownership proceeded at a slower pace than market liberalization. Such asynchronicity gave rise to the new and untested arrangement of partially state-owned enterprises regulated by state agencies. However, as empirical observations documenting the performance of the sector under the new arrangements became available, overlooked shortcomings in the ability and expediency of private sector investment to expand advanced communication infrastructures to more rural communities became visible. In response, forms of collective ownership started to make a rebound. Many communities became newly involved in projects to close a perceived investment gap. In the wake of the financial crisis of 2008, governments worldwide were launching stimulus packages, many of which include considerable investment support for broadband networks and services.

This chapter reviews these metamorphoses of the state from heavy involvement in the provision and regulation of telecommunication services to its more indirect role as a regulator to the more recent return of the state. While there may be an appearance of cyclicality, a return of the 'old' state, such parallels are only superficial. The role of the state has adapted in response to a multitude of forces, including new challenges faced by the sector, the evolving economic and technical conditions, changing political conditions, and shifts in the configurations of relevant stakeholders attempting to shape communications policy. Due to the historical differences in sector organization, the specific forms of transformation differed in North America and in Europe. The debate was cast in terms of privatization, liberalization and regulation in Europe, while it revolved around deregulation, liberalization and more recently the renewed involvement of the public sector in North America. The third role of the state as facilitator and stopgap had remained relevant in Europe and Canada throughout this period but has only lately been revived in the USA.

The state as owner and operator

Throughout most of the 20th century, despite the existence of many national differences in the details of sector organization, telecommunications in the predecessor nations of the EU-15 was dominated by state-owned monopolies. The only exceptions were Italy and Spain, where mixed public-private and fully private firms offered services. National fragmentation was seen as a major obstacle to the integration of the European market. In response, beginning in the 1980s, the European Commission, Council and Parliament – supported by decisions of the European Court of Justice – began to harmonize national policies, to liberalize national and trans-European markets and to introduce transparent regulation. Shaped by nearly 30 directives from the European Commission and the Council since 1988, terminal equipment, value-added services, mobile services, cable services and satellite services were liberalized. In 1998, the last remaining monopoly domain, entry into basic services and network infrastructure, was eliminated (Jordana, 2002).[1]

While liberalization measures were binding to the member states, the EU did not stipulate any particular ownership regime but left the choice to national governments (Clifton *et al.*, 2003). Most likely, this is the outcome of the pragmatic attempt to avoid a heated debate among member states on state ownership issues that might have delayed the whole liberalization process. Moreover, it was also compatible with a broad research literature that had pointed out that, while ownership rights mattered, competition was probably more important than ownership for sector efficiency (Vickers and Yarrow, 1988). Given this overall approach, member states had to obey the competition rules of the EU Treaty and establish non-discriminatory and transparent regulation regardless of ownership status.

Despite this acceptance of public ownership, nearly all members of the EU-15 began selling ownership stakes during the 1990s. The UK had already started to privatize British Telecom (now BT) in the early 1980s. In 1990, 12 of the incumbent public telecommunications operators (PTOs) were fully state-owned; one was majority state-owned; and in two cases the state held a minority share (see Table 9.1). National struggles between proponents and opponents of privatization resulted in different patterns and outcomes as 14 nations sold all or part of their PTO to private investors. To avoid stressing the stock market and to bolster sales revenues, privatization typically occurred in multiple tranches over several years. By 2006,

Table 9.1 Public ownership in EU-15 as of 1990 and 2006

Country	Incumbent	State ownership share (%)	
		1990	*2006*
Austria	Telekom Austria	100.0	28.7
Belgium	Belgacom	100.0	50.0
Denmark	Tele Danmark	100.0	0.0
Finland	TeliaSonera	100.0	58.8
France	France Telecom	100.0	32.5
Germany	Deutsche Telekom	100.0	38.2
Greece	OTE	100.0	33.8
Ireland	Eircom	100.0	0.0
Italy	Telecom Italia	40.0	0.0
Luxembourg	P&T Luxembourg	100.0	100.0
Netherlands	KPN	100.0	7.8
Portugal	PT Communicações, SA	100.0	6.9
Spain	Telefónica	32.0	0.0
Sweden	TeliaSonera	100.0	58.8
UK	BT	50.1	0.0

Source: OECD (2007, pp. 39–42).

five countries had divested all ownership. The Netherlands and Portugal had retained a non-controlling stake of less than 25 per cent. Three countries held a minority ownership of more than 25 but less that 50 per cent. Three countries still owned a majority of the stock; only P&T Luxembourg remained in full state ownership. The majority of shares in TeliaSonera, which had been formed by the merger of the Finnish and Swedish incumbents, were held by the two states.

At the same time as the state reduced its ownership stake in the wireline industry, PTOs expanded their presence into wireless services. However, the presence of the state turned out to be less pervasive than in wireless communications. Licences for first-generation, analogue mobile voice service had been issued during the era of monopoly in the 1970s and 1980s and hence went to the incumbent PTOs (Curwen, 2002). During the early 1990s the first digital mobile voice licences were awarded. In contrast to analogue mobile voice, more than one licence was made available, allowing the entry of new competitors. The rapid growth of digital mobile services resulted in additional licence awards during the late 1990s, typically to new entrants. In an increasing number of cases these were based on auctions – an assignment method in which incumbents could not benefit from good relations to government (Gruber, 2005). Some PTOs provide mobile services themselves but many have established a separate subsidiary, which is often only partly owned by the PTO. Consequently, mobile markets evolved in a less concentrated fashion and the share of customers served by state-owned service providers was much lower than in fixed services. Therefore, the role of publicly owned service providers in the mobile market overall is only a fraction of that in the fixed services industry.

In the USA and Canada, telecommunications was historically dominated by investor-owned, regulated service providers. State ownership played a larger role in Canada, where three provinces (Alberta, Manitoba and Saskatchewan) were historically involved in the provision of telecommunication services (Jorgenson, 1990). After World War II Canada's commitment to the Commonwealth resulted in the nationalization of overseas communications in a Crown corporation, the Canadian Overseas Telecommunications Corporation (COTC, which later became Teleglobe). During the late 1980s and early 1990s, most of these companies were sold to private investors, typically in qualified auctions or limited negotiations. For example, in 1987 Teleglobe Canada was sold to Memotec Data, Terra Nova Telecom was sold to BCE in 1988 and Telesat Canada to Alouette Telecommunications in 1992. In 1990, the government of Alberta established Telus Communications as a parent company to facilitate the privatization Alberta's telephone crown corporation (AGT). Shares in Telus were sold to the public in 1990 and 1991. Telus later also purchased another public telephone company, Edmonton Telephones (EdTel), and developed into one of the leading Canadian private carriers.

In comparison, state ownership played less of a role in the USA. Proposals to nationalize the telephone system during World War I failed to gather sufficient support in Congress putting the country on a course of state regulation of investor-owned firms.[2] Municipal enterprises and cooperatives played a supplementary role, mostly in rural areas. They were generally exempt from regulation by state and federal regulatory agencies. US government was prominently involved in designing, rolling out and operating the US Department of Defense's ARPANET (Advanced Research Projects Agency Network). This core network was later expanded to the civilian sector by NSFNET, operated by non-profit organizations, later in collaboration with IBM and MCI, until its full privatization in the mid-1990s.

More recently, however, state and municipal governments have become involved in building backbone networks and municipal wireless networks, or at least in facilitating and coordinating their deployment, often in response to slow roll-out of infrastructure by the private sector. The performance record of these initiatives is mixed. A large number of first-generation projects experienced financial difficulties, caught in a trap of to higher-than-anticipated costs and lower-than-anticipated demand. A second generation of initiatives is based on broader assessments of the total benefits to a community, for example, for the provision of emergency or public safety services. In municipal wireless services, three models seem to be emerging: (1) full subsidy by the public agency to a private operators; (2) anchor tenancy by the agency to provide ascertain the operator of a base level of demand; and (3) public ownership and operation (Huang, 2008). Furthermore, many of the more than 2,000 US municipal electric utilities have entered the provision of broadband services, taking advantage of existing rights of ways and networks needed to operate their power systems. Private industry looked at these municipal initiatives as unfair competition and lobbied state legislatures and Congress to prevent such public endeavours, reaching legislative limitations or outright prohibitions in several states, including Colorado, Florida and Nebraska. Empirical evidence does not seem to support the claim of unfair competition or crowding out. Rather, municipal utilities seem to complement privately owned service providers (Hauge *et al.*, 2008).

Overall, while the state has withdrawn significantly from the ownership and operation of telecommunication services, important countertrends exist. These often are initiated in areas in which market forces, competition and regulation, the three main pillars of the reforms of the 1980s and 1990s, produced outcomes that were deemed unacceptable by the affected communities. The present renaissance of the state can therefore be seen as the response to the disappointment of overly optimistic expectations as to the range of services that decentralized market forces would spawn and of the timeline with which they would deliver them even to remote areas. It is also compatible with research on the role of ownership and privatization, pointing out that private ownership creates clearer incentive structures but that it is not a sufficient condition to achieve lasting efficiency gains.

The state as a regulator

Historically, regulation by specialized agencies was established as an institutional alternative to state ownership. Until the 1980s, regulation of telecommunications by specialized government agencies was a unique US and Canadian institutional arrangement. This does not mean that regulatory functions were absent outside of these nations but they were typically embedded in the operations of the state-owned service provider, resulting in a peculiar blending of operational and quasi-regulatory tasks in one entity. For example, PTOs typically would certify terminal equipment for use on their networks or they would handle customer complaints. The confounding of these roles was probably one of the reasons why initial policy responses to the changing economic and technological landscape of communications were undertaken much later in countries that had historically relied on state-owned monopolies than in the USA, where emerging stakeholders and interest groups had more options to challenge the regulatory *status quo ante*.

A distinction is often made between economic and social regulation. Analytically, this is fuzzy at best, as any economic regulation has social implications and any social regulation economic consequences. Social regulation is primarily concerned with fairness and equity. As efficiency is only defined in a meaningful way with respect to a specific bundle of rights and obligations, one could argue that social concerns of regulation precede economic concerns and that efficient economic regulation can only be achieved once the social objectives are established. In publicly owned firms, these goals were pursued simultaneously but often in ways that raised many principal–agent conflicts between different government units making demands. For example, PTTs were regularly asked by national legislative and executive bodies to pursue universal service goals, to maintain affordable process, to stabilize employment in times of economic downturns (Nowotny, 1982) and to cross-subsidize loss-making operations such as the postal service. These multiple goals were difficult to reconcile and often left management without clear directions. The model reached its limits when massive investments in network upgrades were required in the 1970s and 1980s, at a time when public budgets were strained making additional budget allocations difficult.

The 'internal regulation' model of public ownership allowed taking public policy considerations other than efficiency into account. There are instances in which this arrangement worked, in particular if transparent principal–agency relations were established. The Swedish operator Telia could perhaps be cited as an example (Karlsson, 1998). Overall, however, there are more cases in which the public ownership model suffered from unclear principal agency structures and often conflicting demands (Aharoni, 1986). In contrast, external regulation requires an open and more transparent discussion of these aspects and therefore a somewhat better opportunity to implement economic and social regulatory goals in a compatible and sustainable fashion. Nonetheless, there are also cases when regulatory agencies failed to employ such coherent solutions, for example, when universal service mandates are imposed on commercial operators without explicit compensation.

Three periods may be distinguished in the historical evolution of government regulation of telecommunications: (1) monopoly regulation; (2) transition from monopoly to a more open market structure; and (3) regulatory intervention in unevenly competitive markets. The relevance of these phases, the timeline of the transition from the first to the third phase and the specific tasks assigned to regulation vary depending on the country and the region. In US telecommunications, monopoly regulation was gradually phased out between the late 1950s and the 1980s by releasing market segments deemed structurally competitive from regulatory oversight (Brock, 1981). During the period from the break-up of the Bell System in 1984 until the passage and practical implementation of the Telecommunications Act of 1996, which declared competition as the basic organizational principle of US telecommunications, regulation went through a final pro-competitive transition (Brock, 1994, 2003). The period 2003–5 is a reasonable marker for the beginning of the latest phase. By then, the successor companies of the Bell System all had met the conditions established in the Telecommunications Act as preconditions to enter in-region long-distance markets. At the same time, the stringent unbundling rules that had been imposed on incumbent local exchange carriers (ILECs) in voice markets were significantly curtailed and aligned with the rules applied in other countries.

Furthermore, broadband access markets were successively declared as essentially unregulated information service markets (Nuechterlein and Weiser, 2007).

During the late 1980s, Europe, stirred by a sense that its telecommunications industry was falling behind the US and a few emerging nations in Asia, embarked on an ambitious programme of market structure and regulatory reform. Led by the European Commission, within a relatively brief period of little more than a decade monopolies were abandoned and replaced by a more openly competitive market structure (Michalis, 2006). Like in the USA, terminal equipment, value-added services and mobile communications were successively opened to new entrants. By 1998, all market segments were fully liberalized, with regulation gradually shifting from retail to wholesale markets. In two Communications Reviews, the European Union has continued this process of reducing regulatory intervention and expanding competition. Regulatory tasks in the EU are pursued by National Regulatory Authorities (NRAs). NRAs coordinate with each other, most importantly within the European Regulators Group (ERG), and with the European Commission.

Ex ante regulatory intervention is based on a systematic and periodic assessment by national regulatory authorities and the European Commission of the presence of significant market power. The relevant market segments are delineated and evaluated in a joint procedure. The toolkit of NRAs is limited by a list of remedies deemed appropriate in relevant European legislation. During the latest review of the regulatory framework, the Commission had proposed establishment of a European Regulatory Agency but the idea failed in the European Parliament. Instead, the European Regulators Group (ERG) will play a more systematic role in coordinating national approaches. Given this two-tier system, national regulation is homogenized by joint European efforts but retains a certain degree of national diversity. Whereas the European Commission continues to be concerned about the fragmentation of the European telecommunications industry, such national diversity is not necessarily bad. It may provide an environment that facilitates institutional learning, as countries will be able to learn from each other's experience, a learning process that would not be possible in a fully homogeneous approach.

The gradual privatization process in Europe created a peculiar new and untested arrangement: state-regulated, fully or partially state-owned ('mixed') enterprises (Bauer, 2005). Government regulation was initially designed as a means to exert public control over investor-owned firms. This separation created a clear (but not necessarily unproblematic or efficient) principal–agent relation. In the case of regulated mixed firms, the state is both regulator and part-owner, a dual principal and agent. The overall effect of this multiplicity of roles is difficult to predict. On the one hand, there is a risk that it may be abused to adopt regulatory provisions favourable to the former state-owned service provider (even if they are within the boundaries of acceptable discretionary choices by the regulatory agency). On the other hand, mixed ownership can stabilize investor expectations and serve as a credible signal that the state will not adopt vindictive policies after privatization (Perotti, 1995). A similar argument could be made with respect to regulated mixed firms: state regulatory agencies might err on either side of fair regulation: they might be captured by the part-owner state or, alternatively, attempting to signal independence from government, might be inclined to bias their policies against the former state-owned enterprise. Mixed ownership might provide safeguards against unreasonable regulation (but not against regulatory favours).

Bauer (2005) and Edwards and Waverman (2006) argue and provide empirical evidence that the degree of regulatory independence is an important mediating factor. The risk of capture by the state is lower if the regulatory agency is truly independent from the executive branch of government. Another possible advantage of mixed firms is that they could provide a more effective tool to realize public values that are difficult to implement with regulatory tools. The public owner, it is argued, for example by Eckel and Vining (1985), could commit management to pursue goals such as universal service on its own motivation, whereas private shareholders would ascertain that demands are not unreasonable and compatible with the financial sustainability of the organization. In other words, mixed ownership would provide a more efficient principal–agent structure than full state ownership. Bauer (2005), however, did not find strong evidence that mixed regulated firms provided such quasi-public goods to a higher extent than either public or private regulated firms.

The establishment of regulation also changes the political dynamics of telecommunications policy. Although created as an institutional arrangement to assist in determining and implementing public values by balancing conflicting interests (such as consumer interests in low prices with investor interests in achieving a sufficient return on the invested capital), it has been criticized for failing to achieve that goal. The deregulatory movement in the USA was strongly influenced by political economic theories that diagnosed serious flaws in the working of regulatory agencies. The Chicago School asserted that, due to asymmetric information and transaction costs, regulators openly or inadvertently are captured by well-organized interests, typically the regulated industry. In a different vein, the Virginia School claimed that the existence of regulatory agencies (or government in general) would inevitably lead to rent-seeking activities by stakeholders trying to pursue their own advantage. In the process, potential welfare gains would be reduced or fully dissipated. A sprawling political and economic literature on regulation has explored other aspects of the political dynamics of regulation (Noll, 1989; Bailey and Pack, 1995).

Overall, while many models explain specific facts, none seems well aligned with the broader picture of empirical observations. These suggest that regulation may fall anywhere on the spectrum from regulation in the public interest (as earlier theories had uncritically assumed) to regulation that benefits special interest groups at the expense of others. Where on this spectrum practical regulation is positioned is not least dependent on the institutional set-up of a country and the organization of the regulatory agencies (e.g., their independence from other branches of government). The complexity of the problem to be solved and hence the degree of dependence of the agency on information from the regulated industries will also play a role. Furthermore, the age of the regulatory system may have an influence with mature systems more plagued by inertia and stakeholder lobbying than younger ones. In recent US regulation the locus of influence shifted clearly from potential new market entrants during the 1990s to incumbents (late 1990s until 2009) and, most recently, to content providers and Silicon Valley hi-tech companies (2009 and forward). In Europe, the introduction of national systems of regulation coordinated and shaped by action at the European level has contributed to a significant expansion of lobbying activities. The increasing number of stakeholders, like in the USA, has most likely rendered it more difficult to find feasible and sustainable policies.

Between the late 1980s, when regulatory reform in European telecommunications started, and the early 2000s, the policy model in the USA and in Europe increasingly looked alike. However, this period of regulatory convergence has been succeeded by renewed regulatory divergence, in particular in the area of next-generation networks (broadband and ultrabroadband). In its latest Communications Review in 2007, the EU essentially retained the basic framework introduced a few years earlier based on a three-part test. *Ex ante* regulation is only warranted if: (1) a market is dominated by one firm or jointly by several, (2) competition is not emerging, and (3) competition policy cannot take care of the issue (Marcus, 2003). However, the US Federal Communications Commission, in part in response to court decisions that settled challenges to earlier regulatory policies, since 2003 has adopted a much stronger deregulatory model. Beginning in 2003, the stringent local loop unbundling policy that had been introduced in the wake of the Telecommunications Act of 1996 and which indirectly also had intensified competition in broadband, was curtailed to a more modest approach more in line with international practice. More importantly, after the 2005 *Brand X* decision by the US Supreme Court affirmed the FCC's jurisdiction to classify services, the agency between 2005 and 2007 declared ADSL, wireless broadband and broadband over power lines (BPL) as essentially unregulated information services (Bauer and Bohlin, 2008). These declaratory rulings eliminated the common carrier obligations of the service providers in these markets, freeing them from the requirement to make their services available at just and reasonable prices and non-discriminatory terms and conditions. Abandonment of these rules has triggered a debate on the obligations that network operators should have in their dealings with content and application providers. As European nations did not eliminate openness provisions at the network layer, they do not have such an intense network neutrality debate, at least not at the moment.

Although government regulation is the predominant form of national public control and coordination in telecommunications, a multiplicity of alternative governance arrangements has emerged in the industry. Self-regulation, voluntary agreements between affected stakeholders, and co-regulation by government and non-government players are increasingly used to address coordination issues affecting the internet and new media (Latzer *et al.*, 2003). For example, codes of governance are widely used to address policy issues in new media. The global integration of communications has led to an increasing number of international agreements. With the framework of intergovernmental organizations, the International Telecommunication Union (ITU), the World Trade Organization (WTO) and the World Intellectual Property Organization (WIPO) have negotiated and adopted treaties that have become embedded in national legislation and regulation. These range from agreements on trade in services, to agreements harmonizing telecom regulation (WTO), to treaties governing intellectual property in a digital age (WIPO).

In addition to these realms of global governance, new forms of global multi-stakeholder coordination have emerged in response to the many governance issues raised by the internet. In contrast to intergovernmental approaches, these are often bottom-up processes in which many non-government stakeholders interact. Primary examples are the Internet Corporation for Assigned Names and Numbers (ICANN), the Internet

Governance Forum (IGF) and the two World Summits on the Information Society (WSIS) conferences in Geneva and Tunis, from which these new arrangements emerged (Malcolm, 2008; Bygrave and Bing, 2009). Both intergovernmental forms of coordination and multi-stakeholder forms of governance raise complicated issues. In the first case, the separation between the subject and the object of governance is blurred; in the second case, questions of legitimacy (many of the non-government groups have no formal delegated authority) and implementation arise (likewise, many of the non-government groups lack the authority to enforce rules), but are beyond the scope of this chapter.

The state as a facilitator and stopgap

The European telecommunications liberalization debate has shifted the focus from the state as an owner to its role as a regulator, as most succinctly reflected in the emergence of the notion of a 'regulatory state' (Majone, 1996), a term also used to refer to the corresponding shift in US policy during the early 20th century. Nonetheless, governments on both sides of the Atlantic continued to intervene with other means in the information and communication technology sectors. The economic crisis of 2008 has seen a renewal of some of these efforts, which may be labelled as forms of 'industrial policy' as well as interventions in which the state acts as a 'stopgap' to overcome the weaknesses and deficiencies of an unregulated market economy. The forms and instruments of industrial policy vary widely between the EU and the USA. Policy-makers in European nations and at the European Commission in Brussels have historically placed stronger trust in the ability of the state to enhance the competitiveness of firms and sectors and to facilitate their adaptation to changing economic conditions. In the USA, on the other hand, industrial policy was pursued more indirectly, mostly through programmes related to the military. The internet can be traced back to ARPANET, funded for many years by the US Department of Defense, but many other defence-related programmes have also supported research and development in ICT. As mentioned above, lower-level government agencies (states, municipalities) that had historically played a role in building energy and communications infrastructures are renewing efforts to support investment in advanced telecommunication infrastructure.

European integration has somewhat constrained and narrowed the toolkit available to the member states, as such measures need to be compatible with the overarching principles of the European treaties. Financial aid, subsidies, tax incentives, consolidation measures, or the granting of regulatory exemptions must not contradict the competitive principles and the basic economic freedoms upon which the EU is built. Within these broad constraints, the EU has crafted many programmes to assist the European information and communication technology industry, ranging from efforts to set Europe-wide standards to the facilitation of research and development (R&D) and the reliance on the public sector to generate demand pull for innovation. As a comprehensive overview of these multiple initiatives would far exceed the scope of this chapter, a few pointers must suffice (see European Commission, 2008). Recent efforts received a major push in the Lisbon Agenda (sometimes also referred to as 'Lisbon Strategy'), which had been adopted by the European Council in Lisbon in 2000. This initiative envisioned making Europe into a 'more dynamic and competitive knowledge-based economy' by 2010 (EC 2000).

Two sub-programmes within the Lisbon Agenda, eEurope 2002 and eEurope 2005, focused on advancing access to and use of the internet and the advancement of broadband access, network security and e-government. Based on recommendations in a mid-term review of these plans (High Level Group, 2004), in 2005 the European Union launched the i2010 initiative as a new overarching framework (European Commission, 2005). It comprises efforts in information and communication technology and media, coordinating regulatory policy (discussed in the previous section), research and development efforts, and other forms of public–private partnerships within an overarching set of concerns. The programmes within the i2010 programme fall into four broad categories: (1) measures to support the integration into a Single European Information Space; (2) programmes supporting innovation and investment in ICT research; (3) initiatives to promote inclusion, better quality of life and public service; and (4) focus programmes under the heading of flagship initiatives (e.g., European Digital Libraries, ICT for sustainable development).

Individual EU member states pursue many complementary programmes to these EU-level initiatives. With the increased recent concern about broadband deployment and adoption, many national governments, including France, Greece, Ireland and Italy, have launched or are discussing programmes to support the roll-out of broadband to rural and remote areas. Likewise, several cities and municipalities, for example Stockholm and Amsterdam, are building broadband networks and others are considering building wireless networks, often as public–private partnerships. For example, Berlin, Germany, recently announced the deployment of a WiFi network to cover major parts of the city. These projects are well intended but their impact on the overall investment volume and infrastructure deployment has not been fully examined. Contradictory effects are at work. On the one hand, such projects may increase the incentives of private providers to accelerate their investment plans so as to not face second-mover disadvantages. Such bandwagon behaviour of major private service was, for example, found in a comparative study of four rural US communities (LaRose *et al.*, 2008). On the other hand, such public investment projects weaken the business case for private investors, especially if broadband access is granted free of charge.

In the USA, federal policy for the past few years was dominated by a strong belief in the superiority of market forces. However, even the staunchest advocates for private, market-driven investment recognize that, due to financing constraints and potentially lower private returns on investment, the network infrastructure will only gradually be extended to less densely populated areas. Concerned about being left behind and excluded from the benefits of the information society, many states and municipalities have launched initiatives to accelerate the deployment of advanced communications networks and services. According to information collected by the Alliance for Public Technology (APT) in collaboration with the Communications Workers of America (CWA), by 2008, 32 states operated their own backbone networks and many made capacity on these networks available to third parties; 26 US states had established a total of 29 authorities to support broadband deployment; 24 programmes affecting 27 states existed to provide direct financing of broadband projects; nine public–private partnerships had been founded; seven states supported investment indirectly via tax credits (APT and CWA, 2008). In addition, several hundred municipalities have taken a lead in the roll-out of wireless broadband networks, as described in the second section above.

The federal government took a more active role in the American Recovery and Reinvestment Act (ARRA) of 2008, which earmarked a total of $7.2 billion in the form of loan guarantees, subsidies and ancillary measures to broadband. The funds will be administered by the Rural Utility Service (RUS), an agency within the US Department of Agriculture, which had been instrumental in bringing electricity and telephone services to rural America during the 20th century, and the National Telecommunications Information Administration (NTIA), an agency within the US Department of Commerce. As projects funded by these initiatives will have to voluntarily commit to open network policies, they will probably also constrain the ability of existing, recently deregulated broadband access providers to price differentiate their platform services. Given concerns about network neutrality, such institutional diversity may thus have unanticipated positive effects on the entire ICT ecosystem.

The role of the state reconsidered

The crisis of the financial services industry in 2008 and the following economic downturn have, within a very short period of time, contributed to a redefinition of the role of the state in telecommunications. Recent orthodoxy, that the state ought to focus on designing and implementing an appropriate regulatory framework but neither own nor operate telecommunications networks and services, was superseded by a new pragmatism that attributes a larger and more diverse role to the state. This rethinking does not go so far at to abandon the overall emphasis on the state as a regulator. However, other roles of the state are experiencing a renaissance and are once again accepted as legitimate means of public policy. This is not an overnight development, as criticism on the deregulatory policies, such as the slow expansion of broadband to rural areas if driven by market forces alone, had been latent and increasingly supported by empirical evidence. Pronouncements of the return of a new Keynesianism (Katz, 2009) may be premature.

Nonetheless, the balance between private market forces and government has been realigned in favour of an increased role of the state. There is renewed acknowledgment that under certain conditions the state may be the appropriate organization to pursue public values in infrastructure sectors. This is a learning opportunity for public policy and, if utilized, one may hope that a new generation of policies will be shaped that takes the relative advantages and disadvantages of different institutional arrangements into account. The theory and practice of governance have evolved remarkably since the first onset of the privatization and deregulation movement. Moreover, the experience with and empirical study of alternative governance arrangements has also deepened our understanding of their possibilities and shortcomings.

One of the recurring insights from these studies is that the economic, political and legal context in which reforms take place matters and that it interacts with ownership and regulatory variables. In general, studies agree that liberalization and competition constitute a stronger efficiency-enhancing factor than privatization on performance measures such as retail price, service diffusion and service quality (Megginson and Netter, 2001; Bortolotti *et al.*, 2002). The degree of independence of the regulatory agency also is an important contributor to such efficiency gains. Moreover, the timing and sequencing of reforms matter: if privatization takes place before liberalization and other regulatory reforms are adopted, its effects are often weakened due to inherent trade-offs between the goal of achieving a high sales price and the intensity of competition in the post-privatization market. Where privatization precedes liberalization, as was the case in the UK, it may entail opportunity costs to society. For example, efficiency gains may be delayed if the incumbent is temporarily protected from competitors in an effort to increase its sales value. Based on a broad conceptual comparative analysis of different institutional arrangements, Jones (2009) concludes that external regulation is better suited than state ownership or laissez-faire to secure widely shared public values such as reliability and affordability of service. Several authors have argued that regulatory instruments intended to ease entry by new competitors, such as unbundling and open access, have improved static performance measures such as the number of market entrants and prices (Cave, 2006).

Research is much more ambiguous and split with regard to the policy choices that are most conducive to support investment and innovation in telecommunications. Neither monopoly nor perfect competition but market structures in between are most conducive to dynamic efficiency. Unbundling and other forms of open access policies that increase the intensity of competition therefore will increase the incentives to invest and to innovate as long as competitive intensity is below a critical threshold, but they will decrease these incentives if competitive intensity is increased above it. It is therefore possible that measures aimed at maximizing competitive intensity (and thus static efficiency) inadvertently reduce dynamic efficiency. Several studies have found evidence of this effect (Crandall *et al.*, 2004; Waverman *et al.*, 2007). Similar trade-offs, although with additional complications, hold with respect to the emerging battlefront over vertical network relations, mostly between content and application providers and network operators, as discussed in the network neutrality debate (Bauer, 2007).

These findings suggest that some degree of concentration in telecommunications may work in support of dynamic efficiency. However, given the potentially high economies of scale in the provision of network platforms, concerns about suboptimally high industry concentration are frequently articulated (Trebing, 2004). Of particular concern is the combination of industry concentration and vertical integration in next-generation networks, in which greater diversity is possible in the provision of applications and services. Such arrangements may create incentives for the vertically integrated provider to sabotage a competitor in the services market that needs access to a network. The evidence for such scenarios is limited but is nonetheless of concern. Unfortunately, drafting a set of regulatory rules that would alleviate all concerns is difficult if not impossible to specify. Moreover, it may have new disadvantages for the innovative dynamics of the ICT value net. Some authors have therefore suggested that the most important role of the state is in the safeguarding of broad interoperability rules (Werbach, 2009).

Compared to the early days of heavy government involvement, either as an owner or a regulator, telecommunications governance has become a more multiplex, multilayered, and light-handed arrangement. This is particularly evident if the increasing importance of international and global interdependencies and the expanding role of international governance arrangements are taken into account. The state is only one actor among others. It continues to enjoy a privileged position, even if it is weaker than the traditional view of the omnipotent, omniscient and benevolent force. However, it is certainly not as weak as portrayed in a newly fashionable view that sees the state as a powerless actor on a global stage. In pursuing its role, the state continues to use the whole arsenal of policy instruments in its disposal, including direct ownership and operation of telecommunications infrastructure and services, regulation and other means of public policy, including fiscal, monetary and industrial policy measures. The debate of the past two decades has sharpened our understanding of the advantages and disadvantages of alternative arrangements. Carefully designed policy could utilize these insights and delineate a new hybrid role of the state, in which the newly dominant role as regulator is complemented in certain areas with the old role as an operator and service provider, as well as an orchestrator of self- and co-regulation.

Review and outlook

This chapter has reviewed three roles of the state: as owner and operator of telecommunications infrastructure and services, as regulator of private and more recently also mixed public–private firms and as the proponent of various forms of auxiliary policies intended to nudge the industry onto a more efficient path. In all three areas fundamental transformations have occurred. The 1980s and 1990s were characterized by a shift from the state as owner and industrial policy-maker to the state as a regulator. The past few years have seen a renewed recognition that there are realms in which these traditional roles have a legitimate place. As a result, some rebalancing in the mix of these functions has occurred. Despite the partial return of the state, the wheel of history has not returned to its starting point at the turn from the 19th to the 20th century, when the classical roles of the state first took shape in Europe and North America. Rather, a combination of theoretical insights, practical experience and political changes have interacted to generate a more pragmatic view of the relative roles of the state, markets and innovative other institutional arrangements, including networks and the gift-like economies of groups like the open source or spectrum commons communities. As technology and markets diversify it can be expected that the diversity of institutional arrangements likewise increases, with renewed roles for the state as well.

Notes

1. In recognition of the more significant economic challenges faced by Greece, Ireland, Portugal and Spain, liberalization deadlines were generally staggered.
2. On 24 July 1918, President Woodrow Wilson issued a proclamation placing the US telegraph and telephone systems under the direction of the Post Office Department. This arrangement was effective 31 July 1918 through 1 August 1919.

CHAPTER

Coordinating Internet Policies: The Time has Come

Dom Caristi

Introduction

Whether or not we live in a global village may be debatable, but there is no question we live in a global economy. Not even the largest nations are totally self-sufficient and all sorts of treaties and contracts exist to facilitate international commerce. When it comes to public policy, domestic regulation of some activities is completely ineffective at achieving the necessary goal. Imagine, for example, a large factory that operates up-wind and up-river that pumps out massive amounts of pollutants. If the host country doesn't care and chooses not to regulate the activity, what is the neighbouring nation suffering all the effects to do? Clearly there needs to be some sort of recourse, and through international mechanisms there is.

In some specific areas of commerce, the porous nature of national borders is a commonplace occurrence: so much so that international commissions have been established to deal with the regular need to coordinate efforts. The International Telecommunications Union has made an important first step in this direction by establishing the World Telecommunication Policy Forum (WTPF) in 1994, and the group met in 1996, 1998, 2001 and 2009 to review telecommunications issues. ITU was founded in 1865 as a coordinating council for international telegraphy (ITU, 2009). Its mission expanded as the need for coordination of other electronic communication (notably electromagnetic frequency assignment and satellite coordination) increased. WTPF is the sort of international effort that is necessary to coordinate internet regulation, but it needs to go much further than it has.

The internet is known as a 'free and open' medium of communication, and there is a legion of commentators who advocate against any forms of regulation. Lessig (1999) asserts that the unregulated nature of the internet is the very reason it has served as well as a tool for creativity. Zittrain (2008) warns that the future of the internet is at risk, although he attributes much of the threat to businesses rather than regulation. Batra (2007) sees the marketplace as providing the greatest form of regulation.

But the indisputable fact is that the internet is not like some romanticized version of a digital unregulated Wild West town. Lawsuits have been fought and won over copyright, privacy and defamation suits. In 2009 India's Supreme Court emphatically stated that bloggers are subject to libel laws and cannot defend themselves by allowing anonymous posts and providing a disclaimer that the opinions expressed are not necessarily those of the website operator (Mahapatra, 2009). Child pornographers have been arrested and websites have been shut down. To be sure the laws vary among countries, as does the fervour with which they are pursued, yet regulation of online behaviour is a fact of life around the world.

There is a precedent for international coordination online. If there weren't, locating websites would be a far more complicated process than it is today. The Internet Corporation for Assigned Names and Numbers (ICANN) has, since 1998, coordinated the top-level domain system management. And while it has faced its share of controversies (for example when it imposed a $2 tax on new domains (McCarthy, 2005)) it has operated largely as designed. In 2006 the new top-level domain '.eu' was launched by the European Union and has already registered more than 3 million URLs, making it the ninth most registered domain in 2008 (AP, 2009).

This chapter presents the proposition that, like the pollution analogy, some regulation is inadequate if handled domestically and it makes more sense that international agreements would be implemented to deal with the cross-border issues. We will now look at the specifics of some of these questions.

Cross-border issues

Intellectual property

The music and motion picture industries are claiming huge losses of revenue that they say are the result of illegal file sharing of copyrighted works. Digital copying combined with the internet's ability to distribute work around the globe have made it easy to share copies of people's favourite entertainment without providing any revenue to the copyright holder.

Many users don't even care whether it's legal. According to a Pew study in 2003, two-thirds of those surveyed that downloaded music said they didn't care whether a file they downloaded was copyrighted (Madden and Lenhart, 2003). A more recent survey in Europe showed three-quarters of the respondents know what is legal or illegal, but the majority believed the recording industry had not convinced them that downloading is damaging (*NewMediaAge*, 2009).

Copyright laws within a country are inadequate to deal with the issue. This was recognized long before anyone dreamed of an internet. The Berne Convention of 1886 recognized the need for a coordinated effort and has been somewhat successful in coordinating international copyright issues. The greatest difficulty has occurred in a digital world where the challenges are greater. As new challenges arise, new solutions need to be considered.

Concepts of what constitute fair use vary dramatically online. Google, long an advocate of increased sharing rights, has asserted that fair use has been recognized as important by the United Kingdom but has yet to become part of British law (Frost, 2009). It seems one of the major issues continues to be the roles the various players should assume. While some advocate that internet service providers (ISP) should assume a proactive role in stopping piracy, ISPs argue that they are not the police and it is up to government agencies to do the policing.

In January 2009, the Isle of Man proposed to collect £1 per internet subscriber per month for unlimited music downloads and provide the money to copyright owners (Pfanner, 2009). France considered a similar proposal in 2006 but it never became law. There are other models to be considered. Is the model proposed in Ireland more suitable? There, pirates have their internet services disconnected. The ISP is not required to monitor downloading but must react when notified by those whose works have been pirated. After two warnings, a third offence will result in disconnection (Seaver, 2009). France proposed the same 'three strikes' approach. Late in 2008 the French Senate overwhelmingly voted in favour of a motion that would result in a one-year denial of internet access after warning letters for the first two offences. The problem lies in the fact that cutting off internet service was a solution that the European Union decided was unacceptable just one month earlier, passing a resolution to ban such legislation (Phillips, 2008).

Of course the greatest source of consternation to the motion picture and recording industries are the file sharing sites. 'Person-to-person' (P2P) sharing allows anyone with a digital copy of a file, whether obtained legitimately or illegally, to make the file available to literally millions of others on the internet. Perhaps most famous of these was Napster. When it first appeared online in 1999 it allowed users to share MP3 audio files. A 2001 court order got the service shut down. The name still exists but it operates now as a pay service that provides licensed copies to customers for a fee rather than as an illegal file sharing service. The next generation of file sharing uses '.torrent' files that are situated around the world and can be located using one of many tracking sites. Swedish website 'The Pirate Bay' was found guilty of violating intellectual property rights, yet it defiantly continues. Pirate Bay and other file sharing sites defend themselves on the premise that their sites can be used for lawful purposes, and they should not be held responsible for the illegal activities of their users, just as gun manufacturers are not responsible for the unlawful use of a product that has a lawful use. The approach by different countries, even within the EU, has differed. In late 2008 a Danish appeal court upheld a ruling that Pirate Bay should be blocked in the country by Danish ISP Sonofon. The decision was appealed to the Danish Supreme Court (Ferro, 2009). On the other hand, as mentioned above, Ireland does not want to serve as a police force. Eircom, the country's largest internet service provider, has refused to block Pirate Bay without a court order to do so (Kirk, 2009). In February 2008 Sweden, where Pirate Bay is located, passed legislation to require ISPs to turn over the account information of alleged pirates to copyright holders, who would then inform the pirates to cease their file sharing or face a copyright lawsuit. As might be expected, the Swedish entertainment industry supported the legislation while a majority of the public opposed it (*The Local*, 2008).

But Creative Freedom Foundation (CFF) in New Zealand fought legislation in that country to implement disconnect laws and has convinced the government to delay any action. While CFF recognizes the illegality of pirating movies or music, the group contends disconnect rules assume a party is guilty whenever an accusation is made, and further that a single misbehaving employee might result in an entire business's internet access being denied (NetGuide, 2009).

Social networking sites such as Facebook and MySpace have provided ample opportunity to violate copyright. They may not violate copyright on the level of P2P sites but because of the nature of members 'sharing' all sorts of content (including pictures, music and video), invariably some of that content will be copyrighted material. In 2008 MySpace announced that it would partner with MTV Networks, allowing MySpace members to post copyrighted video from MTV Networks channels in exchange for a portion of the advertising revenues generated from page views (SiliconValley, 2008). There has been a shift in attitude among the MTV executives, as characterized by Forrester Research Analyst James McQuivey: 'Two years ago the solution was "Let's sue YouTube and block this." It really hasn't worked. Now the solution is "Let's create a system where content can drive benefit"' (Guynn, 2008).

In the USA, the recording industry has actively pursued pirates with the threat of lawsuits. The Recording Industry Association of America (RIAA) has initiated more than 30,000 complaints against alleged intellectual property thieves. Only one of all those cases has resulted in a trial: all the others have either been dropped or settled out of court, usually in the form of a payment by the alleged perpetrator, usually for a lesser amount and also avoiding any court costs (*USA Today*, 2008).

The purpose of this chapter is not to assess whether a proposal for ISPs to police intellectual property, or a tax imposed nationwide, or ad revenue to compensate copyright is the most appropriate scheme for policing intellectual property rights, but rather to raise the question as to who should be involved in passing judgment on such proposals. Is it better to have a patchwork of different rules worldwide? Should the owners of intellectual property be the ones having to know what rules apply in each nation? Would it not make more sense to have some international agreement that provides guidance?

Warner Bros. decided that it ought to take on film piracy head on, but not by legal action. Instead, Warner is trying to make it easier for Chinese to purchase newly released films online. The hope is that if they can extract even small legal payments (on the order of 60 cents to $1 per film download) they might be able to cut into the significant market for pirated movies. Estimates are that 93 per cent of movies sold in China are pirated (Chmielewski, 2008). It remains to be seen whether such a strategy will be successful, given the populace's comfort with 'free' downloads.

If China wishes to decrease the amount of movie piracy, perhaps South African entertainment companies may provide a model. In 2008 the South African Federation Against Copyright Theft (SAFACT) successfully prosecuted a man in East London on charges of movie piracy. SAFACT worked with South African police and the justice department in getting the conviction along with a three-year jail sentence (Pillay, 2008). As with the Warner experiment in China, there's no way of knowing yet whether this strategy will lead to a drop in film pirating.

The USA has created an Intellectual Property Rights watch list, where it identifies countries that do not enforce international property rights agreements such as the Berne Convention rules. It is a unilateral effort to coerce cooperation via economic pressures. In January 2009 Taiwan was removed from the watch list because of its increased efforts to police intellectual property theft (Lowther, 2009). Perhaps this system can work for the USA, with its significant economic clout, yet it seems an unsuitable solution for smaller nations.

Books have been slower than movies or music in their move from analogue to digital, but they, too, are beginning to see the transformation. Google has begun a massive initiative to digitize millions of books that have gone out of print. American authors and publishers have struck an agreement with the Book Search service, but people in other countries will not yet be able to purchase the electronic texts (Pfanner, 2008).

Controlling free expression

One of the more innovative uses of the World Wide Web has been the creation of blogs (a new word contracted from 'Web logs'). Estimates are that 184 million people worldwide have started blogs and 346 million people worldwide read blogs (Technorati, 2009). Blogs have been identified in 81 different languages (there could be more). While a good number of these blogs are diaries, personal accounts or other 'light reading' with very small readerships, some blogs have actually become major media, providing large numbers of followers with news of the day. Greek-American Arianna Huffington publishes *The Huffington Post*, a news and commentary website that had more than 6 million unique visitors in January 2009 (Statsaholic, 2009). In Europe 67 per cent of bloggers are college graduates and have been blogging an average of almost three years.

Not all countries are happy to see their citizens exercising free expression so openly to the entire world, and the results have been catastrophic for some bloggers. In Vietnam the government has 'given police broad authority to move against online critics' (Johnston, 2009). The Asia director of Human Rights Watch asserts that 'Vietnam is one of the few countries where people can be locked up on charges of abusing democratic freedoms.' His suggestion is that the country's donors pressure the government to change its policy. While that might be one approach, it might also be helpful to have the force of an international body that could discuss Vietnam's crackdown on online expression.

Even democratic countries have arrested bloggers for exercising their free speech. In South Korea a blogger going by the pseudonym 'Minerva' (named for the Greek goddess of wisdom) was accused by the government of providing false financial information. Minerva asserts he posted information to assist underprivileged people and did not gain financially from anything he posted. International civil rights groups have called for his release from custody (Harden, 2009).

Social networking has grown dramatically, and Facebook has been one of the major beneficiaries of this growth. While a lot of what happens on Facebook is social, some of it can actually be quite political. A number of groups have formed to support or oppose particular government initiatives, and politicians have begun to exploit social networking as a way of communicating with constituents, or potential constituents. Noz Zica

Srebrenica was a Facebook group founded in support of war crimes fugitive Ratko Mladic and celebrating the massacre of 8,000 Muslims, and had more than 900 members. Thousands of Bosnians formed a group demanding the closure of the group and within days Facebook administrators responded, removing the controversial group. Facebook claimed it was a violation of policy and not the controversy that resulted in the removal (Reuters, 2008b). What is important to note in this instance was that the removal was the result of complaints to the provider, who decided that the content ought to be removed, and not some intervention by government officials.

Obscene and indecent content control

Countries have always had different levels of acceptance with regard to sexually oriented content. Magazines produced and sold in some countries are prohibited for sale in other countries. There may be occasional breeches at the borders, but for the most part countries are fairly efficient at keeping out print content that they find unsuitable for their citizens.

The internet provides new challenges for governments trying to protect national morals. China has been active and overt in its efforts to block sites that provide content that it feels threatens public morals. Interestingly, though, China's complaints are not just levelled at 'hard core' pornographic sites but also mainstream search engines including Google and Baidu, China's own major search engine (Hille, 2009).

There are three primary tools a government may use in preventing content it deems indecent from reaching its citizens. First, it can take the approach followed by Singapore and other countries by requiring all ISPs to be registered through a government authority (in Singapore's case, the broadcasting authority). ISPs are then strictly advised on unacceptable content to be blocked. Second, filters can be applied by the government rather than requiring the ISP to control. China regularly blocks sites and indecency is one of the justifications. Third, there may be no restrictions imposed on access, but then subsequent punishment may occur for individuals accessing unacceptable content. In the USA this has been the primary means of regulation. The USA has laws prohibiting obscenity but the sites that the USA would find truly obscene (as opposed to simply 'indecent', which is less restricted) for the most part originate outside the US borders. Repeated attempts to legislate online morality have been found unconstitutional by US courts, so the main recourse has been limited legal action against individuals who create, distribute or access child pornography: the one seemingly universal taboo.

Privacy

As with so many issues, privacy rights are protected to varying degrees in different countries, so one would expect online privacy rights would likewise vary by nation. Multinational companies like Microsoft, Google and Yahoo have found themselves enforcing different standards worldwide.

Google Earth was hailed as a major development when it was released in 2005. Earlier software had allowed internet users to map towns and driving directions from one location to another, but Google Earth enhanced this feature by allowing users to see satellite imagery of the locations they input. All of a sudden people were not just seeing a graphic display of the street where they lived but they were seeing the actual house. Resolutions varied based on location but in some cases it was claimed that people sunbathing in the back yard were visible.

Then in 2008 Google Earth increased the level of controversy by introducing its 'Street View' feature. Instead of satellite imagery, Street View allows users to see locations from ground-level cameras that roam neighbourhoods. The images are not live but they still raise privacy issues. Concern has been expressed because individuals can be identified as they enter liquor stores or other suggestive locations. Automobile licence plates can be identified so identities can be tracked even more. Interestingly, Google has developed technology that allows it to blur both faces and licence plates but says it will do so only when required to do so by a country. In other places, including the USA, no blurring occurs (Weisman, 2007). Japan, Canada and the EU have expressed concerns over Street View's potential invasion of privacy, and the UK has speculated that individuals whose images are shown without consent might be exploited by Google (Hartley, 2009).

Similarly, the length of time data is kept by search engines is regulated in some countries and not in others. Microsoft was under attack from a European Commission advisory panel because MSN Live Search retained search data for 18 months, while the advisory panel wanted data kept for only six months (O'Brien, 2008). While Microsoft was prepared to reduce the length of time it retained data in EU countries if its competitors did the same, it did not universally offer to reduce the length of time it kept search data from all countries.

Google has found itself at the heart of another internationally known news item. In 2006, video from a mobile phone was posted to Italy's YouTube site showing a boy with Down's syndrome being taunted by four male high school students. An advocacy group, Vivi Down, filed a complaint, which led to a 2008 decision by an Italian prosecutor that four Google executives ought to stand trial. In February 2009 a judge declined to dismiss the charges and will allow a criminal trial to proceed (Lyman, 2009). It is unprecedented for criminal charges to be brought against executives of the site for what third parties elected to post. Each defendant faces up to three years in jail.

National security

Google Earth was a concern for more than just sunbathers. Governments around the world were expressing concerns that the satellite imagery posed a security risk by providing enemies with important reconnaissance data that they otherwise would not be able to access. Concerns have been expressed by a number of countries, including Australia (Barlow, 2005), South Korea, Thailand, Sri Lanka and India (Haines, 2005). In the aftermath of the 2008 terrorist attacks in Mumbai, critics pointed out that the terrorists used Google Earth to help them plan their attack. As Security expert Bruce Schneier has asserted, the terrorists also used boats but no one suggests an elimination of them (Schneier, 2008).

'Cyber-terrorism' has become the new term to describe purposeful political attacks on servers, either to hack into them to steal sensitive information or to cause them to shut down. For example, in 2007 an ethnic Russian was fined for blocking a reform party website in Estonia after a Soviet war memorial was removed from the centre of Tallinn (BBC, 2008). The US Department of Defense claims that it regularly needs to guard itself against similar attacks. But this sort of defence posture requires no acts of regulation, whereas fining perpetrators or restricting their internet access does.

Of course 'national security' has been stated as the reason for government censorship on many occasions when in fact the true reason was something else. In 2008 Thailand blocked 1,200 websites and shut down another 400, purportedly for national security reasons. Of the 400 shut down sites, 344 were 'being mean to the Thai royal family' (Barak, 2008).

Blocking websites for other reasons

In addition to national security and obscenity, sites may be blocked by nations for a variety of reasons, and the level of scrutiny in these decisions varies dramatically. The OpenNet Initiative provides an extensive list of web filtering done by a number of countries around the world at http://opennet.net/research/profiles.

In 2008, Germany blocked access to Wikipedia Germany when a German lawmaker claimed the site contained false information about him. A German court temporarily blocked access to all the German Wikipedia entries: a somewhat broad response to a narrow complaint. As Efroni (2009) points out, tech-savvy Germans were still able to access the article, as was the rest of the world, and the end result was that many more people saw the article in question than would have ever accessed it had the legislator not made such a fuss.

China has long been known for its policy of blocking foreign websites that contain content that is illegal under Chinese law. In particular, it routinely blocks any sites that refer to Taiwan as a separate country or that refer to the government opposition in Tibet. As a result major world news sources such as the BBC, Voice of America and Ming Pao News are regularly blocked from Chinese access (Reuters, 2008a).

Early in 2009, Thailand blocked thousands of websites because it claimed the sites insulted the Thai monarchy. Sites blocked included everything from Thai discussion boards where citizens discuss political issues to an *Economist* article claiming the king was involved in political affairs, contrary to Thailand's claims that the monarchy is merely ceremonial (Bell, 2009).

In the USA, online gambling is currently prohibited. Sites are not permitted to operate within the USA and, although not blocked (as they are in some countries), Americans who access international sites are subject to punishment. Both the government and the citizens know that the laws are easily circumvented. One American internet online poker player said it only takes about 'two minutes' to get around the rules (Gaul, 2008).

Restricting searches

In Argentina, search engines are required by law to censor search results for the names of celebrities, including star athletes and fashion models. This is different from blocking access to the sites themselves. Instead, the search engines may not provide search results for websites that exist. Similarly, German law forbids searches for neo-Nazi websites, France prohibits auction sites from displaying Nazi items for sale and the Church of Scientology has been able to prevent Google from providing links to the Church's copyright-protected content (Condon, 2008). Similarly, a battle rages in Europe over whether Google should be allowed to provide links to knock-off websites whenever someone searches for a designer label.

The distinction between blocking access to a site and not even allowing the result to appear in a list of search results is significant. It is one thing to be informed that a site exists but may not be accessed but quite another not even to be aware of its existence. In China, Google filters search results to exclude news sites that would be inaccessible. The company claims it is doing so merely to make searches more efficient (no point in providing broken links), while critics accuse the company of complicity in censorship (WorldNetDaily, 2004).

A proposal

It might be useful to look at what appears to be a model of collaboration between online content creators and international regulators. In February 2009, 17 social networking sites including the prominent Facebook and MySpace signed an agreement with the European Commission to try to prevent 'cyber-bullying' (the online harassment of individuals by groups) and 'grooming' (adults befriending children online with the intention of sexual activity). The voluntary agreement includes making profile information for users under 18 unsearchable, use of a prominent 'report abuse' button on the sites and making underage profiles private by default (Reuters, 2009). Forty-nine US states have signed similar agreements.

If such a policy is a good one, and one that can be agreed to voluntarily by states, nations and content sites, then why should it have to be negotiated all over the world with all different jurisdictions? Wouldn't it make infinitely more sense to have a model agreement established that could be adopted by any jurisdiction? It is hard to imagine that if Facebook agreed to such a policy in the EU and almost all of the USA, it would balk at such a policy whether requested by Afghanistan or Zimbabwe.

Some 'free internet' advocates will undoubtedly cringe at a coordinated regulatory effort, saying it adds an unnecessary level of bureaucracy and increases the threat of regulation, but in fact the opposite is more likely: less regulation may result when efforts are coordinated. Evidence of this is clear in recent developments in Italy, where the country is considering more regulation. Italian ISP founder and technology commentator Stefano Quintarelli stated it succinctly: 'Australia has taken a step to filter the Internet, France a different step, Ireland another and even the United States another, but what is worrying is that Italy is adding them altogether, and that leads to a very restrictive environment' (Sylvers, 2009). If Italy were part of an international consortium that collectively agreed to appropriate responses to challenges, the country might be less willing to add a new restriction for every conceivable threat.

It is helpful to look to existing structures for a model of international coordination. In 1865 the International Telegraph Union was established to standardize interconnection agreements between countries. That organization's scope has expanded over the years and the name has changed to the International Telecommunication Union (ITU). ITU conferences began in 1925 to deal with the delicate issues of international broadcasting. Over the years membership has changed, the organization has become part of the United Nations structure and conferences have at times been contentious, but the basic premise and structure remains the same.

The ITU has included internet on its agenda, but most of its efforts have been focused on bridging the digital divide, as evidenced by conferences on the information society in 2003 and 2005. This proposal contends that the ITU ought to be more proactive in setting forth model regulations that can be followed specifically in areas where consensus exists as to acceptable policy, such as the voluntary cyber-bullying policy mentioned above. In 2009 a World Telecommunication Policy Forum in Lisbon had the potential to begin to form the sorts of international policies being suggested here, but the final resolutions, while endorsing the theory of 'coordination of internet-related public policy issues', provided little in the way of pragmatic regulatory templates. In order for the Forum to lead to the sorts of reforms suggested here, it must commit to proactively proposing specific model policies for member nations to adopt.

One of the major benefits of periodic conferences is that it forces countries and regions to confront their own regulatory issues in advance of the conference and come to some consensus about the positions they will take. Each country at the table may be one vote, but each country represents multiple interests from government, private interests and public interest groups. Certainly not all industry representatives advocate the same policies, and even different government agencies within the same country may have different perspectives (for example, security interests versus commercial exploitation). The European Commission has hosted workshops in advance of World Radiocommunication Conferences to develop 'coherent policy' prior to entering the worldwide negotiations. The US Federal Communications Commission's International Bureau Chief announced that the USA ought to be preparing now, two years in advance of the 2011 conference (Telecom, 2009). A regularly scheduled, periodic world conference to discuss model digital policies would provide motivation for governments to, at minimum, gather the stakeholders in their own countries to discuss relevant policies.

It would be naive to suggest that such a structure would make all digital regulation consistent across all countries. A regular international forum for model regulation would not guarantee that all disputes are resolved, just as the WRC has unresolved issues and exceptions created for different member nations (Caristi, 1993). The important point is to create a structure that would accommodate international discussion and debate, provide a venue for constituents to resolve disputes and to provide nations with a source for model policies when dealing with issues they have never before had to address.

For consistency, to limit unnecessary regulation and to ensure all the stakeholders have a forum for their concerns, a World Digital Media Conference is a suitable solution. It is in the best interest of ITU member nations, and all the varied constituencies in each of those member nations, to work towards developing a regularly scheduled international conference (one that occurs much more often than four times in 15 years, as has the WTPF) on digital media policy that provides pragmatic regulatory models for member implementation.

Framing the Information Society: A Comparison of Policy Approaches by the USA and the EU

Gisela Gil-Egui, Yan Tian and Concetta M. Stewart

After being the subject of intense scrutiny between the late 1990s and early 2000s, the notion of 'digital divide' (DD) seems to be disappearing from the radar screen of scholars and policy-makers as a category to diagnose and address inequalities in the diffusion and use of information and communication technologies (ICTs). However, policy-makers in many countries seem to be only now confronting the socio-economic and cultural complexities involved in effectively promoting an information society.[1] Discourses at different fronts concerning the latter are, thus, gradually readjusting their focus on issues beyond mere access to information and communication infrastructure, such as digital literacy, multimedia content, adequate regulatory initiatives and/or defining the right balance between public and private action.

A longitudinal exploration of the evolution of major policy initiatives in the USA and the European Union since the mid-1990s reveals shifts in governmental actors' definition of priorities and strategies regarding penetration and adoption of ICTs in their respective societies. A first comparison we conducted some years ago between key policy documents on the digital divide produced by the USA and the EU during the 1995–2002 period showed both a common emphasis on internet access and a common progression over time towards framing diffusion of ICTs in essentially economic and market-based terms (Stewart *et al.*, 2006). More recently, however, policy-making on both sides of the Atlantic, but especially in the EU, is signalling a departure from such an approach to the matter. In this chapter, we present the results of a new round of analysis of policies formulated by the same governmental actors between 2004 and 2008. In conducting our study, we were particularly interested in assessing similarities and differences between the two regions' approaches to issues related to access to and uses of ICTs, in light of changing administrative priorities in the USA in connection to the war on terrorism, and political transformations in the EU resulting from its membership expansions in 2004 and 2007.

Our exploration involved comparing key European and American policy documents concerning ICTs, through both a computer-assisted text analysis and a qualitative reading of official reports on the subject released since 2004 by the National Telecommunications and Information Agency (NTIA) in the USA, and by the European Commission's Directorate-General for the Information Society and Media in the EU. Based on the results of our previous analysis of US and EU policy documents, we expected to find a higher reliance on market forces than what was corroborated in our previous study. However, as we explain later, we perceive in the new results an unanticipated reconsideration of the role that the government can play in promoting universal penetration of ICTs, not so much as a direct provider, but rather as generator of plans, subsidies and programmes intended to stimulate private investment in areas or services deemed to either have low revenue potential (e.g., provision of broadband services in rural areas) or need additional support (e.g., technologies strengthening security of information systems).

Beyond this common reconsideration of the government's role, we found, nevertheless, that the specificity of the political contexts in the USA and EU emerge even more clearly in this recent set of policy documents than in the previous one.

Background

Criticism of the technologically deterministic character of early definitions of the digital divide, which informed much policy-making on ICTs from the mid-1990s to the mid-2000s, is moving gradually from the academic realm (e.g., Colombo and Carlo, 2006; Deursen and van Dijk, 2008; McSorley, 2003; Murdock and Golding, 1999) to the 'real' domains of multilateral organizations such as the World Bank. In this move, there has been recognition of theoretical and empirical flaws of proposals aimed at eliminating the gap between enfranchised and disenfranchised populations by merely providing everyone with access to a computer and the internet. Thus, as early as 2003, a background paper commissioned by the World

Bank's programme on ICT for development, *InfoDev*, argued for the need to reframe the notion of the digital divide by pointing out that '[t]he presence or absence of ICTs (the "digital divide") is a symptom, not a cause' (McNamara, 2003: 4). Moreover, the same report breaks with what could be deemed a positivist tradition in the studies performed for and/or by the World Bank, by admitting that

> ICTs are, to some extent, social constructs...Personal computers are...an answer to specific needs and preferences typical of firms, institutions and individuals in developed countries. They will not necessarily be equally well suited to the needs of, or the forms of social and economic organization common to users in other countries, particularly poor countries. (McNamara, 2003: 7–8)

Empirical and theoretical support to critiques of the shortcomings of traditional conceptualizations of the digital divide have been proposed by a number of authors (e.g., Howard, 2007; Livingstone and Helsper, 2007; Sassi, 2005; Strover *et al.*, 2005). In a comprehensive longitudinal analysis on changes on ICTs for 200 countries between 1995 and 2005, Howard concluded that 'a few poor countries have leapt ahead in the development of a few aspects of ICT infrastructure and use' (2007: 1). Sassi (2005) classifies different formulations of DD into four major approaches: a) technocratic (oriented to widening internet access and usage); b) socio-structural (concerned with broader factors marking disparities in society, such as income, education, or ethnicity); c) info-structural/exclusionary (focused on geographical differences in the penetration of IC infrastructure); and d) modernizing capitalist (concerned with the inequalities in the nature of labour and trade created by globalization and the way ICTs tend to accentuate those disparities worldwide). In exploring the way in which thinking on DD has evolved, the author argues that

> The [above described] approaches all have in common an understanding of real disparities in the use of information technologies, but they differ in how they see the significance of the phenomena. In the main, the technocratic approach is a result of the information society 'project' itself and, accordingly, is affirmative of it. The other three approaches...consider the concept of the information society as more an ideological construct than an empirical phenomenon. (Sassi, 2005: 694)

Despite growing questioning of the technocratic approach, ICT policy-making in the developed world still assumes a major goal: the universal availability of information infrastructure and services. According to Falch (2007), developed nations have attempted to ensure widespread penetration of broadband services in recent years by way of three major strategies: (1) direct market intervention (in which the state participates actively and directly in the provision of services); (2) regulation (in which the state creates binding rules and conditions for third parties who provide services); and (3) facilitation (in which the state limits its role to making information about providers available to users and providers, and generating specific market conditions intended to foster competition). In a comparative exploration of broadband penetration in several developed nations, Falch (2007) found that the effectiveness of any of the three policy frameworks is tempered by a set of structural and contingent factors affecting supply and demand, and by dynamics of infrastructure and content development. But beyond these factors, and despite the fact that all the countries explored in his enquiry implemented policies combining direct intervention, regulation and facilitation in different proportions, Falch concludes that

> public policy does matter. Although technical and economic parameters such as income level play a role in the development of broadband services, successful implementation of broadband...depends on the kind of policy measures to be taken. The most important seems to be the creation of a competitive market for provision of broadband services. This may include a wide range of measures, ranging from facilitation to direct intervention. But stimulation of the demand side also seems to be important. This can be done, e.g. through content development and upgrading of ICT skills. (2007: 257)

The mere acceptance of the proposition that direct governmental intervention can, in combination with regulation and market facilitation, be a valid strategy adopted by developed nations for the promotion of ICT infrastructure and services signals a shift in the paradigm that dominated the US and EU policy documents we analyzed in our previous study (Stewart *et al.*, 2006). In that report, we discussed evidence of the gradual colonization of the internet by market-oriented activities and discourses. This argument was later corroborated by the findings of our computer-assisted text analysis, which led us to establish that

> US and EU documents share a converging trend towards consideration of market-based issues as key points of policies related to the digital divide. Such an underlying commonality became apparent after exploring the different ways in which the documents' most frequent terms generate semantic clusters, which in turn provides a preliminary indication of framing patterns for both populations of texts. (Stewart *et al.*, 2006: 744–5)

Rethinking the role of markets and the state

Results from the round of analyses on more recent documents by the USA and the EU performed for this chapter suggest a partial change in discursive approaches by policy-makers, as we explain in the following sections of this chapter,. Such a change parallels in time both the increasing administrative complexities involved in the expansions of the European Union that took place in 2004 and 2007, and the growing irrelevance of one-sided policy formulas in light of the current global economic downturn.

The first of these two phenomena has been explored by Hofmann and Türk (2006), who contend that the European Union's administration has become essentially fragmented and in need of more resources for coordination, as it embraces a model of 'executive federalism'. Consequently, it is to be expected that discursive practices by different bureaucratic and policy-making actors within the EU reflect this need for additional efforts regarding programmatic harmonization.

The second phenomenon relates to the ambiguous results of a decade of techno-deterministic strategies aimed at promoting a global information economy and knowledge society (as illustrated, among others, by Christensen, 2006; Howard, 2007; and McNamara, 2003), and to the need, highlighted by those results, of more nuanced approaches implicating the public sector in a more active role than that of an arbiter at the sidelines of market forces. Moreover, a reconsideration of the role of the state in the implementation of major policies appears to be gaining ground in the context of the global financial crisis, which lends credence to strategies based on better governmental regulation, state interventions in the economy, and/or policy diversity based on the structural and institutional specificity of each country (Rodrik, 1998; Singh, 2007; World Bank, 2005). In this sense, some commentators have been proposing a more proactive governmental role in situations emerging as market failures, from insufficient investment in ICT research and relevant content development (Christensen, 2006), to inefficient labour relations (Howell, 2004), to broader dysfunctions in the global financial sector (Zuckerman, 2008). By suggesting a reconsideration of the role of the public sector in promoting diffusion and/or strategic adoption of ICTs, the findings presented in this chapter not only yield empirical substantiation to those arguments, but also to theories of alternate cycles or paradigms in policy-making (Baumgartner and Jones, 1993; Hall, 1993).

One way of keeping track of such swings is through the identification of salient themes and terms emphasized by policy-makers when defining action plans, as revealed by frame analysis. This analytical strategy, as argued by Miller and Riechert (2001), allows researchers to distinguish rhetorical *schemata* in the construction of issues by highlighting some aspects of them and neglecting others. This, in turn provides ways to understand how different stakeholders to a certain issue structure messages about it and how people perceive them.

Method

Since our previous study on approaches by the USA and the EU to the digital divide involved an exploration of key policy documents produced on both sides of the Atlantic between 1995 and 2002 (Stewart *et al.*, 2006), the present chapter focuses on newer iterations of those policy documents, produced between 2004 and 2008 (no report was produced in 2003), by the US National Telecommunications and Information Agency and the European Commission's Directorate-General for the Information Society and Media. Specifically, the reports analyzed for this study are, for the USA: *A Nation Online* (US Department of Commerce, 2004) and *Networked Nation* (US Department of Commerce, 2007); for the EU: *i2010 Communication* (Commission of the European Communities, 2005a), *i2010 Annual Report* (Commission of the European Communities, 2006), *i2010 Annual Report* (Commission of the European Communities, 2007) and *i2010 Mid-Term Review* (Commission of the European Communities, 2008).

While the disparity in the number of documents produced by both governmental actors within the 2004–8 period may be read as an indicator of dissimilarities in the level of priority assigned to policy-making on the role of ICTs for development, we still consider both sets of documents comparable in terms of size (the US reports were substantially larger than the EU ones) and scope. Moreover, as they provide continuity to periodical diagnoses of ICT's penetration and adoption, they afford us a longitudinal perspective on changes in policy-making on the matter by both actors.

Our goal was to identify the way in which the USA and the EU are framing[2] their strategies towards ICTs in recent years, by replicating the multi-modal approach we applied in our previous study about policies on the digital divide. Such a multimodal approach involved both a qualitative reading of US and EU policy reports and a computer-assisted text analysis of those reports with the support of two programs constituting the Galileo® suite: CatPac® and ThoughtView®.

Being a neural network program, CatPac can identify the occurrences of each concept in a text and reveal the semantic relationships among the concepts through their clustering patterns (Murphy, 2001; Woelfel and Stoyanoff, 2000). A network for a text is composed of neurons (concepts) and the semantic relationships among those neurons (Murphy, 2001; Woelfel and Stoyanoff, 2000). With CatPac, 'the researchers do not pre-specify categories or pre-code words to be found in a text. Instead, the computer program categorizes all meaning-bearing concepts in a text. This increases both the reliability and objectivity of research' (Stewart *et al.*, 2006: 739). ThoughtView, on the other hand, can run multidimensional scaling (MDS) analysis on the text. Concepts semantically related will appear close to one another in a two- or three-dimensional map. This map provides further insights on the relationships among the concepts in the network.

Based on the design of the computer-assisted text analysis we performed in our previous study, we sought to identify the 40 most frequent words in each text and the way they interrelate. Our CatPac analysis yielded two sets of data for each document: a ranked list of its most recurrent terms and a dendogram displaying clustering patterns among those terms. Median method was selected as a clustering criterion to be used by the program, as it proved in our preliminary tests to generate more discrete and easy-to-interpret clusters.[3] The dendograms also generated input files for ThoughtView to create MDS or perceptual maps that show the relationship of terms and clusters in bi-dimensional and tri-dimensional spaces.

The resulting frequency lists, dendograms and MDS maps obtained from the computer-assisted text analysis with the Galileo suite, allowed a systematic exploration of the *visible* constitutive elements of frames in the EU and US documents, which are described in the next section of this chapter. However, elucidation of the cognitive constructions suggested by frames (a possibility proposed by DiMaggio, 1997; Ferree and Merrill, 2000) involves identifying not only the explicit rhetorical components of such frames, but also those that are consistently omitted from them. Therefore, we deemed it necessary to complement the picture presented by our computer-assisted text analysis with a qualitative reading of the documents, in order to holistically interpret the patterns of association among terms as a complex representation of a phenomenon where the excluded elements (terms, semantic associations, propositions) convey as much meaning as those that are included and purposively highlighted.

Results

The four European and two US reports analyzed for this study reveal more differences than commonalities in the two regions' policy-making approach in recent years regarding access and use of ICTs. While the American documents refocus on diagnosis and assessment of infrastructure availability, as was characteristic of the first *Falling through the Net* reports issued by the NTIA in 1995 and 1998, the European ones emphasize administrative and policy coordination among the EU's growing number of member states to advance broader goals concerning the creation of an information society in which both the private and the public sector have important roles to play.

US reports

A Nation Online 2004

In our previous study, the last US report we analyzed, *A Nation Online 2002*, suggested a 'connected' country where rapidly growing levels of internet penetration enabled policy-makers of the new Bush administration to ignore underserved segments of the population, and thereby concentrate, instead, on ways of generating skilled workers for a digital economy. However, the rapid emergence of new generation of information and communication activities involving more immediacy (e.g., RSS feeds), ubiquity (e.g., Wi-Fi and Wi-Max networks), multimodality (e.g., 3G telephony) and content richness (e.g., multimedia messages and digital video downloading) not only demanded more capacity from distribution infrastructures, but seemed to have brought those same policy-makers back to the drawing board, in terms of defining priorities regarding ICTs.

Indeed, as revealed by the policy report *A Nation Online 2004*, the need for a baseline assessment of domestic penetration of broadband infrastructure is apparent, and so the document focuses once again on pulling together basic data, this time related to access to high bandwidth connectivity by different demographic groups and by different geographic areas in the country. The fact that the list of most frequent words for this report includes *internet, broadband, connections, dial, online, speed, cable, available,* and *dsl,* as well as, *households, age, users, rural, census, urban, disabilities* and *Hispanic,* among other terms, lends quantitative support to a similar conclusion from our qualitative reading of the document.

A look at the clustering patterns shown by these terms also supports the argument that US policy-makers in 2004 were concerned with assessing access to broadband connectivity by different populations. As illustrated by the MDS map in Figure 11.1, the large and very tight cluster of words located on the right side of the plane consists mostly of references to infrastructure and hardware,[4] whereas on the opposite side of the plane it is easy to distinguish another cluster made mostly of demographic references. This distribution of terms thus suggests US policy-makers' assessment of populations and information infrastructures as two elements of a binary equation they are trying to elucidate.

Networked Nation (2007)

Three years later, however, the US government restated some of the self-praising and pro-market rhetoric characteristics of the first report on the subject of DD issued by the Bush administration, *A Nation Online 2002*. Thus, US policy-makers 'upgraded' the title of their following report, published in 2007, as *Networked Nation*. The overarching theme, as

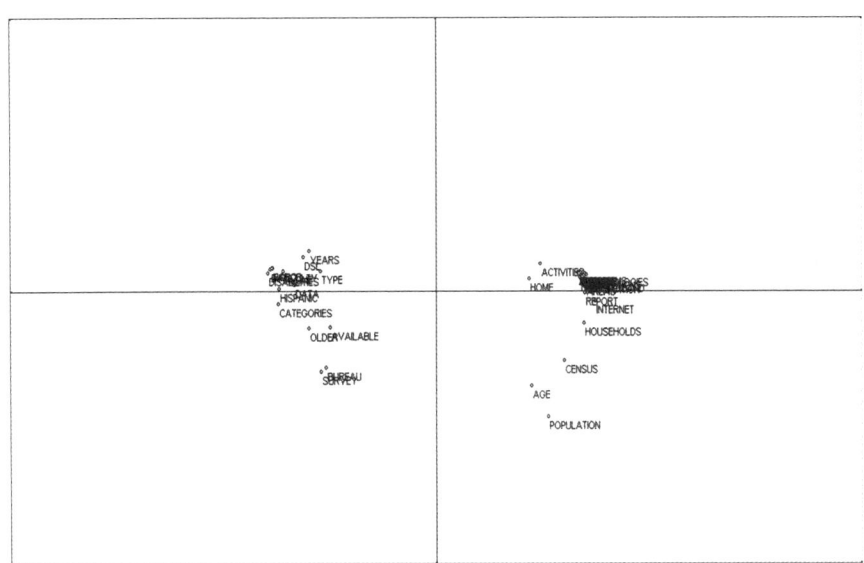

Figure 11.1   MDS map of clustering patterns in *A Nation Online* (2004)

corroborated in a qualitative reading of the document, is accomplishment: that is, most Americans have access to high-speed and affordable communication networks, and those who do not yet will soon be taken care of by the market, thanks in part to specific governmental initiatives aimed at stimulating the 'supply side' of the economy with tax breaks and other financial incentives to serve rural and special populations. Accordingly, a computer-assisted text analysis of this document reveals a preponderance of references to infrastructure, connectivity performance and financing. Any reference to the 'demand side' of the equation gets reduced to a single word, 'consumers', which replaces the term 'users' employed in the previous report, as well as any other demographic marker.

Equally intriguing is the picture presented by the MDS map for this report. As shown in Figure 11.2, a relatively loose collection of references to technology and markets, located on the left side of the plane, faces another much tighter cluster of more generic terms, which frequently accompany statements in the report about the accomplishments of the federal administration and, more specifically, the Bush Administration's vision of a telecommunications market where private providers grow thanks to pro-market governmental incentives.

In general, both US documents reiterate some of the market-based, pro-business elements emerging from the documents we analyzed in our previous study. However, unlike those documents, the US reports analyzed in this report are not intended to set comprehensive strategies or goals

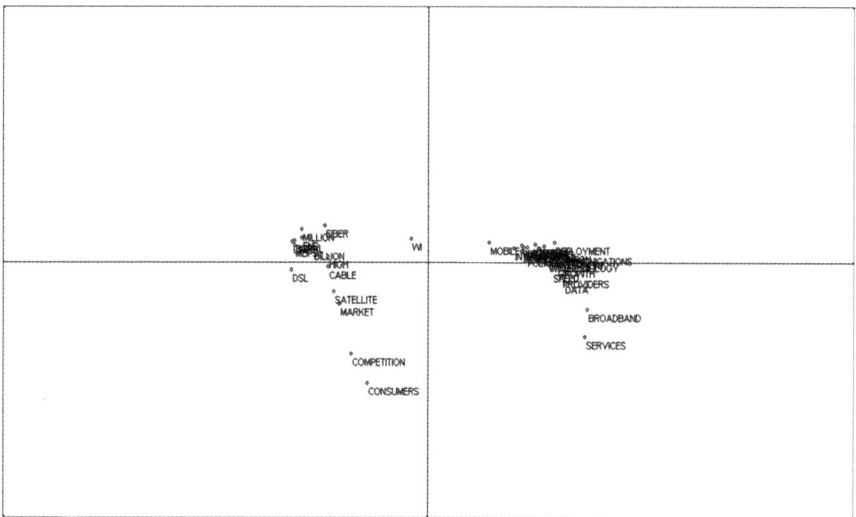

Figure 11.2   MDS map of clustering patterns in *Networked Nation* (2007)

concerning the role ICTs are to play for the US society in the medium and long term. They are rather an inventory of perceived market opportunities and policy accomplishments. Table 11.1 illustrates this observation by comparing the list of most frequent terms in *A Nation Online 2004* and *Networked Nation* (2007).

European reports

i2010 Communication (2005)

In contrast with the clearly neo-liberal trend we noticed in the eEurope[5] policy documents during our previous study, our recent analysis of the European series of *i2010*[6] reports from 2005 to 2008 shows a slightly more balanced picture in terms of the roles that the private and public sectors are to play in ensuring the creation of an pan-European information society. While both series of documents are conceived as policy frameworks, rather than as direct public expenditure programmes, both series differ in their priorities. On the one hand, the eEurope series dealt mostly with basic ICT and internet access as a means to participate more effectively in the world's information economy. The *i2010* series, on the other hand, starts from the assumption that broadband connectivity has reached critical mass within the European Union and, consequently focuses on efforts to harmonize the regulatory environment for ICTs across the Union's member states, in order to expedite the convergence of multimedia services in the region, as

Table 11.1 Comparison of list of most frequent terms for US policy documents

A Nation Online (2004)	Networked Nation (2007)
Internet	Broadband
Broadband	Services
Households	Technology
Home	Wireless
Connections	Speed
Age	Cable
Users	Access
Population	Deployment
Dial	Network
Rural	Providers
Access	Fiber
Information	Data
Areas	Million
Census	Spectrum
Online	States
Speed	Growth
Urban	Investment
High	Administration
Technologies	High
Report	DSL
Service	Mobile
Cable	FCC
Difficulty	Internet
Service	United
Available	Billion
Activities	Number
Categories	Years
Bureau	Rural
DSL	WI
Force	Competition
Labor	MBPS
Number	Telecommunications
Older	Market
Type	Satellite
Years	Areas
Americans	Lines
Data	President
Alone	Policies
Disabilities	Consumers
Hispanic	End

well as foster research and innovation in information and communication technologies.

The subtitle of the first *i2010* document, *A European Information Society for Growth and Employment*, displays something of a legacy from the policy approach adopted in the eEurope series, but, most importantly, it also shows an evident connection with the Lisbon Programme, which was a set of structural policies defined by the European Commission (EC) in 2005 to address social, economic and environmental challenges faced by the European Union. To that end, the EC designated funds and resources to ensure harmonization of policies aimed at supporting knowledge and innovation, making Europe a more attractive place to invest and work, and creating more and better jobs (Commission of the European Communities, 2005a). Consequently, the first *i2010* document reflects an effort by the European Commission to translate the broader plans of the Lisbon Programme into ICT-oriented strategies, and thus the list of most frequent words in that text combine, in similar proportions, terms related to infrastructure, the economy, policy-making and areas of alternate responsibilities or collaboration between the private and public sectors.

Such a mixed picture is also revealed by the MDS map of the document (Figure 11.3), in which we see one large and fairly tight cluster of terms on the right side of the plane, involving words apparently dealing with two main policy goals stated in the *i2010 Communication*, namely the creation of a single European information space and reinforcing investment in ICT research. On the opposite side, we see another cluster comprising terms that

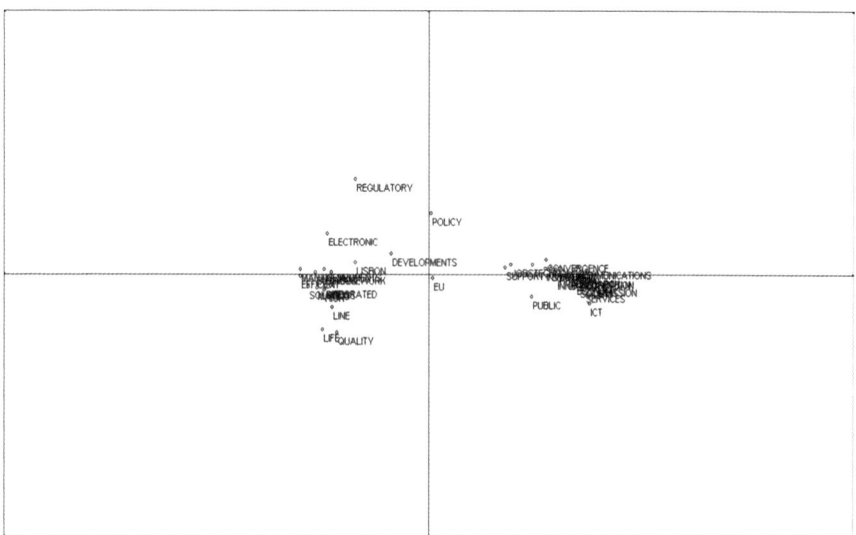

Figure 11.3   MDS map of clustering patterns in *i2010* (2005)

are probably associated with the third major goal stated by *i2010*, that is, inclusion and better quality of life through an efficient use of ICTs. There are also a few loose terms (perhaps bridging notions) floating between the two clusters we just described: *regulatory, policy, developments, EU*. We were initially surprised by the fact that two words usually associated with market-based rhetoric, *business* and *solutions*, emerged as a distinctive sub-cluster within the group of words reflecting the third goal of *i2010*, which is likely to involve more intervention from the public sector than the other two goals. However, a qualitative reading of the document reveals that an important component of the EC's vision regarding quality of life is that of generating environmentally sustainable industries, with a particular emphasis in automobiles and transportation. Therefore, the document refers a number of times to the need for conciliating sustainable development with economic growth, and thus it makes the private sector responsible for generating alternative ways of working that are both financially and environmentally sound.

i2010 Annual Report (2006)

By the time the first annual progress report following the *i2010 Communication* was published (May 2006), the European Union was entering the second year of its expansion to 25 members, after incorporating the Czech Republic, Cyprus, Estonia, Latvia, Lithuania, Hungary, Malta, Poland, Slovenia and Slovakia. Results from the first assessment of initiatives aimed at harnessing ICTs to advance the broad agenda of the Lisbon Programme show some achievements with respect to digital convergence and broadband penetration. However, economic growth and productivity are still lagging behind the European Commission's expectations, and the blame is laid on insufficient levels of investment on ICTs by most EU state members, in comparison to the USA, China and Japan.

Consistent with the urgent tone of the report, which insists on prioritizing a number of actions to strengthen Europe's competitiveness regarding ICTs, our computer-assisted text analysis of the *i2010* report in 2006 reveals a list of most frequent terms that revolve around the public sector and policy coordination, technological challenges and economic references (this time fewer than in the previous *i2010* document: *growth, jobs, investment, competitiveness*), among others. This picture resonates with some of the most interesting findings yielded by our qualitative reading of the document: an emphasis on the role that governmental and public services could play in stimulating demand for online content and development of multimedia applications. So, it is not surprising that the MDS map for this document shows a lot of overlapping among words, and clusters that are not as discrete as those of the previous text (Figure 11.4).

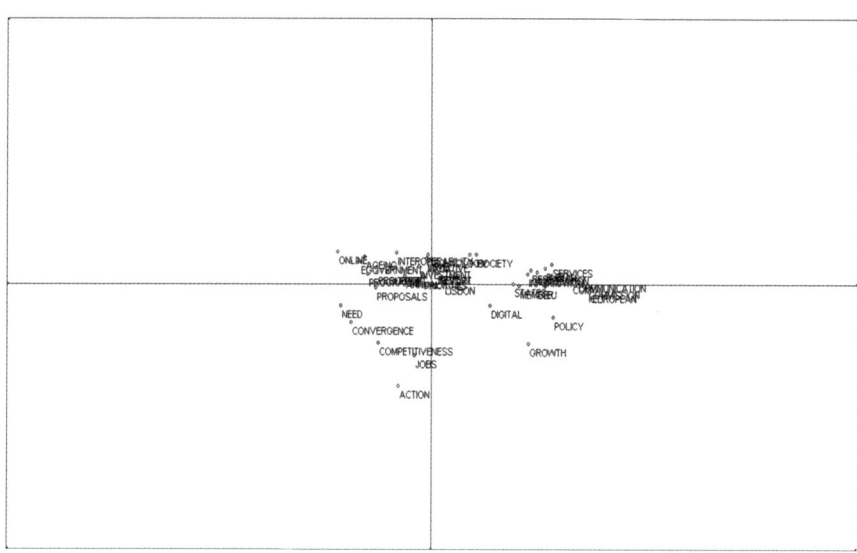

Figure 11.4   MDS map of clustering patterns in *i2010* (2006)

i2010 Annual Report (2007)

The governmental priorities and challenges highlighted in the 2006 report were apparently understood by many EU member states, as the *i2010 Annual Report* of 2007 has a decidedly more optimistic tone than its predecessor. According to the report, broadband penetration continues growing and the EU member states are rapidly embracing new information technologies and services. Consequently, the report now tries to bring attention to issues that go beyond access to infrastructure and the creation of a common regulatory framework. Action is suggested on areas such as information security, more efficient management of the electromagnetic spectrum, identification of factors hindering the provision of online services at a pan-European level and on how to adapt policy-making to technologies and content that are increasingly user-centred.

In line with the themes identified in the qualitative reading of the 2007 report, the computer-assisted analysis of the document generated a list of frequent terms that shows, in comparison to the previous report, (1) a substantial reduction of economic references (and the remaining ones appearing at the bottom half of the list: *market* and *economic*); (2) a higher number of terms related to policy coordination, the public sector and governance; (3) equal number of references to ICT hardware and software; and (4) for the first time in the history of the *i2010* documents, inclusion of the word 'users' as a recurrent term. The growing importance of coordinated regulation, long-term strategies and consistent policy-making as factors promoting the creation of an information society across the EU becomes

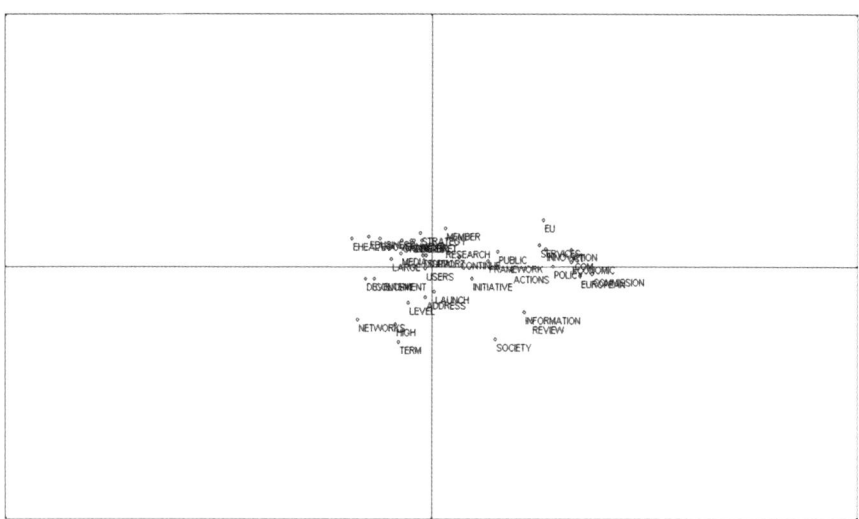

Figure 11.5 MDS map of clustering patterns in *i2010* (2007)

visible in the MDS map for this report. As illustrated by Figure 11.5, a central cluster of references to content (*e-business, e-government, e-health, content, media*) is closely surrounded by a variety of terms, many of which refer to governmental action. A second, loose cluster located on the right side of the plane can be seen close to the central one we just described, comprising words that are mostly about policy and policy-making agents (*EU, European, commission, policy, action*), in combination with the terms 'services' and 'innovation'.

i2010 Mid-Term Review (2008)

The *i2010* report published in 2008 presents a preliminary assessment of the goals and priorities set in the first document of the series, in light of the rapid pace of technological change. While the report maintains some of the optimistic tone of the previous year, it acknowledges disparities among member states that, left unattended, could lead to the emergence of a new digital divide with respect to the latest generation of ICTs (Commission of the European Communities, 2008).

The report also adopts a more economic-oriented rhetoric than the previous two iterations of the *i2010* series, in the sense that most of the issues considered strategic to ensure that Europe becomes an information society are framed in terms of markets, economic growth and competitiveness. Surprisingly, however, the list of most frequent words for this document includes only three clearly economic references: *market* (the fourth most recurrent word), *economic* and *consumer* (which replaces the term 'user' adopted by the previous year's report). Following the trend of preceding years, the 2008 document also shows many references to policy coordination, governance and public agents. Yet, unlike previous years in this series, our computer-assisted analysis shows a surge of terms related to infrastructure, content and connectivity as well. Our qualitative reading of the document corroborates that, indeed, such an increase in ICT-related terms correlates with the document's concern about the rapid emergence of new technologies and the EU's ability to adapt its ICT policy-making accordingly, in order to 'lead the transition to next-generation networks while not slacking off in its efforts to overcome the digital divide' (Commission of the European Communities, 2008: 5). The revival in this report of the forgotten notions of the internet and the digital divide, which had not been used since the days of the eEurope initiative, are particularly telling about the way this document synthesizes what appears to be a new mindset in the European Council: one that wants to continue focusing on economic growth, but which also seems to acknowledge the limits of the market in achieving the broader goals of an information society by itself. Thus, for all its economic and technocratic discourse, the mid-term review of the *i2010* plan also addresses important social issues such as digital inequalities among EU member states, users' rights (albeit most of the times expressed as 'consumer rights') and universal inclusion of different social groups and linguistic communities in the enjoyment of the benefits of an information society. The interweaving of all the themes described above is illustrated by the MDS map for this document (Figure 11.6). The absence of any particularly tight cluster

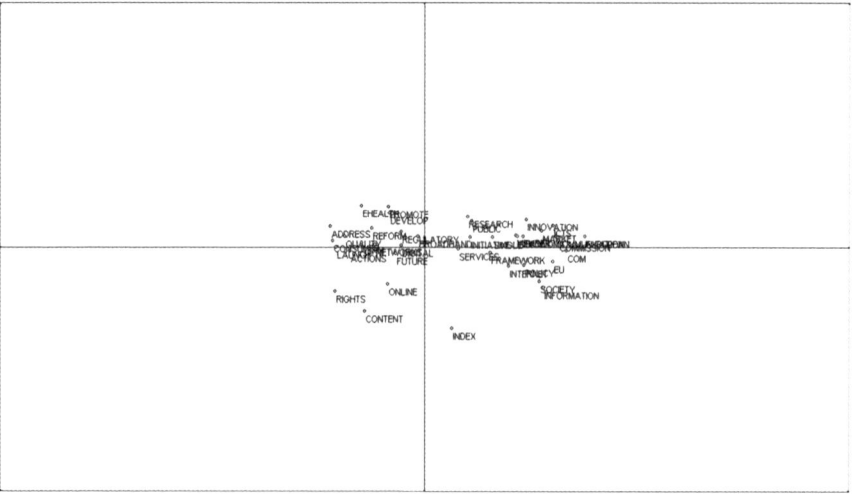

Figure 11.6   MDS map of clustering patterns in *i2010 Mid-Term Review* (2008)

Table 11.2 Comparison of list of most frequent terms for EU policy documents

i2010 (2005)	i2010 (2006)	i2010 (2007)	i2010 (2008)
ICTS	ICT	ICT	European
European	European	Commission	ICTS
Services	Commission	Services	EU
Research	Services	Policy	Market
Information	EU	EU	Internet
Commission	Policy	Innovation	Information
Societal	Public	Information	Society
Digital	Innovation	European	Innovation
Growth	Growth	Review	Policy
Strategy	Research	Society	States
Economy	Digital	Public	Commission
Media	Communication	Actions	Economic
Public	Information	Member	Initiative
Technology	Member	Online	Member
Content	States	Framework	Research
Communications	Lisbon	Content	Framework
Innovation	Society	State	Content
Support	Initiative	Initiative	Online
Investment	Interprobability	Users	Services
Convergence	Level	High	Single
Jobs	Report	Market	COM
Lisbon	Review	Research	Communication
Quality	Key	Continue	Public
Policy	Action	Digital	Digital
Key	Jobs	Launch	Future
Life	Progress	Level	Index
EU	Annual	Media	Broadband
Regulatory	E-government	Support	Regulatory
Solutions	Investment	Term	Rights
Business	Priorities	E-business	Develop
Developments	Technology	Network	Launch
Efficient	COM	Sector	Networks
Electronic	Competitiveness	Strategies	Promote
Framework	Convergence	Address	Term
High	Need	COM	Actions
Instruments	Online	Development	Consumer
Integrated	Programme	Economic	E-health
Line	Proposals	E-government	Quality
Making	Support	E-health	Reform
Management	Ageing	Large	Address

(except for a few couples of terms on the right side of the plane, mostly alluding policy-making entities or outcomes), and the relative proximity of most of the words to each other, highlights the fact that different themes, actors and goals are seen as interdependent and are equally prioritized by the authors of the report.

A comparison of the lists of most frequent terms for all the *i2010* major documents supports our argument about more attention to government than was the case in the eEurope series, as evidenced by Table 11.2.

In general, it is possible to perceive, by looking at these frequency lists, an effort by EU policy-makers to ensure state-led coordination and cohesiveness throughout the *i2010* documents, a fact highlighted by the consistent presence of terms such as *public*, *policy*, *framework*, *support*, *action(s)* and *initiative*. A clear sense of direction for this state-led strategy becomes apparent when comparing these frequency lists, since words denoting goals or developmental issues are also present among the most recurrent terms in all the European documents analyzed in this study: *innovation*, *research*, *communication(s)*, *services*, *information*, *society*. Notably, one aspect that differentiates the EU set of policy documents from the US ones is that, in the former, the establishment of an information society supposes addressing interoperability across ICT infrastructures, but not assuming such infrastructures as ends in themselves. This idea, on the other hand, seems to pervade the US documents, whose frequency lists are largely populated by infrastructure related terms (see Table 11.1).

Discussion and conclusions

While our previous comparison of US and EU documents revealed a common movement towards a neo-liberal rhetoric concerning access to ICTs, the analysis of more recent documents on the subject performed for this chapter shows governmental actors at both sides of the Atlantic now taking divergent paths in their respective approaches to DD issues.

The technologically deterministic denominator of the American documents *A Nation Online 2004* and *Networked Nation* (2007) represents not only a return to the initial assessment purposes of the first two NTIA *Falling through the Net* reports (National Telecommunications and Information Administration, 1995, 1998), but also a regression in terms of policy-making vision, as no real medium- or long-term public strategies are outlined to harness ICTs for the promotion of domestic development. Whereas *A Nation Online 2004* dedicates most of its pages to providing an inventory of availability of broadband technologies in the USA, *Networked Nation* attempts to showcase how any shortcomings in such availability have been addressed by the government, through stimulus to private providers via tax breaks and a policy of minimum to no public intervention beyond the renegotiation of spectrum allocations.

The administrative and plan-based discourse of the recent set of European documents, on the other hand, deviates slightly from the pro-market tone of previous reports by the EU, by proposing specific policies and benchmarks intended to harmonize regulatory frameworks, and by identifying specific areas within the ICT sector where direct state intervention or joint public–private action may be necessary to attain objectives agreed upon by EU state members. Stemming from broader structural goals defined by the Lisbon Programme of 2005, these targets require involvement from different agents at different levels of decision-making. Consequently, we were able to identify in both our qualitative and computer-assisted text analyses of the *i2010* reports a consistent interconnection of issues, areas and roles that underscores the need for shared responsibilities by governmental and non-governmental agents, as well as the importance of ensuring coordination among them.

An exploration of possible relations between the respective policy-making trends in the USA and the EU concerning the digital divide, and the immediate historical context in which the reports were produced, can add further explanatory value to the findings of this study. On the US side, the arrival of the Bush administration in 2000 brought about not only a more laissez-faire approach (compared to the Clinton administration's) regarding the role of the state in the economy, but also a reorganization of the governmental agenda where universal access to ICTs took a secondary place behind priorities such as the 'war on terrorism', providing stimulus to the 'supply' side of the economy, and a few social programmes, such as the Medicaid reform or the 'no child left behind' education initiative. On the EU side, the incorporation of new member states and the prospects of further expansion of the bloc, with its concomitant externalities in terms of bureaucratic, commercial, cultural and human flows, have brought about pressures to ensure governability, policy harmonization and some minimal degree of homogeneity across basic economic and developmental indicators...all while the bloc deals with the legacy of free market competitiveness inherited from the liberalization wave that took over telecommunication and media services in Europe between the late 1980s and mid-1990s.

The different approaches adopted by the USA and the EU in recent policy documents, concerning strategies for the promotion of an information society, are illustrative of the three major models of policy-making in telecommunications identified by Falch (2007): direct intervention, regulation and facilitation. While none of these models is found in 'pure' state and isolated from the others in any polity, we argue that the US documents analyzed for this study show a preponderance of facilitation over direct intervention and regulation. In this sense, the US preserves the market-based approach revealed by documents analyzed in our previous study, but incorporates some elements of governmental involvement beyond regulation, through the provision of tax breaks and other economic stimuli. Conversely, the EU documents we analyzed this time reflect a combination of regulation, facilitation and direct intervention, with the latter two acquiring a more prominent role than was the case in the European policy reports explored in our previous project. This is evidenced, for example, on calls for expanding European broadband networks through content development via direct provision of enhanced public services online.

These new results suggest, in our view, a gradual distancing from the neo-liberal paradigm that dominated telecommunications policy-making in the western hemisphere from the late 1980s to the early 2000s. While it is too early to determine, at the time of writing this report, whether such a shift is pointing towards a new era of direct state intervention and re-regulation, it could at least be read as an initial realization of the limits of free markets in achieving broader social developmental goals such as that of inclusiveness.

In a similar fashion to the current regulatory revision that is taking place within the financial sector in many countries, the relationship between governmental and private actors in connection with national plans involving ICTs might be starting a period of reassessment. Further longitudinal analyses of key policy documents in the USA and the EU have the potential of contributing valuable evidence in this regard. In any event, the results presented in this chapter underscore the value of combining qualitative and quantitative methods of text analysis for the uncovering of underlying patterns of semantic associations and discursive strategies, in connection to complex and polysemic notions such as that of the 'digital divide'.

Notes

1. The complexities begin with a lack of conceptual consensus on the meaning of the notion 'information society' (Webster, 2002), and continue with the emergence of controversies about the potential ideological, techno-deterministic agenda underlying it (Sassi, 2005).
2. For a discussion of framing as discursive strategy, see Schön and Rein, 1994; Nelson*et al.*, 1997; Miller and Riechert, 2001; Reese, 2003.
3. Researchers use median method for cluster analysis to avoid weighting the mean vectors according to cluster size (Rencher, 2002).
4. Although the tightness of the cluster makes it difficult to read its elements, due to so many overlapping terms, we were able to deduct its components by looking at other clusters and by comparing the MDS clusters from those emerging from the dendograms generated by CatPac.

5. The eEurope initiative was launched in 2000, after a report published by the European Commission in 1999, which claimed as a major goal 'accelerating Europe's transition towards a knowledge based economy and to realize the potential benefits of higher growth, more jobs and better access for all citizens to the new services of the information age' (European Commission, 2002, http://ec.europa.eu/information_society/eeurope/2002/index_en.htm).

6. The series began with the *i2010 Communication*, published in 2005, which set the EU policy framework and strategies for the region with regards to ICTs up to the year 2010. Since the publication of that first communication, consecutive annual reports have kept track of achievements and shortcomings by EU members with respect to three major goals: the creation of a 'single European information space', the promotion of 'investment and innovation on ICT research' and the improvement of quality of life, inclusion and public services through ICTs (European Commission, n.d.: http://ec.europa.eu/information_society/eeurope/i2010/strategy/index_en.htm).

Endnote: Prospects for Communications Policy Research

Stylianos Papathanassopoulos and Ralph Negrine

As we have seen in these chapters, the study of communications policy and the communication policy process is a complex affair. On the one hand, it deals with multifaceted and large-scale policy problems and, on the other, problems that are influenced by a good number of forces and actors. Although it has often been argued that communications policy has been largely technology-driven, most of the decisions taken to deal with change are framed by political, economic and institutional dimensions as well as by international factors. The importance of communications policy lies in its linkage with politics, with technology and with economics. The globalization of capital, markets and competition, and the convergence of the media and the entry of new and global actors both private and public, makes the study of communications policy a relevant and an exciting research field.

But we need to be continually aware of the complex forces that come into play when policies are being made. As many of the chapters in this volume demonstrate, a range of forces feed into the ways policies are determined (see the chapters by Alison Harcourt and Robert McChesney, for example, for contrasting illustrations of the different types of actors who can be involved in policy-making) and/or should be determined (see, for example, the chapters by Marc Raboy *et al.*, Sandra Braman and Jackie Harrison).

In all these ways, communications policy research seeks to explore how regulators, governments and public policies shape the communications-information industries and social practices. The same, more or less, applies to policy research. Within this sort of framework, most of the studies in the field of communications policy have focused on the changes, if not the effects, that have been brought about by privatization, liberalization and competition in communication industries.

However, we have to bear in mind, that a good deal of the substantive knowledge required in problem-oriented policy analyses comes not only from political science and media studies, but also from other disciplines such as economics, law and international relations. When one considers the increasingly international character of technological and communication changes, it is plain to see that the researcher's task gains added complexity. But it is a task that needs to be undertaken and the challenge of explaining processes of policy generation and implementation remains one that we should all take on board. By and large, the fact that policy emerges out of a continuing conversation between what is and what should be, and who has a right to participate in that conversation, makes the field of study of especial interest.

In the age of media convergence, digitalization and globalization, communications policy will remain an area of great importance. As governments and vested interests, citizens and consumers all grapple with how to deal with major developments, be it the 'digital divide', digital switchover or the 'digital nation', we can begin to see the significance of sound policy-making for economic/industrial as well as political reasons and considerations of the public good.

Within this context, one has also to take into account the implications of globalization in communications policy, as noted in Chapter 1. Many of the changes which have taken place in the communications landscape came about as a result of numerous interconnecting factors and can be understood as part of larger processes that have rendered the communications landscape global. They have become global in the sense of being better understood as contextualized with larger transnational processes (see also Katz, 2005). As Marc Raboy has noted (2007) we have entered an era of 'global media policy' which in contrast to 'its conventional "national" counterparts', 'is not "made" in any clearly definable political space, and it involves the oddest imaginable assortment of actors'. Raboy's point is that in the era of globalization and communication globalization in particular, a 'global framework for media policy is emerging' (Raboy, 2007: 343). Indeed, global pressures, structures, practices and institutions increasingly affect the national communication systems. International agreements in the ITU or international organizations like the European Union have affected not only national media policy, but also cognitive assumptions about national policy models. As noted by Harcourt in this book, Europeanization has also been used as a 'smokescreen for domestic political strategies'. EU member states and candidate countries are 'forced' to align their media systems to EU directives. In effect, changes in EU regulations and treaties have modified national traditions of policy-making, and the freedom of manoeuvre of national decision-makers. This can be demonstrated in the policy domains of monopoly public services and industrial policy. But even in the cases of the introduction of the new media, such as HDTV or mobile TV, national states in the EU follow a common approach directed by the Commission. One particularly obvious instance is the effect of the common legal framework of the European Union, which tends to impose a universalistic rational-legal framework (one that is at least at this point heavily skewed towards market-oriented policies) on individual countries. When the Spanish government, for example, attempted to favour its media allies in setting technical standards for digital TV decoders, the rival company appealed to Brussels, which ruled against the government. This also applies to other countries and other policy areas such as intellectual property, media concentration and information flows. In effect, it is increasingly difficult nowadays to understand these processes and practices by simply referring to a state, even to a larger one. As Raboy notes:

> This situation poses a particular challenge not only to internationalizing media studies, but far more importantly, to the ongoing development of citizenship and democratic public life. For that reason alone, it demands our attention. Defining the field of global media policy studies at this stage means 'mapping' the global media policy environment, developing a theoretical understanding of the object, and establishing an empirical base from which to explore the issues and processes involved. It means developing a conceptual and analytical framework for studying media policy that takes account of corporate globalization, multilateral politics, the changing role and nature of the national state, and the emergence of civil society as an actor on the world stage. (2007: 343–4)

As noted at the beginning of this book, the study of communications policy is complex and any attempt to force policy into any narrow theoretical frame should be looked at with some degree of scepticism, especially in an age where 'public policy has undergone some rather fundamental changes over the past couple of decades in terms of policy design, selection of policy instruments and the role of the state in society more broadly' (Peters and Pierre, 2006: 2). Although policy 'has become less interventionist, controlling and obtrusive' (Peters and Pierre, 2006: 3), one could also argue that media globalization has given rise to a new model of communications policy analysis. Communications policy and global media policy demand a critical, multidisciplinary and comparative approach. Within this context we might ask the following questions:

- What is the problem to which the globalization of media is a solution?
- Whose problem is it and what can public policy/ies do for it?
- Are different media governance regimes the outcomes of bargaining among political institutions and societal actors or of bargaining in the international arena?

- Should media policies, whether national or global, address the need for non-commercial spaces for civic communication?
- Do we need policies to protect local/domestic cultures in a globalized, commercial and multifaceted environment?
- Should media policies address issues related to communication in-equalities in society?
- What changes in society and culture are being driven by the globalization of the media and their practices?
- Who benefits from global media systems and who does not, and should this also be addressed?
- Should media policies, whether national or global, look beyond issues of competitiveness and commercialism and highlight issues of social need and social benefits?

To address these questions, and countless others, we need to develop a way of understanding those forces and pressures that give shape to the communication system as is and to ask whether other, and better, ways to meet the aims and objectives of industries and publics, of commerce and culture, are possible. In raising these questions we also need inevitably to ask questions about the role of international bodies, of states of industries and of publics in creating different visions of what communication systems should look like and aim to do. Without doubt, the future of communications policy studies will almost certainly be more global and comparative in orientation. We hope that the chapters in this volume will contribute to the development of this field and towards a better understanding of the key issues at play.

References

Aharoni, Y. (1986) *The Evolution and Management of State-owned Enterprise*. Cambridge, MA: Ballinger.

Alexander, J. (2006) *The Civil Sphere*. Oxford: Oxford University Press.

Alexander, J. (2007) 'On The Interpretation of the Civil Sphere: Understanding and Contention in Contemporary Social Science'. *The Sociological Quarterly* 48(4): 641–59.

Allison, G.T. (1971) *Essence of Decision*. Boston: Hill Brown.

Allor, M. (1988) 'Relocating the Site of the Audience'. *Critical Studies in Mass Communication*, 5(3): 217–33.

Ang, I. (1991) *Desperately Seeking the Audience*. London: Routledge.

AP (2009) 'EU Web Address Racks Up 3 Million Registrations'. *FindLaw.com*, 14 January.

APT and CWA (2008) *State Broadband Initiatives: A Summary of State Programs Designed to Stimulate Broadband Deployment and Adoption*. Washington, DC: Alliance for Public Technology, Communications Workers of America.

Aslama, M. and T. Syvertsen (2007) 'Public Service Broadcasting and New Technologies: Marginalization or Re-monopolization?', in E. de Bens (ed.) *Media Between Culture and Commerce*. Bristol: Intellect: 167–78.

Atkinson, D. and M. Raboy (1997) *Public Service Broadcasting: The Challenge of the Twenty-first Century*. Reports and Papers on Mass Communication 111. Paris: UNESCO.

Aufderheide, P. (1999) *Communications Policy and the Public Interest*. New York: Guilford Press.

Aufderheide, P. (2002) 'Tactical Media', Tactical Media: Virtual Case Book. Available at: //www.nyu.edu/fas/projects/vcb/

Bailey, D. and A. De Ruyter (2007) 'Globalisation, Economic Freedom and Strategic Decision-Making'. *Policy Studies* 28(4): 383–98.

Bailey, E.E. and J.R. Pack (eds) (1995) *The Political Economy of Privatization and Deregulation*. Aldershot: Elgar.

Bangemann, M. (1994) *Europe and the Global Information Society*. Brussels: European Commission.

Bar, F. and C. Sandvig (2008) 'US Communication Policy after Convergence'. *Media Culture Society* 30(4): 531–50.

Barak, S. (2008) 'Thai Government Censors Internet for "National Security"'. *Secure Computing*, 4 September.

Bardoel, J. and L. d'Haenens (2008) 'Reinventing Public Service Broadcasting in Europe: Prospects, Promises and Problems'. *Media, Culture & Society* 30(3): 337–55.

Barlow, K. (2005). 'Google Earth Prompts Security Fears'. *ABC News Online*.

Batra, N. (2007) *Digital Freedom: How Much Can You Handle?*. Lanham, MD: Lowman & Littlefield.

Bauer, J.M. (2005) 'Regulation and State Ownership: Conflicts and Complementarities in EU Telecommunications'. *Annals of Public and Cooperative Economics* 76(2): 151–77.

Bauer, J.M. (2007) 'Dynamic Effects of Network Neutrality'. *International Journal of Communication* 1(1): 531–47.

Bauer, J.M. and E. Bohlin (2008) 'From Static to Dynamic Regulation: Recent Developments in US Telecommunications Policy'. *Intereconomics: Review of European Economic Policy* 43(1): 38–50.

Baumgartner, F.R. and B.D. Jones (1993) *Agendas and Instability in American Politics*. Chicago: Chicago University Press.

BBC (2008) 'Estonia Fines Man for "Cyber War"'. *BBC News*, 25 January.

Bell, D. (1985) 'Gutenberg and the Computer: On Information, Knowledge and Other Distinctions'. *Encounter* LXIV(May): 15–20.

Bell, D. (1999) [1973] *The Coming of Post-Industrial Society: a Venture in Social Forecasting*. New York: Basic Books.

Bell, T. (2009) 'Thailand Blocks Thousands of Websites for "Insulting" King'. *The Telegraph*, 7 January.

Belluzzi, M. (1994) 'Cultural Protection as a Rationale For Legislation: The French Language Law of 1994 and the European Trend Toward Integration in the Face of Increasing US Influence'. *Dickenson Journal of International Law* 14: 127–39.

Bennett, T. (1992) 'Putting Policy into Cultural Studies', in L. Grossberg, C. Nelson and P. Treichler (eds) *Cultural Studies*. London: Routledge: 23–37.

Berki, R. (1979) 'State and Society: An Antithesis of Modern Political Thought', in J.E.S. Hayward and R.N. Berki (eds) *State and Society in Contemporary Europe*. Oxford: Oxford Martin Robertson: 1–20.

Beyer C. (2007) 'Non-Governmental Organizations as Motors of Change'. *Government and Opposition* 42(4): 513–35.

Biggam, R. (2000) 'Public Service Broadcasting: The View from the Commercial Sector'. *Intermedia*, 28(5): 21–3.

Bishop, T. (2003) 'FCC May Drop Rules Limiting Media Ownership in a Single Market'. *Seattle Post-Intelligencer*, 29 April.

Black, A. (2001) 'The Scope of the Syllabus of Information Society Studies'. *Education for Information* 19(3): 245–52.

Black Commentator (2003) 'Who Killed Black Radio News?'. May. Available at: http://www.blackcommentator.com/

Blom-Hansen, J. (1997) 'A "New Institutional" Perspective on Policy Networks'. *Public Administration* 75(4): 669–93.

Blumler, J.G. (1992) 'Vulnerable Values at Stake', in J.G. Blumler (ed.) *Television and the Public Interest: Vulnerable Values in Western European Broadcasting*. London: Sage: 22–42.

Boliek, B. (2003a) 'FCC Majority Set on Rules Rewrite'. *Hollywood Reporter*, 9 May.

Boliek, B. (2003b) 'House Panel Votes to Roll Back Ownership Cap'. *Hollywood Reporter*, 16 July.

Bortolotti, B. *et al.* (2002) 'Privatization and the Sources of Performance Improvement in the Global Telecommunications Industry'. *Telecommunications Policy* 26(5–6): 243–68.

Börzel, T. (2001) 'Towards Convergence in Europe? Institutional Adaptation to Europeanisation in Germany and Spain'. *Journal of Common Market Studies* 37(4): 573–96.

Börzel, T. and T. Risse (2000) 'When Europe Hits Home: Europeanization and Domestic Change. European Integration On-line Papers, 4(15). Available at: http://papers.ssrn.com/sol3/papers.cfm?abstract_id=302768

Bovens, M. (2002) 'Information Rights: Citizenship in the Information Society'. *Journal of Political Philosophy* 10(3): 317–41.

Braman, S. (1995) Horizons of the State: Information Policy and Power. *Journal of Communication* 45(4): 4–24.

Braman, S. (2003) 'Introduction', in S. Braman (ed.), *Communication Researchers and Policy-making*. Cambridge, MA: MIT Press: 1–9.

Braman, S. (2004a) 'Where Has Media Policy Gone? Defining the Field in the Twenty-First Century'. *Communication Law and Policy* 9(2): 153–82.

Braman, S. (ed.) (2004b) *The Emergent Global Information Policy Regime*. Basingstoke: Palgrave Macmillan.

Braman, S. (2007) *Change of State: Information, Policy, and Power*. Cambridge, MA: MIT Press.

Braman, S. and S. Lynch (2003) 'Advantage ISP: Terms of Service as Media Law'. *New Media & Society* 5(3): 422–48.

Brants, K. and K. Siune (1992) 'Public Service Broadcasting in a Public of Flux', in K. Siune and W. Tuetzschler (eds) *Dynamics of Media Politics: Broadcasts and Electronic Media in Western Europe*. London: Sage: 101–15.

Broadcasting & Cable (2002) 'The Antithesis of What the Public Interest Demands'. 14 October: 16.

Broadcasting & Cable (2003) 'The New Fairness Doctrine'. 3 November: 40.

Brock, G.W. (1981) *The Telecommunications Industry: The Dynamics of Market Structure*. Cambridge, MA: Harvard University Press.

Brock, G.W. (1994) *Telecommunications Policy for the Information Age: From Monopoly to Competition*. Cambridge, MA: Harvard Business School Press.

Brock, G.W. (2003) *The Second Information Revolution*. Cambridge, MA: Harvard University Press.

Browne, M. (1997a) 'The Field of Information Policy 1. Fundamental Concepts'. *Journal of Information Science* 23(4): 261–75.

Browne, M. (1997b) 'The Field of Information Policy 2. Redefining the Boundaries and Methodologies'. *Journal of Information Science* 23(5): 339–52.

Brunt, R. (1992) 'Engaging with the Popular: Audiences for Mass Culture and What to Say About Them', in L. Grossberg, C. Nelson and P. Treichler (eds) *Cultural Studies*. London: Routledge: 69–76.

Bulmer, S.J. (1998) 'New Institutionalism and the Governance of the Single European Market'. *Journal of European Public Policy* 5(3): 365–86.

Bulmer, S. and M. Burch (2001) 'The "Europeanisation" of Central Government: the UK and Germany in Historical Institutionalist Perspective', in G. Schneider and M. Aspinwall (eds) *The Rules of Integration*. Manchester: Manchester University Press: 73–96.

Burger, R.H. (1993) *Information Policy: A Framework for Evaluation and Policy Research*. Norwood, NJ: Ablex.

Bygrave, L.A. and J. Bing (eds) (2009) *Internet Governance: Infrastructure and Institutions*. New York: Oxford University Press.

Calhoun, C. (2003) 'The Democratic Integration of Europe Interests, Identity, and the Public Sphere', in M. Berezen and M. Schain (eds) *Europe without Borders: Remapping Territory, Citizenship, and Identity in a Transnational Age*. Baltimore and London: Johns Hopkins Press: 243–74.

Calhoun, C. (2007) *Nations Matter: Culture, History and the Cosmopolitan Dream*. London: Routledge.

Canada (1991) *Statutes of Canada, Broadcasting Act*, 38–39 Elizabeth II, 1991, c. 11.

Caristi, D. (1993) 'The 1992 World Administrative Radio Conference: A Survey of the US Delegation and Recommendations for the Future'. *Telecommunications Policy* 17: 407.

Castells, M. (1996) *The Rise of the Network Society*. Oxford: Blackwell.

Castells, M. (1998) *The Power of Identity*. Oxford: Blackwell.

Castells, M. (2000) *The End of the Millennium*. Cambridge: Polity/Blackwell (2nd edition).

Cave, M.E. (2006) 'Encouraging Infrastructure Competition through the Ladder of Investment'. *Telecommunications Policy* 30(3–4): 223–37.

Cave, M. and W. H. Melody (1989) 'Models of Broadcast Regulation: The UK and North American Experience', in C. Veljanovski (ed.) *Freedom in Broadcasting*. Westminster: Institute of Economic Affairs: 224–55.

Cave, M., L. Prosperetti, and C. Doyle (2006) 'Where are We Going? Technologies, Markets and Long-range Public Policy Issues in European Communications'. *Information Economics and Policy* 18: 242–55.

Chakravartty, P. and K. Sarikakis (2007) *Globalization and Media Policy: History, Culture, Politics*. Edinburgh: Edinburgh University Press.

Chang, S.J. (1995) 'Concepts of Information Society, Cultural Assumptions and Government Information Policy: a Case Study of the USA'. *Journal of Information, Communication and Library Science* 2(1): 25–49.

Cherry, C. (1985) *The Age of Access: Information Technology and Social Revolution: Posthumous Papers of Colin Cherry*, ed. W. Edmondson. London: Croom Helm.

Chmielewski, D. (2008) 'Warner Bros. to Offer Legal Movie Downloads in China'. *Los Angeles Times*, 4 November.

Christensen, M. (2006) 'What Price the Information Society? A Candidate Country Perspective within the Context of the EU's Information Society Policies', in J. Servaes and N. Carpentier (eds) *Towards a Sustainable Information Society: Deconstructing WSIS*. Bristol: Intellect: 129–49.

Clifton, J. *et al.* (2003) *Privatisation in the European Union: Public Enterprises and Integration*. Dordrecht, Boston: Kluwer Academic.

Cobley, P. (1994) 'Throwing Out the Baby: Populism and Active Audience Theory'. *Media, Culture and Society* 16(4): 677–87.

Collins, R. (1994) *Broadcasting and Audiovisual Policy in the European Single Market*. London: John Libbey.

Collins, R. (1998) 'Public Service Broadcasting and the Media Economy: European Trends in the Late 1990s'. *Gazette* 60(5): 363–76.

Colombo, F., and S. Carlo (2006) 'Multidimensional Approaches to Media and Cultural Frameworks of the Digital Divide'. Paper presented at the World Political Forum's International Seminar Media between Citizens and Power. Venice, Italy.

Commission (2001) *Communication on a new framework for cooperation on activities concerning the information and communication policy of the European Union.* COM(2001) 354.

Commission (2002) *Communication on an information and communication strategy for the European Union.* COM(2002) 350 final/2.

Commission (2004) *Communication on implementing the information and communication strategy for the European Union.* COM(2004)196.

Commission (2005a) *Action Plan to improve communicating Europe by the Commission.* SEC (2005) 985 final.

Commission (2005b) *Plan-D for Democracy, Dialogue and Debate.* COM(2005)494 final.

Commission (2006) *White Paper on a European Communication Policy.* COM(2006)35 final.

Commission (2007) *Communication on Communicating Europe in Partnership.* COM(2007) 568 final.

Commission (2008a) *Debate Europe – building on the experience of Plan D for Democracy, Dialogue and Debate.* COM(2008)158/4.

Commission (2008b) *Communication on Communicating Europe through audiovisual media.* SEC (2008b)506/2.

Commission of the European Communities (2005a) *i2010 – A European Information Society for Growth and Employment.*

Commission of the European Communities (2005b) *Lisbon Action Plan Incorporating EU Lisbon Programme and Recommendations for Action to Member States for Inclusion in Their National Lisbon Programmes.*

Commission of the European Communities (2006) *i2010 – First Annual Report on the European Information Society.* COM 229 final.

Commission of the European Communities (2007) *i2010 – Annual Information Society Report.*

Commission of the European Communities (2008) *Preparing Europe's Digital Future – i2010 Mid-Term Review.*

Commission Staff Working Paper (2008) *Review of the Broadcasting Communication summary of the replies to the public consultation.* Brussels.

Competition Policy newsletter (2000) Commission Decisions. Available at: http://ec.europa.eu/competition/publications/cpn/cpn2000_1.pdf

Condon, S. (2008) 'Argentine Judge: Google, Yahoo Must Censor Searches'. *CNET,* 11 November.

Corner, J. (1991) 'Meaning, Genre and Context: The Problematics of 'Public Knowledge' in the New Audience Studies', in J. Curran and M. Gurevitch (eds) *Mass Media and Society.* London: Edward Arnold: 267–84.

Copps, M.J. (2002) *Re: In the Matter of Applications for Consent to the Transfer of Control of Licenses from Comcast Corporation and AT&T Corp. Transferors, to AT&T Comcast Corporation. Transferee MB Docket No. 02–70.* Dissenting Statement, November.

Copps, M. (2003) 'Crunch Time at the FCC'. *Nation*, 3 February: 5.

Crandall, R.W. *et al.* (2004) 'Do Unbundling Policies Discourage CLEC Facilities-Based Investment'. *Topics in Economic Analysis and Policy* 4(1): 1–23.

Craufurd Smith, R (2001) 'State Support for Public Service Broadcasting: The Position Under European Community Law'. *Legal Issues of Economic Integration* 28: 3.

Cuilenburg, J. van and D. McQuail (2003) 'Media Policy Paradigm Shifts; Towards a New Communications Policy Paradigm'. *European Journal of Communication* 18(2): 181–207.

Cunningham, S. (1992) *Framing Culture: Criticism and Policy in Australia.* Sydney: Allen & Unwin.

Curry, G.E. (2003) 'FCC Decision Curbs Dissent'. *Final Call.com News*, 22 June.

Curwen, P. (2002) *The Future of Mobile Communications: Awaiting the Third Generation.* New York: Palgrave.

Dahl, R.A. (1961) *Modern Political Analysis.* New Jersey: Prentice-Hall.

Dahlgren, P. (1995) *Television and the Public Sphere: Citizenship, Democracy and the Media.* London: Sage.

De Witte, B. (1995) 'The European Content Requirement in the EC Television Directive – Five Years After'. *The Yearbook of Media and Entertainment Law 1995.* New York: Oxford University Press: 101–27.

deLeon, P. and L. deLeon (2002) 'What Ever Happened to Policy Implementation? An Alternative Approach'. *Journal of Public Administration Research and Theory* 4: 467–92.

Della Sala, V. and A. Kreppel (1998) 'Dancing Without a Lead: Legislative Decrees in Italy', in J. Carey and M.S. Shugart (eds) *Executive Decree Authority.* Cambridge: Cambridge University Press.

Deursen, A. and J. van Dijk (2008) 'Measuring Digital Skills: Performance Tests of Operational, Formal, Information, and Strategic Internet Skills Among the Dutch Population'. Paper presented at the annual conference of International Communication Association, Montreal, Canada.

DiMaggio, P. (1997) 'Culture and Cognition'. *Annual Review of Sociology* 23: 263–87.

Donders, K. and C. Pauwels (2008) 'Does EU Policy Challenge the Digital Future of Public Service Broadcasting? An Analysis of the Commission's State Aid Approach to Digitization and the Public Service Remit of Public Broadcasting Organizations'. *Convergence* 14(3): 295–311.

Donges, P. (2007) 'The New Institutionalism as a Theoretical Foundation of Media Governance'. *Communications* 32(3): 325–30.

Doyle, G. (2002) *Understanding Media Economics.* London: Sage.

Duff, A.S. (2000) *Information Society Studies.* London: Routledge.

Duff, A.S. (2002) 'Social Democracy and Information Media Policy', in B. Rockenbach and T. Mendina (eds) *Ethics and Electronic Information: A Festschrift for Stephen Almagno.* Jefferson, NC: McFarland: 154–65.

Duff, A.S. (2004) 'The Sickness of an Information Society: R.H. Tawney and the Post-Industrial Condition'. *Information, Communication & Society* 7(3): 403–22.

Dunleavy, P. and B. O'Leary (1987) *Theories of the State: The Politics of Liberal Democracy.* London: Macmillan.

Dutheil, G. and D. Psenny (2009) 'La fin de la publicité sue les chaînes publiques ne profite ni a TF1 ni a M6'. *Le Monde*, 27 January: 15.

Dyson, K. and P. Humphreys (eds) (1990) *The Political Economy of Communications: International and European Dimensions*. London: Routledge.

Eckel, C.C. and A.R. Vining (1985) 'Elements of a Theory of Mixed Enterprise'. *Scottish Journal of Political Economy* 32(1): 82–94.

Edwards, G. and L. Waverman (2006) 'The Effects of Public Ownership and Independence on Regulatory Outcomes'. *Journal of Regulatory Economics* 29(1): 23–67.

Efroni, Z. (2009) 'German Court Orders to Block Wikipedia.de Due to Offending Article'. *Center for Internet and Society*. Available at: http://cyberlaw.stanford. edu/node/5928

Entman, R.M. and S.S. Wildman (1992) 'Reconciling Economic and Non-economic Perspectives on Media Policy: Transcending the "Marketplace of Ideas" ' *Journal of Communication* 42(1): 5–19.

European Commission (1994) *Communication to Parliament and Council: Follow-up to the Consultation Process Relating to the Green Paper on 'Pluralism and Media Concentration in the Internal Market – An Assessment of the Need for Community Action'*. COM (94) 353 Final, Brussels: 5 October.

European Commission (2000) *Europe's Information Society. i2010 in context: ICT and Lisbon Strategy*. Available at: http://ec.europa.eu/information_society/ eeurope/i2010/ict_and_lisbon/index_en.htm

European Commission (2001) *Communication of the Commission on the Application of the State Aid rules to Public Service Broadcasters*. Brussels, November, 15 2001. EC 320/11.

European Commission (2005) Lisbon Agenda. Available at: http://www.euractiv. com/en/future-eu/lisbon-agenda/article-117510

European Commission (2008) *Review of the Communication from the Commission on the Application of State Aid Rules to Public Service Broadcasting*. Brussels. Available at: http://ec.europa.eu/avpolicy/info_centre/library/legal/ index_en.htm

European Commission (2009) *Communication from the Commission on the Application of State Aid Rules to Public Service Broadcasting (Text with EEA Relevance)*. Brussels. Available at: http://ec.europa.eu/avpolicy/info_centre/ library/legal/index_en.htm

European Institute for the Media (1994) *La Transparence dans Le Contrôle des Médias*. Prepared for DG XV – E5, November.

Everard, J. (2000) *The Internet and the Boundaries of the Nation State*. London: Routledge.

Falch, M. (2007) 'Penetration of Broadband Services: The Role of Policies'. *Telematics and Informatics* 24: 246–58.

Featherstone, K. and C. Radaelli (eds) (2003) *The Politics of Europeanization*. Oxford: Oxford University Press.

Feintuck, M. (1999) *Media Regulation, Public Interest and the Law*. Edinburgh: Edinburgh University Press.

Ferree, M.M., and D.A. Merrill (2000) 'Hot Movements, Cold Cognition: Thinking About Movements in Gendered Frames'. *Contemporary Sociology* 29(3): 454–62.

Ferro, C. (2009) 'Danish ISPs Await Pirate Bay Appeal Decision'. *Billboard Biz*, 13 February.

Fine, J. (2003) 'FCC Chief: Media Consolidation Serves Public'. 28 April 2003. Available at: http://www.adage.com/

Flew, Terry (2006) 'The Social Contract and Beyond in Broadcast Media Policy'. *Television and New Media* 7(3): 282–305.

Follesdal, A. and S. Hix (2006) 'Why There is a Democratic Deficit in the EU: A Response to Majone and Moravcsik'. *Journal of Common Market Studies* 44(3): 533–62.

Frost, V. (2009) 'Google Calls for UK Copyright Reforms'. *Guardian*, 22 January.

Fuchs, C. (2008) *Internet and Society: Social Theory in the Information Age.* London: Routledge.

GAH Group (1993) *Audience Measurement in the EC.* Internal report for DG XV – E5, September.

GAH Group (1994) *Feasibility of Using Audience Measures to Assess Pluralism.* Internal Report for DG XV – E5, November.

Galperin H. (2004a) *New Television, Old Politics: The Transition to Digital TV in the United States and Great Britain.* Cambridge: Cambridge University Press.

Galperin, H. (2004b) 'Beyond Interests, Ideas, and Technology: An Institutional Approach to Communication and Information Policy'. *The Information Society*, 20(3): 159–68.

Gandy, O. (ed.) (1995) 'Colloquy on Political Economy and Cultural Studies'. *Critical Studies in Mass Communication* 12: 60–100.

Garnham, N. (1986) 'Contribution to a Political Economy of Mass Communication', in Collins *et al.* (eds) *Media, Culture and Society: A Critical Reader.* London: Sage: 9–32.

Garnham, N. (2000) '"Information Society" as Theory or Ideology: A Critical Perspective on Technology, Education and Employment in the Information Age'. *Information, Communication and Society* 3(2): 139–52.

Gaul, G. (2008) 'Prohibition vs Regulation Debated as US Bettors Use Foreign Sites'. *Washington Post*, 1 December.

Gelders D., R. De Cock, P. Neijens and K. Roe (2007) 'Government Communication About Policy Intentions: Unwanted Propaganda or Democratic Inevitability? Surveys Among Government Communication Professionals and Journalists in Belgium and the Netherlands'. *Communications* 32: 363–77.

Glasner, J. (2003) 'Media More Diverse? Not Really'. *Wired*, 30 May. Available at: http://www.wired.com/news/

Goggin, G. (2003) 'Prometheus Unbound: 20 Years of Communication Policy Research'. *Prometheus* 21(4): 487–96.

Golding, P., and G. Murdock. (1991) 'Culture, Communications, and Political Economy', in J. Curran and M. Gurevitch (eds) *Mass Media and Society.* London: Edward Arnold: 15–32.

Goldmann, K. (2005) 'Appropriateness and Consequences: The Logic of Neo-Institutionalism'. *Governance* 18(1): 35–52.

Gomery, D. (1993) 'The Centrality of Media Economics'. *Journal of Communication* 43(3): 190–8.

Gourevitch, P. (1978) 'The Second Image Reversed: The International Sources of Domestic Politics'. *International Organization* 32(4): 881–912.

Gray, A. and W. Jenkins (1985) *Administrative Politics in British Government*. Sussex: Wheatsheaf.

Green, L. (2002) *Communication, Technology and Society*. London: Sage.

Greenaway, J., B. Salter and S. Hart (2004) 'The Evolution of a "Meta-Policy": The Case of the Private Finance Initiative and the Health Sector'. *British Journal of Politics and International Relations* 6(4): 507–26.

Grieves, M. (ed.) (1998) *Information Policy in the Electronic Age*. London: Bowker-Saur.

Gruber, H. (2005) *The Economics of Mobile Telecommunications*. Cambridge and New York: Cambridge University Press.

Guardian (2000) 'Patenting Life: Special Report'. 15 November.

Guynn, J. (2008) 'MTV Networks in Deal to Monetize Uploaded Videos'. *Los Angeles Times*, 3 November.

Habermas, J. (1989) *Structural Transformation of the Public Sphere*. Cambridge, MA: MIT Press.

Habermas, J. (1992) 'Further Reflections on the Public Sphere', in C. Calhoun (ed.) *Habermas and the Public Sphere*. Cambridge, MA: MIT Press: 421–61.

Habermas, J. (1996) *Between Facts and Norms: Contributions to a Discourse Theory of Law and Democracy*. Cambridge: MIT Press.

Habermas, J. (2001) 'So, Why Does Europe Need A Constitution?'. Available at: http://www.iue.it/RSCAS/e-texts/CR200102UK.pdf

Habermas, J. (2006) *The Divided West*. Cambridge: Polity Press.

Habermas, J. (2008) *Between Naturalism and Religion*. Cambridge: Polity Press.

Hagins, J. (1996) 'The Inconvenient Public Interest: Policy Challenges in the Age of Information'. *Journal of Applied Communications Research*, 24(2): 83–92.

Haines, L. (2005). 'Google Earth Threatens Democracy'. *The Register*, 13 September.

Hall, P.A. (1986) *Governing the Economy*. Polity: Oxford.

Hall P.A. (1993) 'Policy Paradigms, Social Learning, and the State: The Case of Economic Policymaking in Britain'. *Comparative Politics* 25(3): 275–96.

Hall P.A. and P.J.W. McGinty (1997) 'Policy as the Transformation Of Intentions: Producing Program From Statute'. *The Sociological Quarterly* 38(3): 439–67.

Hallin, D.C. and P. Mancini (2004) *Comparing Media Systems; Three Models of Media and Politics*. Cambridge: Cambridge University Press.

Hallin, D.C. and S. Papathanassopoulos (2002) 'Political Clientelism and the Media: Southern Europe and Latin America in Comparative Perspective'. *Media, Culture & Society*, 24(2): 175–95.

Halloran, J.D. (1986) 'The Social Implications of Technological Innovations in Communications', in M. Traber (ed.) *The Myths of Information Revolution*. London: Sage.

Ham, C. and M. Hill (1984) *The Policy Process in the Modern Capitalist State.* Sussex: Wheatsheaf.

Hammersley, M. (1992) *What's Wrong with Ethnography? Methodological Exploration.* London: Routledge.

Hanberger, A. (2001) 'What is the Policy Problem? Methodological Challenges in Policy Evaluation'. *Evaluation* 7(1): 45–54

Harden, B. (2009) 'Prescient Young Blogger Did What South Korea Couldn't – Foresee Global Financial Crisis'. *Washington Post*, 24 January.

Harrison, J. (2009) 'European Social Purpose and Public Service Communication', in C. Bee and E. Bozzini (eds) *Mapping the European Public Sphere: Institutions, Media and Civil Society.* Aldershot: Ashgate: 97–113.

Harrison, J. and L. Woods. (2007) *European Law and Broadcasting Policy.* Cambridge: Cambridge University Press.

Hartley, D. (2009) 'Japan Challenges Google's Street View'. *IT Examiner*, 5 January.

Hartley, J. (1988) 'The Real World of Audiences'. *Critical Studies in Mass Communication* 5(3): 234–8.

Hauge, J.A. *et al.* (2008) 'Bureaucrats as Entrepreneurs: Do Municipal Telecommunications Providers Hinder Private Entrepreneurs?'. *Information Economics and Policy* 20(1): 89–102.

Héritier, A. and S. Eckert (2008) 'New Modes of Governance in the Shadow of Hierarchy: Self-regulation by Industry in Europe'. *Journal of Public Policy* 28(1): 113–38.

Héritier, A. and C. Knill (2001) *Differential Europe: The European Union Impact on National Policy-making.* Oxford: Rowman & Littlefield.

Hernon, P. and H.C. Relyea (1991) 'Information Policy', in A. Kent, H. Lancour and J.E. Daily (eds) *Encyclopaedia of Library and Information Science*, vol. 48, New York: Marcel Dekker: 176–204.

High Level Group (2004) *Facing the Challenge: The Lisbon Strategy for Growth and Employment.* Brussels: Commission of the European Communities.

Hill, M.W. (1995) 'Information Policy: Premonitions and Prospects'. *Journal of Information Science* 21(4): 273–82.

Hille, K. (2009) 'China Cracks Down on "Vulgar" Internet Content'. *Financial Times*, 5 January.

Hills, J. and M. Michalis (2000) 'Restructuring Regulation: Technological Convergence and European Telecommunications and Broadcasting Markets'. *Review of International Political Economy* 7(3): 434–64.

Hirsch, M. and V.G. Petersen (1998) 'European Policy Initiatives', in D. McQuail and K. Siune (eds) *Media Policy; Convergence, Concentration and Commerce.* London: Sage: 205–17.

Hix, S. (2008) *What's Wrong with the European Union and How to Fix it.* Cambridge: Polity.

Hofferbert, R. (1974) *The Study of Public Policy.* Indianapolis: Bobbs-Merrill.

Hoffmann, S. (1983) 'Reflections on the Nation-state in Western Europe Today', in L. Tsoukalis (ed.) *The European Community: Past, Present and Future.* Oxford: Basil Blackwell.

Hofmann, H. and A. Türk (2006) *EU Administrative Governance.* Cheltenham: Edward Elgar.

Homet, R.S. Jr (1979) *Politics, Cultures and Communication*. Westport, CT: Praeger.

Howard, P. (2007) 'Testing the Leap-frog Hypothesis: The Impact of Existing Infrastructure and Telecommunications Policy in the Global Digital Divide'. *Information, Communication and Society* 10(2): 133–57.

Howell, D.R. (2004) 'Labor Market Institutions and Unemployment: An Assessment', in D.R. Howell (ed.) *Fighting Unemployment: The Limits of Free Market Orthodoxy*. Cambridge, MA: Oxford University Press: 310–42.

Huang, K.C. (2008) 'Can City-wide Municipal WiFi be a Feasible Solution for Local Broadband Access in the US? An Empirical Evaluation of a Techno-Economic Model'. PhD dissertation, University of Pittsburgh, Pittsburgh, PA.

Hultén, O. (2007) 'Between Vanishing Concept and Future Model: Public Service Broadcasting on the Move', in M. Werner and J. Trappel (eds) *Power, Performance and Politics*. Baden-Baden: Nomos: 197–221.

Humphreys, P. (2007) 'The EU, Communications Liberalization and the Future of Public Service Broadcasting'. *European Studies*, 24: 91–112.

Hutchison, D. (1999) *Media Policy: An Introduction*. Oxford: Blackwell.

Hyder, M. (1984) 'Implementation: The Evolutionary Model', in D. Lewis and H. Wallace (eds) *Policies into Practice*: *National and International Case Studies in Implementation*. London: Heineman.

Independent Television Commission (n.d.) *Culture and Communications: Perspectives on Broadcasting in the Information Society*. London: ITC.

International Herald Tribune (2008) 'British Regulator Begins Review of Public Broadcasting'. 11 April.

Iosifidis, P. (2007a) 'Digital TV, Digital Switchover and Public Service Broadcasting in Europe'. *Javnost/The Public*, 14(1): 5–20.

Iosifidis, P. (2007b) *Public Television in the Digital Era, Technological Challenges and New Strategies for Europe*. London: Palgrave Macmillan.

Iosifidis, P. (2007c) 'Public Television in Small European Countries: Challenges and Strategies'. *International Journal of Media and Cultural Politics* 3(1): 65–87.

IRIS Special Series (2007) 'The Public Service Broadcasting Culture'. Strasbourg: European Audiovisual Observatory.

Ito, Y. (1981) 'The "Johoka Shakai" Approach to the Study of Communication in Japan', in G.C. Wilhoit and H. de Bock (eds) *Mass Communication Review Yearbook*, vol. 2. Beverly Hills, CA: Sage: 671–98.

ITU (2009) 'ITU's History', www.itu.int

Jakubowicz, K. (2003) 'Ideas in Our Heads: Introduction of PSB as Part of Media System Change in Central and Eastern Europe'. *European Journal of Communication* 19(1): 53–75.

Jakubowicz, K. (2007a) 'Public Service Broadcasting: A Pawn on an Ideological Chessboard', in E. De Bens (ed.) *Media between Culture and Commerce*. Bristol: Intellect: 115–50.

Jakubowitz, K. (2007b) 'Systemic Parallelism; The Public Service Broadcasting Culture'. *IRIS Special Series* European Audiovisual Observatory: 16–17.

Japan Computer Usage Development Institute (JACUDI) (1974) 'The Plan for an Information Society: A National Goal Toward Year 2000'. *Ekistics* 226(September): 175–82.

Jensen, K.B. and K.E. Rosengren (1990) 'Five Traditions in Search of the Audience'. *European Journal of Communication* 5(2/3): 207–38.

Johnston, T. (2009) 'Vietnamese Authorities Rein in the Country's Vigorous Blogosphere'. *Washington Post*, 18 January.

Jones, D.N. (2009) 'Matching Regulatory Arrangements with Public Values in the Provision of Energy and Telecommunications: One View'. *International Journal of Public Policy* 4(5): 435–48.

Jordana, J. (ed.) (2002) *Governing Telecommunications and the New Information Society in Europe*. Cheltenham: Elgar.

Jordana J., D. Levi-Faur and I. Puig (2006) 'The Limits of Europeanization: Regulatory Reforms in the Spanish and Portuguese Telecommunications and Electricity Sectors'. *Governance: An International Journal of Policy, Administration, and Institutions*, 19(3): 437–64.

Jorgenson, J.J. (1990) 'Managing Privatization and Deregulation: The Telecommunications Sector in Canada', in D.J. Gayle and J.N. Goodrich (eds) *Privatization and Deregulation in a Global Perspective*. Westport, CT: Quorum: 394–412.

Kahin, B. and C. Nesson (eds) (1997) *Borders in Cyberspace: Information Policy and the Global Information Infrastructure*. London: MIT Press.

Kant, I. (1999) *Practical Philosophy*. Cambridge: Cambridge University Press.

Karlsson, M. (1998) *The Liberalisation of Telecommunications in Sweden: Technology and Regime Change from the 1960s to 1993*. Linköping, Sweden: LTAB.

Katz, E., J.G. Blumler and M. Gurevitch (1974) 'Utilization of Mass Communication by the Individual', in J. Blumler and E. Katz (eds) *The Uses of Mass Communication: Current Perspectives on Gratifications Research*. Sage Annual Reviews of Communication Research, vol. III. Beverly Hills, CA: Sage: 19–332.

Katz, E., M. Gurevitch and H. Haas (1973) 'On the Use of the Mass Media for Important Things'. *American Sociological Review* 38: 164–81.

Katz, R. (2009) 'The World Economic Crisis: The Return of Keynesian Economics to the New Communications Networks'. *Telos* 78: 13–27.

Katz, Y. (2005) *Media Policy for the 21st Century in the United States and Western Europe*. Cresskill, NJ: Hampton Press.

Keohane, R.O. and J.S. Nye (1998) 'Power and Complex Interdependence in the Information Age'. *Foreign Affairs* 77(5): 81–95.

Kerr, D.H. (1976) 'The Logic of "Policy" and Successful Policies'. *Policy Sciences* 7: 351–63.

Kirk, J. (2009) 'Irish ISP: We Won't Block the Pirate Bay'. *PC World*, 24 February.

Kizza, J.M. (1998) *Civilizing the Internet: Global Concerns and Efforts toward Regulation*. Jefferson, NC: McFarland.

Klein, A. and D.A. Vise (2003) 'Media Giants Hint They Might Be Expanding'. *Washington Post*, 3 June.

Knill, C. and D. Lehmkuhl (1999) 'How Europe Matters. Different Mechanisms of Europeanization'. *European Integration Online Papers* 3(7).

Knill, C. and D. Lehmkuhl (2002) 'The National Impact of European Union Regulatory Policy: Three Europeanization Mechanisms'. *European Journal of Political Research* 41(2): 255–80.

Koenig, M.E.D. (1995) 'Information Policy: The Mounting Tension (Value Additive versus Uniquely Distributable "Public Good")'. *Journal of Information Science* 21(3): 229–31.

Krasner, S.D. (1988) 'Sovereignty: An Institutional Perspective'. *Comparative Political Science* 21(1): 66–84.

Krasnow, E.G. and D.L. Longley (1973) *The Politics of Broadcast Regulation.* New York: St Martin's Press.

Krebber, D. (2002) *Europeanisation of Regulatory Television Policy: The Decision-making Process of the Television without Frontiers Directives from 1989 and 1997.* Baden-Baden: Nomos.

Kroes, N. (2008) 'Broadcasting Communication Review'. Speech given at the Strasbourg Seminar, Strasbourg, 17 July.

Kurian, G.T. and G.T.T. Molitor (eds) (1996) *Encyclopaedia of the Future*, vols 1 and 2. New York: Simon & Schuster/Macmillan.

Labaton, S. (2003) 'Senators Move to Restore FCC Limits on the Media'. *New York Times*, 5 June.

LaRose, R. *et al.* (2008) *Closing the Rural Broadband Gap. Study supported by the US Department of Agriculture.* East Lansing, MI: Michigan State University.

Latzer, M. *et al.* (2003) 'Regulation Remixed: Institutional Change through Self and Co-regulation in the Mediamatics Sector'. *Communications & Strategies* 50: 127–57.

Lee, J. (2003) 'On Minot, ND, Radio, a Single Corporate Voice'. *New York Times*, 31 March.

Leeson, K.W. (1984) *International Communications: Blueprint for Policy ('The Leeson Report').* Amsterdam: North-Holland.

Lerner, P. and H.D. Laswell (1951) (eds) *The Policy Sciences.* Stanford, CA: Stanford University Press.

Lessig, L. (1999) *Code and Other Laws of Cyberspace.* New York: Basic.

Lessig, L. (2001) *The Future of Ideas.* New York: Random House.

Levy, D. (1997) 'Regulating Digital Broadcasting in Europe: The Limits of Policy Convergence'. *West European Politics* 20(4): 24–42.

Levy, D.A. (1999) *Europe's Digital Revolution: Broadcasting Regulation, the EU and the Nation State.* London: Routledge.

Library House of Commons Standard Note SN/IA/2888 (2008) *Internal Affairs and Defence Section.*

Linder, C. (2003) 'FCC Dems Hear from Deregulation Opponents'. *Hollywood Reporter*, 28 May.

Livingstone, S. (1996) 'Rethinking Audiences: Towards a New Research Agenda'. Paper presented at the International Communications Association conference, Chicago, May.

Livingstone, S. (2002) *Young People and New Media: Childhood and the Changing Media Environment.* London: Sage.

Livingstone, S. and E. Helsper (2007) 'Gradations in Digital Inclusion: Children, Young People and the Digital Divide'. *New Media and Society* 9(4): 671–96.

Llorens-Maluquer, C. (1998) 'European Responses to Bottlenecks in Digital Pay-TV'. *Cardozo Arts & Entertainment Law Journal* 16(2): 425–49.

Loader, B.D. (ed.) (1998) *Cyberspace Divide: Equality, Agency and Policy in the Information Society*. London: Routledge.

Lowther, W. (2009) 'US Removes Taiwan from IPR Watch List'. *Taipei Times*, 18 January.

Lull, J. (1996) 'The Political Correctness of Cultural Studies'. Paper presented at the International Association of Mass Communications Research conference, Sydney, August.

Lyman, E. (2009) 'Google Sued in Italy over Uploaded Video Content'. *USA Today*, 18 February.

MacBride, S. (1980) *Many Voices, One World: The MacBride Report*. Paris: UNESCO.

Machlup, F. (1962) *The Production and Distribution of Knowledge in the United States*. Princeton, NJ: Princeton University Press.

MacPherson, C.B. (1973) *Democratic Theory: Essays in Retrieval*. Oxford: Oxford University Press.

Madden, M. and A. Lenhart (2003) 'Music Downloading, File Sharing and Copyright'. Pew Internet & American Life Project, July.

Mahapatra, D. (2009) 'Bloggers Can Be Nailed for Views'. *The Times of India*, 24 February.

Majone, G. (ed.) (1996) *Regulating Europe*. European Public Policy Series. London and New York: Routledge.

Malcolm, J. (2008) *Multi-Stakeholder Governance and the Internet Governance Forum*. Wembley, Australia: Terminus Press.

Malm, K. and R. Wallis (1992) *Media Policy and Music Activity*. London: Routledge.

Malo, G., and L. Giroux (1998) 'La mesure industrielle des auditoires', in S. Proulx (ed.) *Accusé de réception: le téléspectateur construit par les sciences sociales*. Quebec City: Les Presses de l' Université Laval: 15–46.

March, J.G. and J.P. Olsen (1996) 'Institutional Perspectives on Political Institution'. *Governance* 93: 147–264.

March, J.G. and J.P. Olsen (1998) 'The Institutional Dynamics of International Political Orders'. *International Organization* 52: 943–69.

Marcus, J.S. (2003) 'The Potential Relevance to the United States of the European Union's Newly Adopted Regulatory Framework for Telecommunications', in L.F. Cranor and S.S. Wildman (eds) *Rethinking Rights and Regulations: Institutional Responses to New Communication Technologies*. Cambridge, MA: MIT Press: 397–428.

Mattelart, A. (2003) *The Information Society: An Introduction*. London: Sage.

May, B.E., J.-C. V. Chen and K.-W. Wen (2004) 'The Differences of Regulatory Models and Internet Regulation in the European Union and the United States'. *Information & Communications Technology Law* 13(3): 259–72.

May, T. and A.B. Wildavsky (1978) *The Policy Cycle*. Beverly Hills: Sage.

McCarthy, K. (2005) 'ICANN Imposes $2 Internet Tax'. *The Register*, 31 March.

McClintock, P. (2003) 'FCC to Tackle Ownership Rules'. *Variety*, 20–6 January 2003: A11.

McConnell, B. (2003) 'Ownership Reg Faces Murky Outcome'. *Broadcasting & Cable*, 22 September: 3.

McLuhan, M. (1964/1994) *Understanding Media: The Extensions of Man.* Cambridge, MA: MIT Press.

McNamara, K. (2003) 'Information and Communication Technologies, Poverty and Development: Learning from Experience'. A background paper for the *infoDev Annual Symposium*, World Bank.

McQuail, D. (1986) 'Is Media Theory Adequate to the Challenge of New Communications Technologies?', in M. Ferguson (ed.) *New Communication Technologies and the Public Interest.* London: Sage: 1–17.

McQuail, D. (1987) *Mass Communication Theory: An Introduction.* London: Sage.

McQuail, D. (1992) *Media Performance.* London: Sage.

McQuail, D. (1994) 'Media Policy Research: Conditions for Progress', in C.J. Hamelink and O. Linné (eds) *Mass Communication Research. On Problems and Policies. The Art of Asking the Right Questions. In Honor of James D. Halloran.* Norwood, NJ: Ablex: 39–51.

McQuail, D. (2003) *Media Accountability and Freedom of Publication.* London: Sage.

McQuail, D. (2005) *McQuail's Mass Communication Theory.* London: Sage.

McQuail, D. (2007a) 'Introduction: Reflections on Media Policy in Europe', in W. Meier and J. Trappel (eds) *Power, Performance and Politics.* Baden-Baden: Nomos: 9–19.

McQuail, D. (2007b) 'The Current State of Media Governance in Europe', in G. Terzis (ed.) *European Media Governance: National and Regional Dimensions.* Bristol: Intellect: 17–26.

McQuail, D. and K. Siune (eds) (1986) *New Media Politics: Comparative Perspectives in Western Europe.* London: Sage.

McQuail, D., and K. Siune (eds) (1998) *Media Policy: Convergence, Concentration and Commerce.* London: Sage.

McRobbie, A. (1996) 'All the World's a Stage, Screen or Magazine: When Culture is the Logic of Late Capitalism'. *Media, Culture and Society* 18: 335–42.

McSorley, K. (2003) 'The Secular Salvation Story of the Digital Divide'. *Ethics and Information Technology* 5(2):75–87.

Media Institute (2003) 'Remarks of Michael J. Powell'. Media Institute.

Megginson, W.L. and J.M. Netter (2001) 'From State to Market: A Survey of Empirical Studies on Privatization'. *Journal of Economic Literature* 39(2): 321–89.

Melody, W.H. (1990) 'Communication Policy in the Global Information Economy: Whither the Public Interest?', in M. Ferguson (ed.) *Public Communication: The New.* London: Sage: 16–39.

Mendina, T. and J.J. Britz (eds) (2004) *Information Ethics in the Electronic Age: Current Issues in Africa and the World.* Jefferson, NC: McFarland.

Merton, R.K. (1955) 'A Paradigm for the Study of the Sociology of Knowledge', in P. Lazarsfeld and M. Rosenberg (eds) *The Language of Social Research: A Reader in the Methodology of Social Research.* New York: Free Press: 498–510.

Merton, R.K. (1981) 'Remarks on Theoretical Pluralism', in P.M. Blau and K. Merton (eds) *Continuities in Social Inquiry.* London: Sage: i–xi.

Michalis, M. (2006) *European Governance: Communications. From Unification to Coordination.* Lanham, MD: Lexington.

Miege, B. (1987) 'The Logics at Work in the New Cultural Industries'. *Media, Culture and Society* 9: 237–89.

Miller, E.A. and J. Banaszak-Holl (2005) 'Cognitive and Normative Determinants of State Policymaking Behavior: Lessons from the Sociological Institutionalism'. *Publius* 3: 191–215.

Miller, M.M. and B.P. Riechert (2001) 'The Spiral of Opportunity and Frame Resonance: Mapping the Issue Cycle in News and Public Discourse', in S.D. Reese, O.H. Gandy Jr and A.E. Grant (eds) *Framing Public life: Perspectives on Media and Our Understanding of the Social World.* Mahwah, NJ: Lawrence Erlbaum: 107–22.

Miller, P. and N. Rose (1992) 'Political Power Beyond the State: Problematics of Government'. *British Journal of Sociology* 43(2): 173–205.

Miller, T. (1996) 'Cultural Citizenship and Technologies of the Subject, or Where Did You Go, Paul Dimaggio?'. *Culture and Policy* 7(1): 141–56.

Millward, R. (2005) *Public and Private Enterprise in Europe: Energy, Telecommunications and Transport, 1830–1990.* Cambridge and New York: Cambridge University Press.

Moe, H. (2008) 'Public Service Media Online? Regulating Public Broadcasters' Internet Services – a Comparative Analysis'. *Television New Media*, 9(3): 220–38.

Molsky, N. (1999) *European Public Broadcasting in the Digital Age.* London: FT Media and Telecoms.

Moore, N. (1997) 'The Information Policy Agenda in East Asia'. *Journal of Information Science* 23(2): 139–47.

Moore, N. (1998) 'The British National Information Strategy'. *Journal of Information Science* 24(5): 337–44.

Moravcsik, A. (2002) 'In Defence of the "Democratic Deficit": Reassessing Legitimacy in the European Union'. *Journal of Common Market Studies* 40(4): 603–24.

Moravcsik, A. (2005) *Europe without Illusions: A Category Mistake.* Available at: http: //www.prospect-magazine.co.uk/article_details.php?id=6939

Moravcsik, A. (2006) *What Can We Learn from the Collapse of the European Constitutional Project?.* Available at: http: //www.princeton.edu/~amoravcs/library/PVSO4.pdf

Moravcsik, A. (2008a) 'The European Constitutional Settlement'. *The World Economy* 31(1): 158–83.

Moravcsik, A. (2008b) *European Integration: Looking Ahead.* Available at: http: //www.princeton.edu/~amoravcs/library/decisions.pdf

Morley, D. (1992) *Television, Audiences and Cultural Studies.* London: Routledge.

Morris, M. (1988) 'Banality in Cultural Studies'. *Discourse* X 2: 3–29.

Mosco, V. (1988) 'Toward a Theory of the State and Telecommunications Policy'. *Journal of Communication* 38 (1): 107–24.

Mosco, V. and A. Herman (1980) 'Communication, Domination and Resistance'. *Media, Culture and Society* 3: 351–65.

Mouffe, C. (ed.) (1992) *Dimensions of Radical Democracy: Pluralism, Citizenship, Community*. London: Verso.

Mueller, M. (1995) 'Why Communication Policy is Passing "Mass Communication" By: Political Economy as the Missing Link'. *Critical Studies in Mass Communication* 12(4): 457–72.

Mueller, M. and B. Lentz (2004) 'Revitalizing Communication and Information Policy Research'. *The Information Society* 20(3): 155–8.

Murdock, G. (1992) 'Citizens, Consumers and Public Culture', in M. Skovmand and K. Schroder (eds) *Media Cultures: Reappraising Transnational Media*. London: Routledge: 17–41.

Murdock, G. (2000) 'Digital Futures: European Television in the Age of Convergence', in J. Wieten, G. Murdock and P. Dahlgren (eds) *Television across Europe: A Comparative Introduction*. London: Sage: 35–77.

Murdock, G. and Golding, P. (1977) 'Capitalism, Communication and Class Relations', in Curran *et al.* (eds) *Mass Communications and Society*. London: Arnold: 12–43.

Murdock, G. and Golding, P. (1999) 'Common Markets: Corporate Ambitions and Communication Trends in the UK and Europe'. *Journal of Media Economics* 12(2): 117–32.

Murphy, P. (2001) 'Affiliation Bias and Expert Disagreement in Framing the Nicotine Addiction Debate'. *Science, Technology, Human Values* 26(3): 278–99.

Napoli, P.M. (1999) 'The Marketplace of Ideas Metaphor in Communications Regulation'. *Journal of Communication*, 49(4): 151–69.

Napoli, P.M. (2001) *Foundations of Communications Policy: Principles and Process in the Regulation of Electronic Media*. Cresskill, New Jersey: Hampton Press.

National Telecommunications and Information Administration (1995) *Falling Through The Net: A Survey of the 'Have Nots' in Rural and Urban America*. Available at: http://www.ntia.doc.gov/ntiahome/fallingthru.html

National Telecommunications and Information Administration (1998) *Falling Through the Net: Defining the Digital Divide*. Available at http://www.ntia.doc.gov/ntiahome/fttn99/

Negrine, R. (1989) *Politics and the Mass Media in Britain*. London: Routledge.

Negrine, R. and S. Papathanassopoulos (1990) *The Internationalisation of the Television*. New York: Pinter.

Nelson, T.E., R.A. Clawson and Z.M. Oxley (1997) 'Toward a Psychology of Framing Effects'. *Political Behavior* 19(3): 221–46.

Nerone, J.C. (ed.) (1995) *Last Rights: Revisiting Four Theories of the Press*. Urbana and Chicago: University of Illinois Press.

NetGuide (2009) 'Applause for Delay on 92A'. Available at: http://www.techday.co.nz/netguide/news/applause-for-delay-on-92a/1004/

NewMediaAge (2009) 'Nearly Half of Web Users Have Illegally Downloaded Music'. Available at: http://www.nma.co.uk

Niec, H. (1998) 'Cultural Rights at the End of the World Decade for Cultural Development'. Paper presented at the Virtual Conference on the Right to Communicate and the Communication of Rights.

Nikoltchev, S. (2007) 'European Backing for Public Service Broadcasting'. *IRIS Special*. Strasbourg: European Audiovisual Observatory.

Nilsen, K. (2001) *The Impact of Information Policy: Measuring the Effects of the Commercialization of Canadian Government Statistics*. Westport, CT: Ablex.

Noam, E.M. (1992) *Telecommunications in Europe*. New York: Oxford University Press.

Noam, E. (1993) 'Reconnecting Communications Studies With Communications Policy'. *Journal of Communication* 43(3): 199–206.

Noam, E. (2007) 'Public Telecoms 2.0: The Return of the State'. *Financial Times*, 25 April.

Noll, R.G. (1989) 'Economic Perspectives on the Politics of Regulation', in R. Schmalensee and R.D. Willig (eds) *Handbook of Industrial Organization. Volume 2*. Amsterdam, Oxford and Tokyo: North-Holland: 1253–87.

Nora, S. and A. Minc (1980) *The Computerization of Society: a Report to the President of France*. Cambridge, MA: MIT Press.

Nord, L. (2009) 'What is Public Service on the Internet? Digital Challenges for Media Policy in Europe'. *Observatorio Journal*, 9: 24–39. Available at http://obs.obercom.pt

Nordlinger, E.A. (1981) *On the Autonomy of the Democratic State*. Cambridge, MA: Harvard University Press.

Nowotny, E. (1982) 'Nationalized Industries as an Instrument of Stabilization Policy: The Case of Austria'. *Annals of Public and Co-operative Economy* 53(1): 41–57.

Nuechterlein, J.E. and P.J. Weiser (2007) *Digital Crossroads: American Telecommunications Policy in the Internet Age Cambridge*. MA: MIT Press.

O'Brien, K. (2008) 'Microsoft Offers to Reduce Search Data in Europe'. *New York Times*, 9 December.

OECD (2007) *Communications Outlook 2007*. Paris: Organization for Economic Cooperation and Development.

Offe, C. (2000) *Is There, or Can There Be, a 'European Society'?* http://www4.soc.unitn.it:8080/poloeuropeo/content/e64/e385/e395/offe-Europeansociety_ita.pdf

Offe, C. (2002) *The Democratic Welfare State: A European Regime Under the Strain of European Integration*.http://www.eurozine.com/articles/2002–02-08-offe-en.html

Open Society Institute (2008) *Television across Europe: More Channels, Less Independence*. Open Society Institute. Available at http://www.soros.org/initiatives/media/articles_publications/publications/television_20090313

Oppenheim, C. (1996) 'An Agenda for Action to Achieve the Information Society in the UK'. *Journal of Information Science* 22(6): 407–21.

O'Regan, T. (1992) 'Some Reflections on the "Policy Moment"'. *Meanjin,* 51(3): 517–32.

Ostrow, J. (2003) 'Musicians Blast FCC Plan'. *Denver Post*, 23 May.

Pace, M. (2007) 'The Construction of EU Normative Power'. *Journal of Common Market Studies* 45(5): 1041–64.

Padovani, C. and M. Tracey (2003) 'Report on the Conditions of Public Service Broadcasting'. *Television & New Media*, 4(2): 131–53.

Papathanassopoulos, S. (2002) *European Television in the Digital Age, Issues, Dynamics and Realities*. Cambridge: Polity Press.

Papathanassopoulos, S. (2007) 'Financing Public Service Broadcasters in the New Era', in E. de Bens (ed.) *Media between Culture and Commerce*. Bristol: Intellect: 151–66.

Perelman, M. (2002) *Steal this Idea: Intellectual Property Rights and the Corporate Confiscation of Creativity*. New York: Palgrave Macmillan.

Perotti, E.C. (1995) 'Credible Privatization'. *American Economic Review* 85(4): 847–859.

Peters, G. and J. Pierre (2006) 'Introduction', in G. Peters and J. Pierre (eds) *Handbook of Public Policy*. London: Sage: 1–10.

Pfanner, E. (2008) 'Digital Revolution Comes to the Printed Word'. *International Herald-Tribune*, 7 November.

Pfanner, E. (2009) 'Isle of Man Plans Unlimited Music Downloads'. *New York Times*, 26 January.

Phillips, C.F., Jr (1993) *The Regulation of Public Utilities: Theory and Practice*. Arlington, VA: Public Utilities Reports.

Phillips, L. (2008) 'French Internet Law Clashes with EU Position'. *EU Observer*, 31 October.

Picard, R.G. (2003) 'Research Note: Assessing Audience Performance of Public Service Broadcasters'. *European Journal of Communication* 17(2): 227–35.

Pillay, V. (2008). 'House Arrest for Film Pirate'. Available at http://www.news24. com/News24/South_Africa/News/0,,2-7-1442_2419112,00.html

Pool, I. de Sola (1983) *Technologies of Freedom*. Cambridge, MA: Belknap Press.

Porat, M.U. (1977) *The Information Economy*, vols I–IX. Washington, DC: US Department of Commerce/Office of Telecommunications.

Powell, M.K. (2003) 'Should Limits on Broadcast Ownership Change?'. *USA Today*, 21 January.

Prado E. and D. Fernández (2006) 'The Role of Public Service Broadcasters in the Era of Convergence; A Case Study of Televisión de Catalunya'. *Communications & Strategies* 62: 49–69.

Price, M.E. (1995) *Television, the Public Sphere, and National Identity*. Oxford: Oxford University Press.

Proulx, S., G. Stoiciu, J.-P. Laurendeau, D. Maillet and R. Ouimet (1993). *Usages de la télévision et qualité de la vie familiale: construction et validation d'instruments de recherche dans une perspective ethnosociologique*. Montreal: Université du Québec à Montréal.

Raboy, M. (1998) 'Public Broadcasting and the Global Framework of Media Democratization'. *Gazette* 60(2): 167–80.

Raboy, M. (1999) 'Communication Policy and Globalization as a Social Project', in A. Calabrese and J-C Burgelman (eds) *Communication, Citizenship, and Social Policy: Re-thinking the Limits of the Welfare State*. Totowa, NJ: Rowman & Littlefield: 293–310.

Raboy, M. (2007) 'Broadening Media Discourses: Global Media Policy Defining the Field'. *Global Media and Communication* 3(3): 343–61.

Raboy, M. and B.D. Abramson (1998) 'Grasping an Enigma: Cultural Policy and Social Demand'. *Cultural Policy* 4(2): 1–27.

Raboy, M. and S. Proulx (2003) 'Viewers on Television: Between Policy and Uses'. *Gazette* 65: 4–5.

Raboy, M., S. Proulx and P. Dahlgren (eds) (2003) 'Media Policy and Social Demand: A Transnational Perspective'. Theme issue of *Gazette* 65(4–5): 323–9.

Raboy, M., B.D. Abramson, S. Proulx and R. Welters (2001) 'Media Policy, Audiences and Social Demand: Research at the Interface of Policy Studies and Audience Studies'. *Television and New Media* 2(2): 95–115.

Raboy, M., I. Bernier, F. Sauvageau and D. Atkinson (1994) 'Cultural Development and the Open Economy: A Democratic Issue and a Challenge to Public Policy'. *Canadian Journal of Communication* 19(3/4): 291–315.

Radaelli, C. (1997) 'How does Europeanization Produce Policy Change?'. *Comparative Political Studies* 30(5): 553–75.

Radaelli, C (2000) 'Whither Europeanization? Concept Stretching and Substantive Change'. *European Integration Online Papers* 4(8).

Reese, S.D. (2003) 'Framing Public Life: A Bridging Model for Media Research', in S.D. Reese, O.H. Gandy Jr, and A.E. Grant (eds) *Framing Public Life: Perspectives on Media and Our Understanding of the Social World*. Mahwah, NJ: Lawrence Erlbaum: 7–32.

Reich, S. (2000) 'The Four Faces of Institutionalism: Public Policy and a Pluralistic Perspective'. *Governance* 13(4): 501–22.

Reinard, J.C. and S.M. Ortiz (2005) 'Communication Law and Policy: The State of Research and Theory'. *Journal of Communication* 3: 594–631.

Rencher, A.C. (2002) *Methods of Multivariate Analysis*. New York: Wiley-Interscience.

Reuters (2008a) 'China Says Within Rights to Block Some Websites'. 16 December.

Reuters (2008b) 'Facebook Removes Group Celebrating Bosnian Killings'. 15 December.

Reuters (2009) 'Social Websites Sign EU Pact vs 'Cyber-Bullying'. 10 February.

Rimlinger, G. (2003) 'Feingold Leads Charge against New FCC Rules'. *Capital Times*, 16 July.

Roberts, D. (2001) 'FCC Chief "Working Himself Out of a Job"'. *The Financial Times*, 25 May.

Rodrik, D. (1998) 'Why Do More Open Economies Have Bigger Governments?'. *Journal of Political Economy* 105(5): 997–1032.

Rose, F. (2002) 'Big Media or Bust'. *Wired*, March.

Roszak, T. (1994) *The Cult of Information: A Neo-Luddite Treatise on High Tech, Artificial Intelligence, and the True Art of Thinking*, 2nd edn. Berkeley, CA: University of California Press.

Rowland, W.D. (1986) 'American Telecommunications Policy Research: its Contradictory Origins and Influences'. *Media, Culture and Society* 8: 159–82.

Rowland, W.D. (1993) 'The Traditions of Communication Research and Their Implications for Telecommunications Study'. *Journal of Communication* 43(3): 207–17.

Rowlands, I. (1996) 'Understanding Information Policy: Concepts, Frameworks and Research Tools'. *Journal of Information Science* 22(1): 13–25.

Rowlands, I. (1999a) 'Patterns of Author Co-citation in Information Policy: Evidence of Social, Collaborative and Cognitive Structure'. *Scientometrics* 44(3): 533–46.

Rowlands, I. (1999b) 'Patterns of Scholarly Communication in Information Policy: a Bibliometric Survey'. *Libri* 49(2): 59–70.

Runciman, D. (2008) *Political Hypocrisy: The Mask of Power, from Hobbes to Orwell and Beyond*. Princeton, NJ, and Oxford: Princeton University Press.

Sabatier P.A. (1991) 'Toward Better Theories of the Policy Process'. *PS: Political Science and Politics* 24(2): 147–56.

Sadeh, T. and D. Howarth (2008) 'Economic Interests and the European Union: A Catalyst for European Integration or a Hindrance?'. *British Journal of Politics and International Relations* 10(1): 1–8.

Safire, W. (2003) 'Regulate the Media'. *New York Times*, 16 June.

Sanders, E. (2003) 'Hollywood Guilds Band Together to Defend Media Ownership'. *Los Angeles Times*, 13 January.

Sarikakis, K. (2004) *Powers in Media Policy: The Challenge of the European Parliament*. Bern: Peter Lang.

Sassi, S. (2005) 'Cultural Differentiation of Social Segregation? Four Approaches to the Digital Divide'. *New Media and Society* 7(5): 684–700.

Saulauskas, M.P. (2005) 'On the Concept of "Information Society": Counterfactuality, Ideology and Public Discourse', in J. Baranova (ed.) *Contemporary Philosophical Discourse in Lithuania*. Washington, DC: Council for Research in Values and Philosophy.

Saunders, P. (1981) *Social Theory in Urban Question*. London: Hutchinson.

Scazzieri, R. (1993) *A Theory of Production: Tasks, Processes, and Technical Practices*. Oxford: Clarendon Press.

Schement, J.R. and T. Curtis (1995) *Tendencies and Tensions of the Information Age: the Production and Distribution of Knowledge in the United States*. New Brunswick, NJ: Transaction.

Schiller, D. (2007) *How to Think about Information*. Urbana, IL: University of Illinois Press.

Schlesinger, P. (2004) *The Babel of Europe?*. Available at http: //www.arena.uio.no/cidel/ WorkshopStirling/PaperSchlesinger.pdf

Schlesinger, P. (2007) 'A Cosmopolitan Temptation'. *European Journal of Communication* 22(4): 413–26.

Schneier, B. (2008) 'Schneier on Security'. 8 December. Available at http://www.schneier.com/blog/archives/2008/12/mumbai_terroris.html. Accessed 25 February 2009.

Schön, D. and M. Rein (1994) *Frame Reflection: Toward the Resolution of Intractable Policy Controversies*. New York: Basic.

Seaver, M. (2009) 'Across Irish Sea: Two Bold Tactics Against Music Piracy'. *Christian Science Monitor*, 5 February. Retrieved 19 February 2009 from LEXIS-NEXIS Academic Database.

Selian, A.N. (2004) 'The World Summit on the Information Society and Civil Society Participation'. *The Information Society* 20(3): 201–15.

Sevastopulo, D. (2003) 'Senators Deploy Veto to Attack Media Rules'. *Financial Times*, 16 July.

Shipan, C.R. (1997) *Designing Judicial Review: Interest Groups, Congress, and Communications Policy*. Michigan: University of Michigan Press.

Shiver, J. Jr, R. Simon and E. Sanders (2003) 'FCC Ruling Puts Rivals on the Same Wavelength'. *Los Angeles Times*, 9 June.

Shulz, W. and T. Held, (2004) *Regulated Self-regulation as a Form of Modern Government*. Luton: Luton University Press.

SiliconValley (2008) 'MySpace Ad Deal Lets Members Use Copyright Video'. http://www.siliconvalley.com

Sillince, J.A.A. (1994) 'Coherence of Issues and Coordination of Instruments in European Information Policy'. *Journal of Information Science* 20(4): 219–36.

Simon, R. and J. Hook (2003) 'FCC Rule May Bring a Veto Standoff'. *Los Angeles Times*, 25 July.

Singh, K. (2007) 'International Investments: Is Policy Pendulum Swinging Back?'. *Global Politician*. Available at http://www.globalpolitician.com/23192-business

Siune, K. (1998) 'Is Broadcasting Policy Becoming Redundant?', in K. Brants, J. Hermes and Liesbet van Zoonen (eds), *The Media in Question: Popular Cultures and Public Interests*. London: Sage: 18–26.

Slevin, J. (2000) *The Internet and Society*. Cambridge: Polity Press.

Smith, A. (1989). 'The Public Interest'. *Intermedia* 17(2): 10–24.

Snoddy, R. (1997) 'UK: EU Raises Doubts on Digital TV Licence Bid', *Financial Times*, 4 June.

Statsaholic (2009) 'Website Traffic Graphs for Huffingtonpost.com'. Available at http://www.statsaholic.com/huffingtonpost.com

Sterling, T.D. (1986) 'Democracy in an Information Society'. *The Information Society* 4(1/2): 9–47.

Stewart, C.M., G. Gil-Egui, Y. Tian and M.I. Pileggi (2006). 'Framing the Digital Divide: A Comparison of US and EU Policy Approaches'. *New Media & Society* 8(6): 731–51.

Storsul, T. and T. Syvertsen (2007) 'The Impact of Convergence on European Television Policy; Pressure for Change – Forces of Stability'. *Convergence* 13(3): 275–91.

Strover, S., K. Gustafson, K. Inagaki and M. Fuentes-Bautista (2005) 'Critically Evaluating Market Diffusion Policy and the Digital Divide in Texas 2000–2004'. Conference paper at the International Communication Association.

Sugaya, M. (2000) 'Media Convergence Policy in Japan: Coping with Multimedia'. *Keio Communication Review* 22: 31–40.

Sylvers, E. (2009) 'Italy Moves to Place Controls on Internet Content'. *International Herald Tribune*, 9 March.

Syvertsen, T. (1999) 'The Many Uses of the Public Service Concept'. *Nordicom Review* 1: 5–12.

Syvertsen, T. (2003) 'Challenges to Public Television in the Era of Convergence and Commercialization'. *Television and New Media* 4(2): 155–75.

Taylor, C. (1989) 'Cross-purposes: The Liberal Communitarian Debate', in N. Rosenblum (ed.) *Liberalism and the Moral Life*. Cambridge, MA: Harvard University Press: 159–82.

Technorati (2009) State *of the Blogosphere 2008*. Available at: http://technorati.com

Telecom, A.M. (2009) '2011 World Conference is So Important the FCC is Getting Ready Now'. 27 February.

Television Week (2003) 'FCC, Powell Must Bring the Public into the Process'. 21 April: 8.

Thatcher, M. (2004) 'Varieties of Capitalism in an Internationalized World: Domestic Institutional Change in European Telecommunications'. *Comparative Political Studies* 37: 751–69.

The Local (2008) 'Swedish Parliament Passes Copyright Bill'. 25 February.

Thomas, A.M. (1960) 'Audience, Market and Public: An Evaluation of Canadian Broadcasting'. *Canadian Communications* 1(1): 16–47.

Thompson, J.B. (1990) *Ideology and Modern Culture: Critical Social Theory in the Era of Mass Communication*. Cambridge: Polity.

Thompson, J.B. (1995) *The Media and Modernity: A Social Theory of the Media*. Cambridge: Polity.

Times Literary Supplement (1995) 'The Hundred Most Influential Books since the War'. 6 October: 39.

Timms, D. (2003) 'US Media Bill Faces Further Revolt'. *Guardian*, 16 July. Available at http://media.guardian.co.uk

Traquina, N. (1998) 'Western European Broadcasting, Deregulation, and Public Television: The Portuguese Experience'. *Journalism and Mass Communication Monographs* 167.

Trautmann, C. (1998) Speech given by the French Minister for Culture at the European Audiovisual Conference, Birmingham, 6–8 April.

Trebing, H.M. (2004) 'Assessing Deregulation: The Clash between Promise and Reality'. *Journal of Economic Issues* 38(1): 1–27.

Tunstall, J. (1986) *Communications Deregulation: The Unleashing of America's Communications Industry*. New York: Basil Blackwell.

Tunstall, J. (2008) *The Media were American*. New York: Oxford University Press.

US Department of Commerce (2004) *A Nation Online: Entering the Broadband Age*. Available at http://www.ntia.doc.gov/reports

US Department of Commerce (2007) *Networked Nation: Broadband in America 2007*. National Telecommunications and Information Administration. Available at: http://www.ntia.doc.gov/reports

USA Today (2008) 'Law Professor Fires Back at Song-Swapping Lawsuits'. 17 November.

Van den Bulck, H. (2007) 'Old Ideas Meet New Technologies: Will Digitalisation Save Public Service Broadcasting (Ideals) from Commercial Death?'. *Sociology Compass* 1(1): 28–40.

Van Steenbergen, B. (ed.) (1994) *The Condition of Citizenship*. London: Sage.

Venturelli, S. (1998) *Liberalizing the European Media: Politics, Regulation, and the Public Sphere*. Oxford: Clarendon Press.

Vickers, J. and G. Yarrow (1988) *Privatization: An Economic Analysis*. Cambridge, MA: MIT Press.

Vogel, S.K. (1996) *Freer Markets, More Rules: Regulatory Reform in Advanced Industrial Countries*. Ithaca, NY: Cornell University Press.

Ward, D. (2003) 'State Aid or Band Aid?'. *Media, Culture & Society* 25: 147–71.

Waverman, L. *et al.* (2007) *Access Regulation and Infrastructure Investment in the Telecommunications Sector: An Empirical Investigation.* LSEConsulting Group /ETNO.

Webster, F. (2002 and 2006) *Theories of the Information Society,* 2nd and 3rd edns. London: Routledge.

Weisman, R. (2007) 'Get Ready for Your Close-Up'. *Boston Globe*, 11 December.

Wessler, H.P., B. Brüggemann, M. Kleinen, K. von Königslöw and S. Sifft (2008) *The Transnationalization of Public Spheres.* London: Palgrave Macmillan.

Werbach, K.D. (2009) 'Higher Standards: Regulation in the Network Age'. *Harvard Journal of Law and Technology*, 23(1): 179–225.

Wheeler, M. (2007) 'Whither Cultural Diversity: The European Union's Market Vision for the Review of Television Without Frontiers Directive'. *European Studies* 24: 227–49.

White Paper (2004) *Safeguarding the Future of the European Audiovisual Market.* Brussels: Association of Commercial Television, European Publishers Council and Association Européenne des Radios.

Wildavsky, A.B. (1979) *Speaking Truth to Power: The Art and Craft of Policy Analysis.* Boston: Little Brown.

Williams, K. (2005) *European Media Studies.* London: Hodder Arnold.

Willmore, L. (2002) 'Government Policies Toward Information and Communication Technologies: A Historical Perspective'. *Journal of Information Science* 28(2): 89–96.

Woelfel, J. and N. Stoyanoff (2000) 'CatPac: A Neural Network for Qualitative Aanalysis of Text'. Paper included in the software CatPac.

World Bank (2005) *Economic Growth in the 1990s: Learning from a Decade of Reform.* Washington, DC: World Bank Group.

WorldNetDaily (2004) 'Google Restricting Search Results in China'. 23 September.

Young, C. and J. Weber (2003) 'Where Media Merger Mania Could Strike First'. *Business Week*, 9 June: 96.

Zittrain, J. (2008) *The Future of the Internet: And How to Stop It.* New Haven, CT: Yale University Press.

Zuckerman, M. (2008) '7 Fixes for a Market Failure'. *US News & World Report.* 9 May.

Index